Africa's Urban Youth

T0384611

Making up 65 percent of Africa's population, young people between the ages of eighteen and thirty-five play a key role in politics, yet they live in an environment of rapid urbanization, high unemployment rates, and poor state services. Drawing from extensive fieldwork in Ghana, Uganda, and Tanzania, this book investigates how Africa's urban youth cultivate a sense of citizenship in this challenging environment and what it means to them to be "good citizens." In interviews and focus group discussions, African youth, activists, and community leaders vividly explain how income, religion, and gender intertwine with their sense of citizen belonging. Though Africa's urban youth face economic and political marginalization as well as generational tensions, they craft a creative citizenship identity rooted in their relationships and obligations both to each other and to the state. Privileging above all the voice and agency of Africa's young people, this is a vital, systematic examination of youth and youth citizenship in urban environments across Africa.

AMY S. PATTERSON is Carl Gustav Biehl Endowed Professor of International Affairs and Professor of Politics at the University of the South. She has authored six books, including *Africa and Global Health Governance* (2018) and *Dependent Agency in the Global Health Regime* (2017), both of which were awarded prizes by the International Studies Association. A two-time Fulbright Scholar, her work has appeared in *African Affairs*, *African Studies Review*, *Journal of Modern African Studies*, *Africa Today*, *International Affairs*, and *Global Public Health*.

TRACY KUPERUS is Professor of Politics at Calvin University. Her research interests include religion and politics, democratization, and citizen mobilization. She has coauthored *When Helping Heals* (2017) and published chapters in edited volumes as well as articles in such journals as *African Affairs*, *Africa Today*, and the *Journal of Modern African Studies*.

MEGAN HERSHEY is Professor of Political Science at Whitworth University. She is the author of *Whose Agency: The Politics and Practice of Kenya's HIV-Prevention NGOs* (2019). A Fulbright-Hays recipient, her work has appeared in such journals as the *Journal of Eastern African Studies*, *Development in Practice*, and *Political Studies Review*.

Africa's Urban Youth

Challenging Marginalization, Claiming Citizenship

AMY S. PATTERSON
University of the South

TRACY KUPERUS
Calvin University

MEGAN HERSHEY
Whitworth University

CAMBRIDGE
UNIVERSITY PRESS

CAMBRIDGE
UNIVERSITY PRESS

Shaftesbury Road, Cambridge CB2 8EA, United Kingdom

One Liberty Plaza, 20th Floor, New York, NY 10006, USA

477 Williamstown Road, Port Melbourne, VIC 3207, Australia

314–321, 3rd Floor, Plot 3, Splendor Forum, Jasola District Centre,
New Delhi – 110025, India

103 Penang Road, #05-06/07, Visioncrest Commercial, Singapore 238467

Cambridge University Press is part of Cambridge University Press & Assessment,
a department of the University of Cambridge.

We share the University's mission to contribute to society through the pursuit of
education, learning and research at the highest international levels of excellence.

www.cambridge.org
Information on this title: www.cambridge.org/9781009235174

DOI: 10.1017/9781009235136

First published 2023

A catalogue record for this publication is available from the British Library.

Library of Congress Cataloging-in-Publication Data
Names: Patterson, Amy S. (Amy Stephenson), author. | Kuperus, Tracy, author. |
    Hershey, Megan, author.
Title: Africa's urban youth : challenging marginalization, claiming citizenship / Amy S.
    Patterson, University of the South, Tracy Kuperus, Calvin University,
    Megan Hershey, Whitworth University.
Description: Cambridge, United Kingdom ; New York, NY : Cambridge University Press,
    2023. | Includes bibliographical references and index.
Identifiers: LCCN 2023004355 (print) | LCCN 2023004356 (ebook) | ISBN 9781009235174
    (hardback) | ISBN 9781009235143 (paperback) | ISBN 9781009235136 (epub)
Subjects: LCSH: Urban youth–Africa–Social conditions. | Urban youth–Political
    activity–Africa. | Citizenship–Africa.
Classification: LCC HQ799.A35 A373 2023 (print) | LCC HQ799.A35 (ebook) |
    DDC 305.235096–dc23/eng/20230207
LC record available at https://lccn.loc.gov/2023004355
LC ebook record available at https://lccn.loc.gov/2023004356

ISBN 978-1-009-23517-4 Hardback
ISBN 978-1-009-23514-3 Paperback

To this generation of African youth

Contents

Figures

Tables

Acknowledgments

Our years of teaching undergraduate students in the United States, as well as our work with African youth on development projects, made us keen to write this book. But the steady erosion of democracy worldwide and the rising mental health and social crises among global youth pressed us further. We wondered: From the vantage point of youth, what is the meaning of citizenship? As one contemplative American youth told one author, "I really don't think you can be a good citizen and a good person." The rules of the political game, she said, get in the way of caring, moral action.

When we engaged African youth, however, the story was a bit different. Some, like the eye-rolling American, were cynical. But the vast majority found alternative paths, leaning into their everyday relationships with others to define their citizen identity. It was not that these African youth were naïve or blindly optimistic: They certainly understood the deep structural problems of poverty and exclusion they often encountered. But these problems didn't erode citizenship; they simply changed its texture.

Just as our youth respondents often understood citizenship to be a communal endeavor, this project has benefited from many people's assistance. We are grateful to Phoebe Kajubi and Joshua Beinomugisha in Uganda, Colman Msoka and Violet Mammba in Tanzania, and Richard Asante and Agnes Doe in Ghana for arranging interviews, translating, transcribing, and guiding us in countless ways. We know that the final product would be weaker (or nonexistent) without their support. In addition, Canon Gideon Byamugisha and Ruth Ninsiima were instrumental in helping Amy Patterson with some Ugandan interviews, while John Masuwa and the Network of Zambian People Living with HIV/AIDS assisted her with the Zambian case study. Thanks to Ntuthuzelo Vika and Siyabonga Vonco for arranging focus groups with little advance notice in Khayelitsha and Zwelihle, respectively. The directors and staff at the Volmoed Youth Leadership

Programme – especially Edwin Arrison, John de Gruchy, Wilma Jacobson, and David Willliam Daniels – graciously welcomed Tracy Kuperus. In Tanzania, Reverend Hiza, Reverend Mbiso, and Anania Ndondole welcomed and connected Megan Hershey to congregations in the Evangelical Lutheran Church in Tanzania.

We owe a huge debt of gratitude to Katherine Theyson for Afrobarometer data analysis, Livia Karoui for NVivo work, and Neil Patterson for a lot of calculations. In addition, Emmanuel Asiedu-Acquah, Rachel Riedl, Mila Dragojevic, and 2019 ISA copanelists shared insights and/or read portions of the work. The very thorough comments from anonymous reviewers made the manuscript much better. At Cambridge, we are grateful to Maria Marsh and Rachel Imrie, as well as to Atifa Jiwa (formerly at Cambridge). Of course, all errors are completely our own.

Several organizations funded fieldwork, writing time, and collaborative meetings: Global Religion Research Initiative's International Collaboration Grant, the Council for Christian Colleges and Universities (CCCU), the US Fulbright Scholars' Program, the University of the South, Calvin University, and Whitworth University. Thank you to Wheaton College (Illinois) for providing workspace for summer meetings and to Nita Stemmler at the CCCU for supporting our project in multiple ways.

We thank our families for accommodating our multiple trips for fieldwork. In addition, thanks to Matt Heun for his unflappable support, patience, and technical assistance. And thanks to Joshua Kistner for his encouragement and support in Tanzania and at home. Thank you, Neil, Sophia, and Isabel Patterson, for putting up with a lot of missed dinners, weekends in the office, and time away from family, as well as for your steadfast interest in Africa (and its youth) over the decades.

Finally, we have enormous gratitude to the hundreds of African youth, as well as the elders who care about them, who over the years have educated us about what it means to be a citizen.

Abbreviations

ANC	African National Congress
ANCYL	African National Congress Youth League
CBO	community-based organization
CCM	*Chama cha Mapinduzi*
CHADEMA	*Chama cha Demokrasia na Maendeleo*
COSAS	Congress of South African Students
CPP	Convention People's Party
DP	Democratic Party
EFF	Economic Freedom Fighters
ELCT	Evangelical Lutheran Church in Tanzania
FBO	faith-based organization
FGD	focus group discussions
GBV	gender-based violence
GNI	gross national income
HDI	Human Development Index
ICGC	International Central Gospel Church
LPI	Lived Poverty Index
NDC	National Democratic Congress
NGO	nongovernmental organization
NHIF	National Health Insurance Fund
NPP	New Patriotic Party
NRM	National Resistance Movement
NYLTP	National Youth Leadership Training Programme
NZP+	Network of Zambian People Living with HIV/AIDS
PF	Patriotic Front
SADC	Southern African Development Community
SJC	Social Justice Coalition
UGCC	United Gold Coast Convention
UPC	Uganda People's Congress
VYLTP	Volmoed Youth Leadership Training Programme
ZANU-PF	Zimbabwe African National Union–Patriotic Front

Introduction
Why Investigate Urban Youth Citizenship in Africa?

This book explores youth citizenship in the African cities of Accra, Kampala, and Dar es Salaam. It places youth stories and perspectives at its heart, building on focus group discussions, interviews, and observations among ordinary youth participants and comparing those with national survey trends. To ensure that readers understand our efforts: This book falls in the sociological tradition of interpreting meanings as opposed to investigating scientifically derived, causal explanations. We rely on thick descriptions that document the ways African youth understand their lives. Our work asserts that there is something special about the way that urban youth, or the individuals we encountered who were eighteen to thirty-five years old, understand their role in their communities and countries. Chapter 1 conceptualizes the contested category of youth, but most youth shared the experience of uncertainty and economic and social instability as they "waited" for adulthood (Honwana 2012). Socioeconomic and political constraints meant many were delayed in achieving some or all of the "adult" milestones of employment, marriage, parenthood, property ownership, stability, and status in the community (Diouf 2003; Honwana 2012; Sommers 2015). They operated in a context of marginalization or an arena without visible boundaries in which contestation and struggle over identity and belonging occurred (Hodgson 2017). Their experiences of being on the economic, social, and political edge mattered for their views of citizenship. Although at times these understandings overlapped with those of their elders, because of their age, economic situation, and particular experiences in a neoliberal context, they approached citizenship somewhat differently. They espoused an "everyday citizenship" (Pailey 2021; Puumala and Shindo 2021), a contested identity of belonging that revolved around their daily actions and experiences as youth. At times this everyday citizenship took on a legalistic tenor, but at other times, it manifested in commitment to others and ideals about one's role in nation building. Everyday

1

citizenship intersected with economic, gender, and religious identities as individuals negotiated their rights and responsibilities in ever-changing communities.

Although there is "no uniform 'youth' politics in Africa's emerging democratic societies" (Van Gyampo 2020, 330), we were struck by the fact that youth across our study countries shared a general conviction that their citizenship was both relevant and puzzling. They reported that citizenship mattered, as they described the creative ways (from graffiti to voting to teaching) that they act out their citizenship. Yet the topic was also puzzling. Some grappled with understanding what it meant to be a citizen in political contexts that purported to be democratic yet still held onto authoritarian practices that shut out their voices (Branch and Mampilly 2015; Cheeseman 2015; Sommers 2015). Others questioned how they could meet their citizenship obligations – from caring for their families to paying taxes – given their overall economic marginalization. Churchgoing youth drew on their faith to define citizenship, while men and women both challenged and affirmed gendered notions of citizen obligations. Through our discussions, it was apparent that citizenship – with all its murky obligations and the ways it intersected with other identities – was salient for the youth we met.

I.1 Urban Youth at a Crossroads

The topic of urban youth citizenship deserves attention for several reasons. The first is that youth themselves think their citizenship is different from that of their elders. Absent our prompting, the youth in this study collectively self-identified as youth, illustrating that being youth is both a personal and collective mindset. In Tanzania, for example, they used the Swahili term *vijana* (youth) often to refer to themselves, while in Uganda they set themselves apart from "older people," and in Ghana they repeatedly referred to themselves as "future leaders." This self-identification drove their understanding of citizenship, and it deepens the often dichotomous and paradoxical ways the literature paints them. Youth are portrayed as violent trouble-makers *or* peaceful activists, prone to peril *or* promise, a challenge to be conquered *or* an opportunity to be seized (Abbink and van Kessel 2005; Honwana 2012; McEvoy-Levy 2013; Seekings 1993). By listening to urban youth, we discover that they exude energy and propose new solutions for societal problems. Their citizenship revolves around a commitment to their relationships with friends and neighbors, concerns about economic survival, and a desire to be heard. They link citizenship to issues that matter to them: employment, the environment, health threats, crime, gender inequality, and their communities' development. Our respondents' distinct positionality and perspective drive us to examine their citizenship in its own right.

The second reason urban youth citizenship deserves attention is purely numeric: Youth comprise a significant portion of African populations, making youth a "powerful category … in academic and policy-related research" (Oinas, Onodera, and Suurpää 2018, 2) and "a preoccupation" (Diouf 2003). In 2020, approximately 60 percent of the continent's population was under twenty-five years old, with one-third being between fifteen and thirty-four years (Rocca and Schultes 2020). Africa is the only world region where rising youth populations will continue for the indefinite future (Resnick and Thurlow 2015, 1). This growth reflects the presence of better health systems in low-income countries, which has led to a 78 percent decline in child mortality rates since 1950 and an increase in life expectancy at birth from roughly fifty years in 1990 to sixty-two years in 2015 (Bollyky 2018, 43–4). Youth is the biggest voting bloc in most countries, and economists predict that, during every year over the next decade, eleven million African youth will join the job market (Bollyky 2018, 130). Figure I.1 illustrates the growth of the continent's youth population, projected through 2040.

A third reason we should investigate urban youth citizenship is because the significant growth of African cities conditions youth opportunities and challenges. In the last two decades, the continent's urbanization rate has been 3.5 percent per year (Paller 2019). Today, 40 percent of Africans live in urban areas, and it is estimated that, by 2030, over 50 percent will (Sommers 2010, 319). Urbanization is not unique to Africa: In 2009 the number of people worldwide living in cities surpassed the number living in rural areas, and by 2050 the United Nations projects that "69 percent of the world's people will live in cities" (Latendresse and Bornstein 2012, 355). However, sub-Saharan Africa is urbanizing faster than any other region, "by 600 per cent in the last 35 years" (Sommers 2010, 319). Neoliberal economic reforms and globalization that capitalizes on urban centers for trade and labor contributed to urbanization during the 1990s as rural

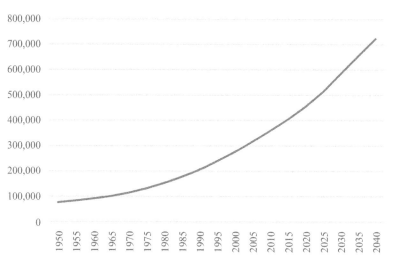

Figure I.1 Growth of Africa's youth population*
*For youth aged fifteen through thirty-four years, in thousands, projected through 2040
Source: UN Department of Economic and Social Affairs (2022)

citizens flocked to cities (Carmody and Owusu 2018). After this initial rural-to-urban migration, urban growth is now primarily determined through reproduction rather than migration, with an estimated "7 out of 10 residents in African cities [being] 30 years old or younger" (Resnick and Thurlow 2015, 7).

Although many analysts agree that urbanization can promote economic and social development through economies of scale for social services, concentrations of industrial labor, and population centers that foster technological innovation, these positive knock-on effects have been less apparent in Africa (Freire, Somik, and Leipziger 2014). Only four out of ten urban Africans had access to improved sanitation in 2015. The majority of urban Africans now live in informal settlements with overcrowded housing, poor service delivery, and uncertain property rights (Bollyky 2018, 133). Eviction, the lack of affordable housing, divorce and/or a partner's death (for women), and housing destruction (due to floods, fire, and razing) lead urban populations to frequently move from one neighborhood to another. Young people without stable jobs and property are most impacted (Tipple and Speak 2009), making some of them susceptible to recruitment by sophisticated criminal networks that may offer economic opportunities

(Scheye and Pelser 2020). One-quarter of surveyed Africans – including one-fourth of youth eighteen to thirty-five years old – say that things have gotten "much worse" or "worse" in the last few years in terms of their personal safety (Afrobarometer 2016/2018).

The youth in this study reported pressures on educational services and a dearth of job possibilities. In 2016, the average number of completed years of schooling in Africa was 5.3 years compared to 1.2 years in 1950 (Bollyky 2018, 99). Universities cannot meet a growing demand, with enrollments increasing by 4.3 percent each year between 1970 and 2013 (Darvas et al. 2017; World Bank 2021). In terms of jobs, the continent's aggregate unemployment rate for youth was 11 percent in 2021 (Statista 2021), but this number can be as high "as 49 to 52 percent ... in places like South Africa" (Resnick and Thurlow 2015, 5). By some estimates, over half of urban African youth are underemployed or unemployed (Bollyky 2018, 100). At the current rate, the World Bank (2016) predicts that sub-Saharan Africa will have over 300 million people searching for work by 2050. Many of them will end up in the informal economy, which, according to some estimates, provides 95 percent of all youth jobs (Scheye and Pelser 2020) and produces an estimated 70 percent of Africa's GDP (Rizzo 2017, 7). The COVID-19 pandemic exacerbated this situation, with its accompanying decline in commodity prices, foreign investment, and, for some countries, tourism. Despite a rebound with a 4.5 percent growth rate in 2021, economies were predicted to decline again in 2022 due to the war in Ukraine, global food shortages, inflationary pressures, and rising debt levels (IMF 2020, 2021, 2022).

A fourth reason to take a closer look at African youth citizenship relates to their distinct experiences with neoliberalism. Born after the mid-1980s, the youth we studied have only known market economies, limited state involvement in their lives, and the notion of individual "responsibilization" that undergirds neoliberal policies (Ferguson 2010). They swim, tread water, and, sometimes, sink in a river of neoliberal ideas and initiatives that color their views of citizenship. Although definitions of neoliberalism are contested and controversial (Venugopal 2015; Whyte 2019), we understand neoliberalism to be both a set of economic principles embodied in public policies and a "sociopolitical project" that those policies demand and produce (Harrison 2005, 1303). Neoliberal structural adjustment policies that many low- and middle-income countries were required to adopt in order to obtain international banking credit in the 1980s and 1990s included fiscal austerity, trade promotion, deregulation, currency devaluation, and privatization (Ferguson 2010, 172; World Bank 1981). Unevenly implemented across the continent (van de Walle 2001), they brought macroeconomic stability to countries such as Ghana, Tanzania, and Kenya (Gyimah-Boadi 1995; Radelet 2010). However, they also contributed to increasing inequality (Harvey 2007), deprived states of funds needed for infrastructure and social services (Hearn 2002), reduced government capacity (Pfeiffer and Chapman 2010; Semboja and Therkildsen 1995), and undermined the social democratic potency of independent political parties (Williams and Taylor 2000). With "wildly unpopular results" (Ferguson 2010, 173), they eroded the social contract between the state and citizens. With "the state, less prone to intrude … neoliberalism [has] left the former subject-targets of a developmental government to fend for themselves" (Schneider 2014, 18). Economic advancement is no longer tied directly to state employment and connections (Asante 2013; Mueller 2018, 71; Resnick 2015), and private enterprise or donor-funded development now drives the growth of Africa's middle class (Rotberg 2013). Neoliberalism has varied over time, as states have selectively intervened in markets, particularly to promote private capital through public-private partnerships in health, education, and public transportation (Rizzo 2017, 15).

As a discourse, neoliberalism includes the principles of self-reliance, individualism, entrepreneurship, responsibility, innovation, and hard work (Escobar 1995; Foucault 2002; Gupta and Ferguson 2002; Harvey 2007; Hearn 2002; Rasmussen 2013; Schertz 2014). As a structural force that shapes lives (Ganti 2014), an "ethic" of faith in the market (Treanor 2005), and a set of "deep core" beliefs (Rushton and Williams 2012, 153), neoliberal themes were frequently espoused by this study's participants. For example, one Ugandan priest described how a young parishioner started a business selling pancakes (sweet cakes) by the roadside. Because of a "strong work ethic, [he's] now rich and he drives several cars! All from pancakes!" (UG Interview 11). A Tanzanian church leader echoed this remark, "[A good citizen] must work … you must struggle … not wait for the government to employ you, you must employ yourself" (TZ Interview 2), while a Ghanaian pastor complained that too many youth think "they can make money easily without working hard. We all know that hard work pays!" (GH Interview 5; see Meyer 2007, 22). Because religious leaders may shape public discourse (McClendon and Riedl 2019), these are more than just one-off admonitions. As Chapter 2 illustrates, some youth equated entrepreneurship and individual responsibility with citizenship. But they also recognized how economic uncertainties, educational and employment pressures, and the daily challenges of urban life undercut this citizenship view and led them to perceive citizenship in light of the dependent relationships they had with friends and neighbors. Given youth's significant numbers and the unique ways that urbanization and neoliberalism have hit them, we must interrogate their experiences to understand how their citizenship may be distinct from that of their elders.

I.2 An Uneven Democratic Context

Although youth and their elders both operate in political systems experiencing uneven democratic transitions, youth have engaged those systems differently, often through informal political involvement rooted in youth-distinct experiences. In the 1990s, multiparty rule replaced authoritarian regimes throughout much of sub-Saharan Africa, and liberal democracy deepened (Cheeseman 2015). Many African states wrote new constitutions that allowed regularly scheduled elections, a free press, and freedom of assembly. Cities were the sites of political opposition and mobilization, with urban, civil society organizations playing a crucial role in demanding the end of one-party states (Bratton and van de Walle 1994; Paller 2018). Youth experienced this "third wave of democracy" through participation in elections, party youth organizations, civic associations, protest politics, and, in some countries (e.g., Uganda), representation through official legislative quotas.

Thirty years after democratic liberalization, levels of democratic deepening vary significantly across the region. Hybrid regimes that hold regular elections but have weak legislatures and judiciaries, elite circulation, weak rule of law, centralization of executive power, elite entitlement to resources, and high rates of corruption are the norm (Bleck and van de Walle 2018, 6–7; Diamond 2015; Ochieng' Opalo 2019). Crackdowns on media outlets and civil society groups, politically motivated internet outages, and presidents who remove term limits are increasingly common (Cheeseman and Fisher 2021; Conroy-Krutz

2020; Gyimah-Boadi 2015). In 2021, only 7 percent of Africans lived in a "free" country, while 49 percent lived in a "not free" country (Freedom House 2022). Five countries experienced a military coup d'état in 2021–2022 (Maclean 2022).[1] Average citizens have felt this tightening of democratic space acutely: Although in its 2016–2018 round of surveys Afrobarometer found that 48 percent of respondents said that they had "somewhat more" or "much more" freedom to say what they think than they did a few years ago, 19 percent said they had the "same" freedom, and 31 percent said they had "somewhat less" or "much less" (Afrobarometer 2016/2018). Afrobarometer did not ask the same question in 2019–2021 surveys, though we suspect that these numbers would indicate even less felt freedom.

The youth in this book maneuver in this uneven democratic context, with many framing their citizenship in light of these constraints. Although some scholars portray African youth as prone to political violence (Honwana 2012; Resnick and Thurlow 2015; Sommers 2015), and post-independence governments and donors have "panicked" over this rising demographic (Lambert 2016), the youth we encountered often debunked assumptions about their destabilizing potential, political apathy, or homogeneity. In Africa's third wave of protests that began in 2013, youth acted as both leaders and foot soldiers, demanding jobs, greater income equality, and good governance (Branch and Mampilly 2015; Mueller 2018). Although urban youth protested in 2020 for free and fair elections in Uganda, Côte d'Ivoire, and Malawi and in 2021 against Sudan's military coup d'état, they are only marginally more involved in protests than their elders (Resnick and Thurlow 2015, 173). The evidence is "weak that the youth bulge alone will lead to instability" (Bollyky 2018, 105) or that unemployed youth will perpetrate violence (Kahl 2006). Although youth are less likely to vote, attend community meetings, or belong to political parties (Lekalake and Gyimah-Boadi 2016; Resnick and Thurlow 2015; Sloam 2011; Sommers 2015) – trends that counter Western models of democratization predicting that increasing levels

---

[1] Numerous factors drive authoritarianism, including colonialism that centralized authority, prevented citizen participation, and denied investment in liberal institutions (Cheeseman and Fisher 2021); economies dependent on natural resource rents (Ross 2015); ruling parties that subsume the state (Morse 2018); and Western backsliding in democracy promotion (Haggard and Kaufman 2021).

of education and urbanization will lead individuals to more political participation (Bratton 2013; Ingelhart and Welzel 2005) – youth are not divorced from political issues or interest. Despite youthful skepticism (Sloam 2011), they do energetically discuss politics (Ingelhart and Welzel 2005; Lekalake and Gyimah-Boadi 2016), as our long conversations with youth in Kampala, Accra, and Dar es Salaam illustrated.

Similar to youth worldwide, some African youth engage in politics through social media (Kamau 2017; Mare 2018; Nyabola 2018) – activities made possible by the region's fifty-fold increase in internet connectivity since the early 2000s (Allen 2021). Afrobarometer (2019/2021) finds that 26 percent of all respondents report using the Internet daily, though this number is 33 percent for people aged eighteen to twenty-five. Youth deploy Whatsapp, Twitter, and Facebook to share information (Diamond 2010), facilitate interactions, discuss politics (Kalyango and Adu-Kumi 2013), create unifying narratives for mobilization (Olorunnisola and Douai 2013), and embolden online participants for public action such as during Nigeria's #EndSARS movement (Uwalaka 2022). Politicians use these tools to target youth for political messaging, to promote themselves as celebrities (Mare 2018), and, in some cases, to justify their hold on power (Doyle 2021). Yet, social media engagement may not lead previously inactive people to political participation (Bosch, Admire, and Ncube 2020), and, for our youth respondents, social media engagement was not central to how they discussed citizenship as a lived experience.

Beyond social media messaging, elders may seek to mobilize youth by capitalizing on their political and economic marginalization. Party leaders may entice youth voters and campaigners through food parcels or stipends (forms of patronage), nationalist rhetoric, and the hope of future positions (Bob-Milliar 2014). They may harness a politics of frustration over political exclusion and limited economic opportunities, as well as a politics of envy that revolves around growing inequality in Africa (McClendon 2018). Elites may use such strategies to control youth labor, promote youth discipline, and foster state building (Burgess 1999; Hodgkinson and Melchiorre 2019; Van Gyampo 2015). Yet, because marginalization signifies the "relational, processual nature of the status of being on the margins" (Hodgson 2017), youth are not without agency in these scenarios. Youth strategically navigate the field of politics by repositioning and aligning themselves with local powerbrokers "to exploit the possible opportunities that emerge" (Dawson 2014, 865). Sometimes purposefully "waiting," they articulate alternative visions of citizenship, maneuver around structural limitations, and devise ways to shape and transform their social realities. For example, they may turn to other forms of public engagement, such as volunteering, leading civil society groups (Brown and Prince 2015; Sloam 2011), and even working in the informal economy (Thieme 2013). The significant presence of nongovernmental organizations (NGOs) and community-based organizations (CBOs) due to neoliberal promotion of private, donor-funded efforts has created opportunities for youth's local engagement (Brass 2016; Dietrich 2013; Hershey 2013).

The youth in this study add additional layers to these aggregate patterns. Many situated their citizenship in the context of neoliberal expectations and partial democratic constraints. They emphasized responsibility, the "boot-strap" mentality, and employment as under-girding citizenship because these paths may enable youth to meet their obligations to family and contribute to society. At the same time, our respondents looked to the government to help alleviate major socio-economic challenges, and they often felt that their governments had let them down. Indeed, 76 percent of youth aged eighteen to thirty-five across all Afrobarometer survey countries (and 76 percent of their elders) think the government is handling job creation fairly badly or very badly (Afrobarometer 2019/2021). Facing democratic constraints and political marginalization, some youth advocated for basic services and demanded better governance (Hern 2019, 95–100; Robins 2014). But most of the youth we encountered did not engage in such actions. Instead, they volunteered for communal projects, loaned neighbors money, and cared for young children or the sick. For them, these were acts of citizenship.

I.3 Youth Agency and Creativity

Studying youth citizenship gives us new insights into agency, particularly in the underappreciated and often unnoticed arenas of the neighborhood, family, and religious community. Agency is the ability of actors to process social experiences and to devise responses. The agent can "cope with life," even with its economic, political, and socioeconomic constraints, because actors are "knowledgeable" and "capable" (Long 1990). Agency refers not to the intention to do things but to the capacity to act (Giddens 1991). This capacity may be embodied in a repertoire of words, deeds, symbols, and cultural practices, and it may only be recognized in hindsight. Agency is constantly negotiated, moving along a continuum in response to constraints. Agents may exhibit more or less dependence on economic or political structures, but they still have capacity to "resist, and sometimes to deflect what seems to be their structural fate" (Lonsdale 2000). The youth we study exemplify elements of "dependent agency" (Anderson and Patterson 2017a): They depend on employment or educational opportunities to get ahead materially; they depend on family or religious organizations to sustain them materially, socially, and emotionally; and they depend on political systems to acknowledge and protect their rights. They face economic, political, and social structures that tell them as young people to "bide their time."

Despite dependency and marginalization, many youth in our study acted to secure their citizen belonging and assert their rights and responsibilities in the community. In the process, they resembled youth in other countries. For example, Senegalese youth in Y'en a Marre used hip-hop music to mobilize against constitutional manipulation in 2011. The #FeesMustFall movement in South African universities used Twitter, Whatsapp, and Facebook, as well as conventional protests and student walk-outs, to galvanize a nationwide movement for equitable resources and a decolonized curriculum in 2016 (Nyamnjoh 2016). Youth have turned to theater, community meetings, and public art to educate about and demand accountability on issues such as corruption, COVID-19, and climate change (Honwana and Honwana 2021; Lambert 2016; Nkrumah 2021). Youth have grasped new leadership roles, such as young Nigerian women who used social media and fundraising skills gained during the Bring Back Our Girls Campaign in 2014 for the #EndSARS movement in 2020 (Olaoluwa 2020). The Not Too Young to Run campaign in Nigeria has recruited youth candidates, and youth politicians such as Julius Malema in South Africa, Diane Rwigara in Rwanda, and Nelson Chamisa in Zimbabwe have challenged ruling party structures.

Many of the youth we encountered exhibited the same energy and creativity at the micro level. Some spoke up at meetings about their lack of jobs; others contributed to community clean-up efforts; one started a group to help other youth facing mental health issues; a few painted graffiti to educate against political violence; most debated politics extensively; and, if they are at all indicative of survey data patterns, the majority voted. The diversity in agentic behaviors highlights how citizenship is dynamic and often contested, but also how youth draw on their own resources in their citizenship. Although we encountered some youth who expressed frustration and anger, the vast majority were not cynical and disaffected. They echoed the results of a 2020 survey that found that African youth were optimistic about their economic future and thought they made crucial contributions to their communities. Youth in the survey leaned into their shared African identity as a resource, just as the youth in this study sought to capitalize on a sense of belonging and responsibility to assist their communities and countries (Ichikowitz Foundation 2020).

Studying youth citizenship challenges us to recognize that citizenship includes daily experiences and relationships in community alongside interactions with the state through a legally defined identity. Finding a job, forming an NGO, and fostering orphan children have the potential for shaping identity and enabling people to claim rights and meet obligations. As the youth in this study show, citizenship is more than voting, protesting, or paying one's taxes: It is how people live their lives.

1 | Theorizing Urban Youth and Everyday Citizenship

A good citizen ... participates in everything going on in the country. He/ she[1] has the country at heart, even if he prays so that God will lift His hands on the country ... Also, he contributes to development ... by paying taxes.

(GH FGD 2)

As a good citizen, you should love the community ... That was the basic given to us by God: that we should love one another ... value and care for one another.

(TZ FGD 2)

Spoken with excitement and strong conviction by youth in this study, these statements portray a citizenship that is multifaceted, active, and rooted in everyday relationships. The Ghanaian stresses participating, praying, contributing, and paying taxes but also brings in emotion and commitment to the country. The Tanzanian stresses love and care of neighbors and believes his faith undergirds his citizenship. Together, they illustrate everyday citizenship, a concept that acknowledges a legal identity tied to the state but, more centrally, reflects how the "give and take between people" builds identity and defines community (Isin and Nielsen 2008, 5; Pailey 2016; von Lieres 2014). This citizenship "permeates everyday life" (Dorman 2020, 465) and emerges through the dense relations among "social beings who coexist ... in and through conflict and cooperation" (Isin and Nielsen 2008). Everyday citizenship signifies belonging and its accompanying rights and responsibilities in local and national communities.

---

[1] When speaking English, most respondents used he/him pronouns, though some used she/her, and a few used he/she. Because many African languages use nongendered pronouns, and some respondents spoke in Twi (Ghana), Swahili (Tanzania), or Luganda (Uganda), we alternate translating the nongendered pronouns to he/him or she/her.

There are theoretical and practical stakes for our analysis of everyday citizenship among urban youth in select African cities. We move beyond the tension between, on the one hand, citizenship as rights claims on the state and, on the other hand, citizenship as ties to the community (Dorman 2020; Ndegwa 1997). For everyday citizens, local connections and daily struggles inform and shape their engagement with the state as voters, advocates, or protestors. Thus, we conceptualize citizenship as more than micro-level engagements *with the state*, and we recognize how engagements *with other individuals* inform citizenship (MacLean 2011). In addition, we expand the concept of everyday politics, which recognizes how social practices generate and reinforce political behavior, by interrogating how such practices shape citizenship identity (Ammann 2016; Bayat 2010; Paller 2021). We deepen knowledge of youth politics through our focus not solely on youth political behavior but, more proximately, on the citizen identity that undergirds that behavior. Through an intersectional analysis, we show how income level, church attendance, and identification as a man or woman shape contestation over citizenship. Our work has practical implications: It provides readers with a "lay of the land" resource to catalyze further questions on the identities and obligations of African youth. It also opens the door to examine the contested nature of micropolitics, thereby facilitating citizenship analysis of other marginalized populations, such as ethnic minority youth or rural youth.

To begin, this chapter first conceptualizes the meaning of youth (Section 1.1), relying on anthropological studies to elucidate youth subjectivity. We then describe the theory of everyday citizenship (Section 1.2). After establishing concepts, we turn to the country contexts in which our youth respondents contested citizenship (Section 1.3), and we describe our multi-method approach of focus group discussions, interviews, case studies, and use of Afrobarometer survey data (Section 1.4). Finally, we outline the book's remaining chapters (Section 1.5).

1.1 The Meaning of Youth

Youth is both a chronological category and a socially constructed identity, with governments and donor agencies focusing on the former. For the United Nations (2022), "youth" refers to persons between the ages of fifteen and twenty-four, though international law has no set definition.[2] The African Union's Youth Charter defines "youth" as those aged fifteen to thirty-five years old, with persons fifteen to seventeen being classified as minors (African Union Commission 2006, 11). Ghana defines "youth" as people between fifteen and thirty-five years (Van Gyampo 2020, 329); Uganda, between twelve and thirty years (Republic of Uganda 2001); and Tanzania, between fifteen and thirty-five years (United Republic of Tanzania 2007, 10). Scholars criticize the chronological perspective because it draws a narrow dividing line between youth and adulthood (Rogers 2003), reflects Western legal traditions (White 2002), ignores youth's diverse experiences with biological transitions (e.g., menstruation), dismisses the divergent social experiences of young people (Clark-Kazak 2009), discounts how such experiences vary across time and space (Christiansen, Utas, and Vigh 2006; La Fontaine 1986; Whiting 1990), and, ultimately, says little about the "social meaning ascribed to biological development" (Clark-Kazak 2009, 1310).

As a socially constructed identity, youth is an elusive, ambiguous category rooted in "social, economic, political, moral and emotional predicaments and embodied processes" (Oinas, Onodera, and Suurpää 2018, 4). It often is set apart from adulthood, with its conventional markers of employment, marriage, parenthood, property ownership, financial independence, assumed knowledge, rights, and stability (Dungey and Meinert 2017; Fredericks 2014; Honwana 2012; Quaynor 2015b; Sommers 2015; Van Gyampo and Anyidoho 2019). Moving from adolescence to adulthood has always been a slippery path (Christiansen, Utas, and Vigh 2006), making "youth" a "social shifter" with deictic and referential functions (Durham 2004).[3] As a reference, "youth" points to a particular identity, but as a deictic, it becomes subjectively linked to structures and situations (Durham 2017). Its meaning is rooted in "relations and constructions of power [that are] refracted, recombined, and reproduced, as people make claims on each other based on age" (Durham 2000, 114). Viewing "youth" as a shifter demystifies the concept for Western audiences,

---

[2] In contrast, the Convention on the Rights of the Child defines children as persons under eighteen.
[3] A deictic is a type of word that is only understood in a particular context so that its meaning constantly shifts. "There" is a deictic, since it is meaningless without knowing the location of "here."

who may question the chronological age ranges presented above, and it allows us to center our respondents' voices as we analyze their citizenship.

The meaning of youth has been associated with waithood,[4] a suspended period of "stuckness" in a "liminal space with no exit" between childhood and the seemingly stable category of adulthood (Dungey and Meinert 2017; Durham 2017; Honwana 2012). Yet, waithood has no finite endpoint, just as adulthood is not necessarily a stable status.[5] Gerontocratic power shapes waithood, with many elders expecting that youth will make current and future contributions to family, community, and the nation. Neoliberalism's entwinement with assumptions about formal employment as adulthood's "unmarked normal" (Durham 2017, 7) means "becoming somebody is no longer taken for granted" (Cruise O'Brien 1996, 58). But as many youth "hustle" as a "last resort" (Thieme 2013), they simultaneously create new social possibilities (Jua 2003). As a subaltern majority, youth are situated awkwardly between an elite (sometimes aligned with transnational economic partners) and the community (Diouf 2003; Ifeka 2006); youth constantly strive to "navigate" these changing spaces and temporalities (Christiansen, Utas, and Vigh 2006). Elites may celebrate youth identity in order to downplay class, religion, or ethnicity (Burgess 1999), but they also may strive to harness youth labor for development (Brennan 2006), seek to control youth's bodies (and sexuality), define youth citizenship (Burgess 2002; Diouf 2003), placate youth through tokenism (Campbell et al. 2009), and mobilize youth via patronage for electoral politics and/or insurgent violence (Kagwanja 2005; Olaiya 2014; Van Gyampo, Graham, and Asare 2017). In Kenya's 2022 presidential election, for example, William Ruto played up his background as a young person "hustling" to survive by selling chickens, a clear appeal to youth voters in that "hustler nation" (Walsh 2022).

Waithood is not a moment of "doing nothing" or "sitting around." Rather, it is a time of creating, improvising, experimenting, and maneuvering to redefine what the future will be (Dawson 2014; Honwana

---

[4] Scholars globally have written about waiting youth, from American millennials "failing to launch" to "parasite singles" in Japan (see Durham 2017, 1).

[5] A fifteen-year-old may be considered an adult because she has a job or a child, just as an eighty-year-old may be considered a child because his dementia prevents self-care.

2012; Utas 2005). Although youth face relational obligations, they remain actors with aspirations and dignity in their own right (Jungar and Oinas 2011). In the political space, many vote, some advocate, a few protest, and most work toward their communities' development (Van Gyampo and Obeng-Odoom 2012). They may actively situate themselves in neopatrimonial networks with their elders, thereby challenging the idea that they are "captured." In pursuit of a new status, they may capitalize on such connections (Iwilade 2013). Being youth may mean challenging social norms, renegotiating social relations, and adopting new identities. Youth embrace new modes for political action: hip hop and rap (Fredericks 2014; Perullo 2005), the mystification of politics (Ifeka 2006), disruptive activities (Iwilade 2020), "hustle as a criticism of government" (Thieme 2013), and social media's global reach (Akor 2017; Iwilade 2013). Youth contest their political identity in the street (Diouf 2003), classroom (Quaynor 2015a), worship space (Gusman 2009), university (Asiedu-Acquah 2019), and on the athletic field (Dyck 2011). As foot soldiers in ethnic movements that shape West African democracies (Olaiya 2014), as protesters who push policy changes (Akor 2017), and as voters who help to determine election outcomes (Resnick 2022), youth often (though not always) realize their power and reach beyond conventional possibilities.

Our analysis mirrors this tension in defining youth, in that we both incorporate a chronological view and recognize the meaning of "youth" as deictic. In order to investigate broad trends in survey data from Afrobarometer, we define "youth" as people aged eighteen to thirty-five years. However, our respondents neither stressed chronological age as foundational for identity nor divorced youth identity from "gender, social class, ethnicity, religion and other social distinctions" (Oinas, Onodera, and Suurpää 2018, 4). Thus, as we analyze our qualitative data, we pay less attention to strict age ranges. Our respondents illustrated that being youth means facing problems they believed to be uniquely theirs while also actively and creatively striving to honor local relationships, meet obligations to the state, and build the nation – all actions they classified as citizenship.

1.2 The Theory of Everyday Citizenship

Scholars have theorized extensively on citizenship in Africa (see Dorman 2020; Dorman, Hammett, and Nugent 2007; Keller 2014;

Manby 2009; Ndegwa 1997; Nyamnjoh 2007; Pailey 2021; Smith 2013). While not denying the richness of this literature, we lean on recent scholarship that emphasizes the everyday nature of politics and citizenship in order to understand the words and deeds of the youth we encountered (see Beveridge and Koch 2019; Guillaume and Huysmans 2018; Jacobs and Sonneveld 2021; Paller 2021; Puumala and Shindo 2021). This literature recognizes the "politics of in-between" – avenues through which marginalized peoples may not embrace formal political processes but view informal actions as having political meaning (Barreto and Muñoz 2003). Benedict Kerkvliet (2005, 22) explains:

Everyday politics ... involves people embracing, adjusting to, or contesting norms and rules regarding authority ... or allocation of resources. It includes quiet, mundane, and subtle expressions and acts ... [it] involves little or no organization. It features the activities of individuals and small groups as they make a living, raise their families, wrestle with daily problems.

This perspective recognizes citizen status, participatory acts at all levels of government and in civil society, and sites of citizen struggle (Gouws 2005). By stressing the everyday, our inductive approach addresses Naila Kabeer's (2005, 1) concern that much of the debate about citizenship occurs in an "empirical void" that reproduces categories imposed from above and not very applicable to the reality of political life.

Everyday citizenship first recognizes that citizenship is a sense of belonging, which in turn shapes one's rights and responsibilities within the community. Definitions of community and belonging are fluid, emerging "in places where seemingly nothing more than ordinary life or mundane, routine-like practices of governance, negotiation, and disruption take place" (Puumala and Shindo 2021, 745). Everyday citizenship is not about scale (e.g., small), site (e.g., local), or practice (e.g., routine) but instead acknowledges that political life is common and abundant, and citizenship is continuously being articulated in "everyday multiple scenes and sites" (Guillaume and Huysmans 2018). As youth conflate "the domestic and public spheres" (Diouf 2003), everyday citizenship disrupts an elite-focused political analysis, recognizes the agency of ordinary people, and urges examination of "the social practices of individuals" (Paller 2021). In adopting everyday citizenship as our guiding principle rather than trying to squeeze the perspectives of our youth participants into a rigid classification system, we emulate the work of Nic Cheeseman, Gabrielle Lynch, and Justin Willis (2020, 52), who view elections as a field of contestation and claims making in which people draw on interconnected concepts for understanding. Thus, everyday citizenship brings in elements from conventional liberal and communal models but recognizes a "flexibility of citizenship" (Nyamnjoh 2007).

As a conceptual guide, everyday citizenship contributes several insights to our study of youth citizenship. First, it blurs the lines between "citizenship-from-above" and "citizenship-from-below" (Puumala and Shindo 2021), just as our respondents did. Citizenship-from-above lies in relation to the state – a territory with sovereignty and the legitimate monopoly on the use of force (Nyamnjoh 2007). The state sets the boundaries for citizenship by codifying citizen legal requirements in constitutions and documenting citizen belonging through legibility. With a passive legal status that sets basic citizen obligations, this vertical relationship (encapsulated in the liberal citizenship model) focuses on autonomous individuals who are linked to a state that is supposed to uphold their rights and allow citizens to make legitimate claims for rights protection (Isin and Turner 2007, 5–17; Keller 2014, 19; Patterson 1999, 4). When individuals participate in the political process to select leaders and demand state accountability, they engage in citizenship-from-above (Bratton 2013; von Lieres 2014).

Citizenship-from-above reflects Western views of political identity that do not fully align with Africa's political history (Ekeh 1975; Ndegwa 1997). Under colonialism most individuals were subjects incorporated into the governing apparatus through state-enforced customary order. They were not recognized as citizens with rights, and they had no opportunities to claim rights through participation (Mamdani 1996). After independence, African ruling elites embraced some notions of liberal citizenship as they propagated a universal national identity and assumed that legally defined citizens would meet their obligations to the state in exchange for the state's protection of rights (Dorman 2020). This promulgated "civic public" remained distant from most Africans' sense of obligations and rights, making it "immoral" in the eyes of many and leading people to give to it only "grudgingly" (Ekeh 1975, 108). This citizenship-from-above paid little attention to the realm of "primordial groupings, ties, and sentiments" rooted in moral imperatives and influential for the public interest (Ekeh 1975, 92). In contrast, citizenship-from-below encompasses the arena of neighborhoods, villages, ethnic groups, and family lineages (Peter Ekeh's "primordial public") to which the citizen "gives out and asks for nothing in return" (Ekeh 1975, 108). This citizenship reflects how people's responsibility toward the community is wrapped up in the very ways their identity is defined by that community (Geschiere 2009). Ethnic patterns of voting, the loyalty some feel toward religious organizations, and mobilization through CBOs in urban neighborhoods indicate that citizenship-from-below can play a role in fostering belonging (Hershey 2013; Sommers 2010).

By blurring the line between citizenship-from-above and citizenship-from-below, we echo Ekeh's point about the dialectical relationship between the civic and primordial publics. Everyday citizens may engage in state-oriented processes such as elections in which their legal status permits participation. They may even do so partially to hold the state accountable and express policy preferences (Hern 2019). But everyday citizens also may vote in order to bring patronage to the community (Bratton 2008; Ferree and Long 2016; McCauley 2012). Responsibilities to the local community (citizenship-from-below) may lead some to demand rights protection from the state (citizenship-from-above) – a practice we saw when youth voted, advocated, and formed organizations rooted in their communal concerns.

A second insight that the concept of everyday citizenship brings is recognition that ordinary people continuously contest citizen identities and definitions of community. As a result, the community stretches beyond the state to include neighborhood organizations, sites of religious worship, and the marketplace. Contestation occurs at different scales and within particular historical and political contexts. Subjectivity shapes these processes, as citizenship is "as much a question of individual and reciprocal perception, events, and struggles as a political and legal status" (Puumala and Shindo 2021, 745; see also Caglar 2015, 640; Casey 2008, 66; Guillaume and Huysmans 2018). Subjectivity and contestation mean that legal views of citizenship are insufficient, for they do not acknowledge how other identities such as race, class, gender, ethnicity, sexuality, and/or nationality matter for citizen belonging (Nyamnjoh 2007; Yuval-Davis 2007). Contestation occurs when some use informal and formal political processes to define identity in ways that extend rights and resources while excluding or perpetrating violence against those considered to be noncitizens (Bøås 2009; Dorman, Hammett, and Nugent 2007; Mamdani 1996;

Manby 2009). Kenya's 2007 post-election violence, the legal exclusion of "outsiders" in Côte d'Ivoire, and South Africa's race-exclusive political parties illustrate this contestation at the macro level (Englebert 2009; Holmes 2020; Whitaker 2005). At the micro level, contestation over community and identity occurs through words and deeds (Isin and Nielsen 2008, 2; Isin and Turner 2007, 16; Pailey 2016) by which ordinary people show agency as they claim rights, act to marginalize others, or choose not to act at all (Puumala and Shindo 2021, 747).

Third, everyday citizenship recognizes the multiplicity of activities that constitute citizenship. This dynamic involves "processes of transforming and becoming" (Bird 2016, 263; Isin and Nielsen 2008, 2) through context-specific "repertoires of citizenship" (Caglar 2015). These may include actions to target the state through state-ordained processes (e.g., voting) and state-rejected activities (e.g., protesting), as well as micro-level deeds such as creating jobs, paying school fees, or caring for the sick (Kershaw 2010; Lister 1997; Pailey 2016; Patterson 2019). Because citizenship-from-below and citizenship-from-above are blurred, micro acts may inform how citizens engage in explicitly political spaces. For example, communal labor, cultural organizations, and even sports clubs in impoverished neighborhoods may lead some to embrace contentious politics as they come face-to-face with local power structures (Diouf 1999).

Acknowledging a diversity of citizenship acts adds a twist to the portrayal of Africans as subjects who delegate authority to leaders, not citizens who actively claim their rights (Bratton 2013; Gyimah-Boadi 2015). Surveys done around the time of our fieldwork show that, although an average of 68 percent of Africans report voting in the most recent election, far fewer engage in political actions such as contacting a government official or working with others to press government to address a problem (Afrobarometer 2016/2018). By viewing citizenship through the lens of the everyday, we can question *why* people chose other citizen avenues. They may perceive that the state lacks legitimacy and capacity because of its colonial foundation (Bezabeh 2011; Englebert 2009). As an entity "under construction" (Dorman, Hammett, and Nugent 2007), the state is a "twilight institution" that jockeys with donors, subnational governments, NGOs, CBOs, faith-based organizations (FBOs), religious leaders, and traditional leaders to assert public authority, extract material and political resources, and disperse benefits (Chabal and Daloz 1999; Lund 2006). Everyday citizens engage with these authority structures, even those that "might not be measurable or observable" (Paller 2021), to negotiate citizen belonging (Jabril 2013; Oduro 2009; Piper and von Lieres 2015). As agents, these everyday citizens amplify, define, and contest their reciprocal ties to such authorities, thereby stretching these relations beyond conventional patronage politics. Our examination of youth everyday citizenship highlights the complexity and potentially positive aspects of interpersonal politics.

Everyday citizenship is distinct from other concepts. It is not nationalism, though it may at times be expressed as patriotism, "love of the nation," or an obligation to "build the nation" (Zembylas 2014, 8; see Young 2007). In surveys, high numbers of Africans report a national identity, despite the state's artificial, colonial-era borders, its inclusion of diverse populations (Joseph 2003), its insufficient provision of public goods, and its minimal authority over territory (Herbst 2000). This "nationalism paradox" may result from elites who drum up national identities to achieve political goals (Englebert 2009; Miguel 2004; Posner 2005), citizens who instrumentalize such identities to access state resources (Englebert 2009, 203), or communities that link citizenship to familyhood and ancestry (Bhandari and Mueller 2019, 299). Nationalism is often (though not always) circumscribed to a geographic entity, but everyday citizenship emphasizes that community and identity are contested through acts that generate belonging in multiple geographic spaces.

Everyday citizenship is not synonymous with the concepts of civil society, political values, or social capital. Civil society is the collection of organizations outside the realm of the state, market economy, and family that people establish around a shared interest (Bratton 1989; Gyimah-Boadi 1996; Obadare 2011, 2016; VonDoepp 2020). In contrast, everyday citizenship is a contested identity rooted in quotidian actions that define rights and responsibilities in community. Citizenship contestation might occur in a civil society organization, but also in the family, marketplace, house of worship, or courthouse. In addition, political values may undergird, but be distinct from, everyday citizenship as they shape how community is understood, who is perceived "to belong," and who has rights and responsibilities. For example, the "civic culture" of allegiance to authority, belief in institutional legitimacy, and trust in society may lead people to perceive citizenship to include paying taxes, following the law, and voting (Almond and Verba 1963). Similarly, values such as respect for traditional authorities and family responsibility may matter for how people understand and act out their citizenship (Chabal and Daloz 1999; Ekeh 1975). Finally, everyday citizenship is not social capital. A criticized concept (see Harriss and de Renzio 1997), social capital has been variously defined as webs of trust, solidarity, and reciprocity (Putnam 1994; Woolcock 1998); as a by-product of social position that undergirds power (Bourdieu 1986); and as a collective asset that emerges from networks and interactions (Coleman 1988). Social capital is often viewed to "be productive" because it helps individuals or communities achieve political power, democracy, development, and/or service delivery (Putnam 1994, 167). As an action-oriented, contested identity, everyday citizenship is not the asset of social capital, although – through processes of citizenship contestation over belonging – social capital may emerge.

In summary, as Robtel Neajai Pailey (2016, 2) writes, citizenship is not just a "bundle of rights embedded in constructions of local, national, and cultural identity, but it is also a set of practices and interactions embodied in the life-worlds." For the youth in this study, everyday citizenship includes practices (or active elements) and "a set of relations" (or interactive elements). It is a dynamic sense of belonging that transverses the public and private realms; occurs at multiple levels; and is rooted in words, deeds, and emotions.

1.3 Case Selection and Within-Study Variation

Our focus on Ghana, Tanzania, and Uganda (with secondary cases from South Africa and Zambia) echoes a research trend in African politics that has tended to privilege more populous, wealthier, Christian-majority anglophone countries, while francophone, smaller, and Muslim-majority states have been underrepresented (Briggs 2017). Despite this limitation, our study countries are broadly representative of different regions, rates of urbanization, levels of economic development, and political freedoms. Our findings may not extend to francophone or lusophone countries, Muslim majority countries, or rural areas. However, we were struck by the fact that – although on some elements of citizenship, country context seemed to matter – the vast majority of youth we encountered held many common citizenship views across our countries of study. Scholars working in underrepresented countries could consider these trends in future work.

Table 1.1 illustrates several general similarities in the study countries. First, although they differ in the percentage of the population that is urban, they all have significant annual urban population growth rates. Second, they are relatively similar in measures of economic development, although Ghana has achieved a higher gross national income (GNI) per capita and Human Development Index (HDI) than Tanzania or Uganda. Despite their relatively low economic freedom measures, all espouse neoliberal policies such as trade promotion, reliance on the private sector, and improved competitiveness (Government of Ghana 2020; USAID 2021, 8–10; World Bank 2020c, 2022). In addition, all are Christian-majority countries. We deliberately sought such countries because churches are a significant social outlet for youth. Across Africa, 23 percent of youth aged eighteen to thirty-five say they are "active members" of religious organizations compared to 17 percent for community or volunteer organizations (Afrobarometer 2016/2018). Churches have deliberately appealed to youth through programming on everything from leadership training to community outreach (Boyd 2014; Kalu 2008; Marshall 2009). In addition, some churches are outspoken on political and development issues and provide social services – factors that may shape how youth understand citizenship (Gifford 1998; McCauley 2012; McClendon and Riedl 2019; Patterson and Kuperus 2016).

The most notable difference between the countries lies in political regime type. Freedom House (2022) classified Ghana as a "free" country, Tanzania as "partly free," and Uganda as "not free." This within-study variation allows us to draw out differences in views on citizenship among these countries' youth that may relate to the political context. For example, youth respondents in Tanzania and Uganda referenced the lack of freedom more often than youth in Ghana. The within-study variation also enables us to assess similarities among youth respondents regardless of political context. Country context can provide useful insights when we analyze everyday citizenship across income levels (Chapter 4), frequency of church attendance (Chapter 5), and gender identification (Chapter 6). Because citizenship is not divorced from the political arrangements under which youth live (Senay 2008, 974–75), we provide more background on each country's political experiences, focusing on the postcolonial period up until

Table 1.1 *Country case comparisons*

Country	Region	Urban (%) (annual growth %)	Human Development Index (ranking)*	GNI per capita	Economic freedom ranking**	Religious makeup***(%)	Freedom House ranking
Ghana	West	57 (3.3)	0.611 (138)	USD 5,269	110	Christian (71) Muslim (18) Traditional (6)	Free
Tanzania	East	35 (5.0)	0.529 (163)	USD 2,600	126	Christian (63) Muslim (34) Other (3)	Partly free
Uganda	East	25 (5.7)	0.544 (159)	USD 2,123	125	Protestant (45) Catholic (39) Muslim (14) Other (1)	Not free

* Using a scale of 0–1, HDI includes life expectancy, school enrollment, and GNI per capita. Higher numbers mean higher development. Country ranks are out of 189, with a higher rank indicating lower development.

** Of 167 countries, with a higher rank indicating less freedom

*** Historic divisions between Protestants and Catholics in Uganda mean these two Christian groups are often reported separately.

Sources: Freedom House (2022); Index Mundi (2021); Legatum Institute (2021); UNDP (2021); World Bank (2021), compiled by the authors

fieldwork in 2018 and centering on key themes that our youth respondents emphasized: democratic accomplishments and political stability in Ghana; state paternalism, national unity, and uncertain freedoms in Tanzania; and military autocracy in Uganda.

1.3.1 Ghana: Democratic Accomplishments and Political Stability

Ghana has been referred to as the "success story of liberal democracy in Africa" (Cheeseman, Lynch, and Willis 2020, 60) because of its transition from military rule to a competitive two-party system. A precolonial history of landowning elites, state development, and a broad appreciation for public authority provided a foundation for Ghana's state system. Throughout British colonialism, these elites constituted an African economic and professional establishment, and, through the United Gold Coast Convention (UGCC), they initiated negotiations toward independence in the 1950s. Economically conservative and tied to traditional leaders, this Danquah tradition (named for J. B. Danquah of the UGCC) is embodied in today's New Patriotic Party (NPP). The UGCC was poised to rule after independence, but Kwame Nkrumah mobilized workers, teachers, market women, clerks, and urban youth to win a key 1951 election and then gained the upper hand in negotiations for independence in 1957 (Apter 1968; Cheeseman, Lynch, and Willis 2020).

As president, Nkrumah sought to bring associational life (trade unions, cocoa farmers, professional organizations) under party control and to centralize economic policies. The adoption of a one-party state in 1964, increasing corruption, economic stagnation, and behind-the-scenes Western support helped the military stage a coup d'état in 1966. A 1969 election brought Kofi Busia (of the Danquah tradition) to power, but economic challenges led the military to intervene again in 1972. With an election scheduled for 1979, Flight Lieutenant Jerry Rawlings staged a coup d'état but then handed power to Hilla Limann (Chazan 1992). In 1981, Rawlings again staged a coup d'état, and his military government ruled until public pressure and donors' nudging led Rawlings to agree to multiparty elections in 1992 (Cheeseman, Lynch, and Willis 2020, 69; Gyimah-Boadi 1994), a contest his National Democratic Congress (NDC) easily won (and won again in 1996). Even though our respondents were children during the

Rawlings era, several spoke positively about his populist vision for a more equitable Ghana and his willingness to honor the constitutional limit of two presidential terms (Cheeseman, Lynch, and Willis 2020, 60; GH Interviews 9, 10).

In the 2000 election, the NPP capitalized on a charismatic presidential candidate, a strong campaign organization, significant funding (Nugent 2001), an economic downturn, and charges of NDC corruption to give Ghana its first experience with alternation in power (Gyimah-Boadi 2001). Alternation was repeated in 2008 (when the NPP lost) and 2016 (when the NDC lost and the sitting president John Mahama – who assumed the presidency after the death of President John Evans Atta Mills in 2012 – was denied a second term). Not only have elections become more competitive – the NDC won in 2008 with roughly 50,000 votes and the number of "swing districts" has increased (see Gyimah-Boadi 2009) – but they also have become relatively more peaceful (Lynch, Cheeseman, and Willis 2019). Although some party vigilantes have engaged in property destruction, intimidation, and low-level violence, most have assisted in voter registration and party get-out-the-vote efforts (Bjarnesen 2020; Van Gyampo, Graham, and Asare 2017).

Several factors undergird Ghana's political stability. Political and economic elites have dense networks that facilitate trust across party lines, a professionalized military has little interest in politics (Osei 2018), the middle class demands stability (Hamidu 2015), power is somewhat decentralized to include elites in private businesses and social institutions (Osei 2016), the public supports democracy (Gyimah-Boadi 2009), and electoral institutions have increased in legitimacy. Indeed, when the NPP challenged the 2012 election results, it helped to push needed electoral reforms and improve voter education and election observation efforts (Bob-Milliar and Paller 2018).[6] Perhaps most crucially, Ghana's entrenched, two-party system promotes stability. Parties have strong organizations – as is evident in university party wings, football clubs, and media outlets – and voters often are socialized into party identification through the family. The two-party system and majority-vote for presidential elections

---

[6] The 2020 election, which the NPP incumbent Nana Akufo-Addo won with 51 percent of the vote, indicates continued two-party competition and, despite the NDC's unsuccessful court challenge, a willingness to play by the rules.

incentivize playing by the rules, since each party has the chance to win (Osei 2018), though some youth reported that partisanship had made politics increasingly divisive (see Chapter 7). Although scholars debate if voters are more evaluative or patrimonial, many voters base their decisions on the party's past performance (Cheeseman, Lynch, and Willis 2017; Lindberg and Morrison 2008, 121), the current economic situation (Bob-Milliar and Paller 2018; Gyimah-Boadi 2009), campaign messages, concerns over corruption (Arthur 2009), and a belief that party leaders will institute policy changes (Nathan 2019). Voters increasingly view effective state performance to be a "right of national citizenship" (MacLean et al. 2016). Voting decisions are not primarily ethnically based (Kpessa-Whyte and Abu 2021), although Akan peoples in Ashanti and Eastern regions tend to support the NPP, while northerners and the Ewe tend to support the NDC (Arthur 2009; Dickovick 2008; Driscoll 2020). Ethnicity also shapes grassroots partisan networks that provide access to clientelistic benefits (Nathan 2019).

Ghana has been referred to as a "patronage democracy," with concerns that clientelism and corruption undermine its democratic achievements. Illustrating "competitive clientelism," local officials may direct state resources in ways that ultimately undermine development goals (Abdulai and Hickey 2016). Voters make individual and collective demands on leaders from village chiefs to parliamentarians regardless of party (Lindberg 2010), and political vigilantes may participate in campaigning because they seek personalized goods (Van Gyampo, Graham, and Asare 2017). But the emphasis on these instrumental and private benefits can diminish how recipients couch demands in the language of development and community (Cheeseman, Lynch, and Willis 2020, 73) – a pattern our respondents emulated when they discussed citizenship. In addition, the diffuse, face-to-face, and long-term nature of relations between leaders and local people embodies a deep concern for others' welfare (Paller 2019, 51–53). Our respondents echoed these nuanced views of clientelism, as they situated their citizenship in the context of the country's democratic success and stability.

1.3.2 Tanzania: State Paternalism, National Unity, and Uncertain Freedoms

Tanzania's politics and society remain deeply influenced by the ideas and actions of the first president, Julius Nyerere. Upon independence from Britain in 1961 and the unification of Tanganyika and Zanzibar in 1964, Nyerere emphasized socialism to "build the nation" (*kujenga taifa*) and promote self-reliance (*kujitegemea*). The 1967 Arusha Declaration established the Ujamaa policy (meaning "community-hood" or "familyhood") that included nationalization of privately-owned properties, relocation of peasants to new villages (90 percent of the population was rural), expropriation of land, industrialization, and a mandatory two-year national service program for youth (Boone and Nyeme 2015; Burgess 1999; Green 2010; Scott 1998, 235). Over time, Ujamaa became top-down and coercive, directed by ruling party elites who extracted labor as a form of unregulated taxation on peasants and youth (Phillips 2018, 16, 138; Scott 1998; Shivji 2012). The policy contributed to a culture of conformity, because those who questioned Ujamaa – including party youth – were viewed as "offender[s] against the proper order of things" (Schneider 2014, 49; 58–59). It also emphasized a hierarchical and paternalistic state that perceived its actions as being in citizens' interests (Green 2010) and that framed those actions using a family narrative (Phillips 2018, 20).

Nyerere also sought to promote national identity in a country with approximately 120 ethnic groups and several religious traditions. He banned religiously or ethnically based schools, declared that citizenship would be nonracial, and required that Swahili be used for all official documents and for instruction in most schools (Lofchie 2014). These policies, as well as institutional arrangements that cause individuals to downplay ethnic identities to access land and state services (Boone and Nyeme 2015, 83), contribute to national identity. Indeed, at the time of our fieldwork, 47 percent of Tanzanians said they identified only as Tanzanians, compared to the African average of 33 percent (Afrobarometer 2016/2018). The emphasis on national identity and state paternalism have facilitated unity and stability, but these narratives also may deny legitimate and specific ethnic, religious, and regional concerns, divert responsibility, silence opposition, and minimize civil society activism (Phillips 2018, 15, 21).

After Nyerere voluntarily stepped down in 1985, Tanzania underwent a democratic "transition from above," with political liberalization occurring without protests or violence (Cheeseman 2015, 97). At the same time, the country underwent World Bank required economic liberalization. Between 1995 and 2015, Tanzanians experienced increasing levels of freedom (Becker 2021; Whitehead 2012),[7] although the ruling *Chama cha Mapinduzi* (CCM) (Party of the Revolution) continued to win sizable electoral victories. This one-party dominance reflected the opposition's limited funding, the CCM's credentials as the party of Nyerere, and its grassroots penetration (Bakari and Whitehead 2013). Through formal and informal means, the CCM has become present in all aspects of governance (i.e., local government, public services, security forces), civil society organizations, the media, and business (Whitehead 2012). Despite this dominance, the opposition *Chama cha Demokrasia na Maendeleo* (CHADEMA) (Party of Democracy and Development) gradually expanded its reach, capitalizing on increasing disappointment with the government's poor performance on poverty eradication, rural development, and corruption (Becker 2021; Collord 2019; Paget 2022). CHADEMA's vote grew from 6 percent in 2005 to 40 percent in 2015, a year when, because of internal divisions, the CCM won just 58 percent of the vote. These divisions led John Magufuli – a party stalwart, Minister of Roads, and someone perceived to be outside the party's grand corruption – to become the CCM nominee and then president.

President Magufuli claimed to speak for the downtrodden (*wanyonge*) and for ordinary citizens (*wananchi*), and he capitalized on nostalgia for Nyerere's "good old days" in order to mobilize support for his increasingly nationalistic and authoritarian rule. His "New Tanzania" policy stressed industrialization, state economic intervention, infrastructure development, CCM control over parastatals, and military-owned industries (Collord 2019; Paget 2020a; Thiong'o 2021). He used corruption allegations to target mid-level state officials (portrayed as lazy and corrupt), business leaders (portrayed as greedy cheats), and foreigners (portrayed as exploitative) (Paget 2020a, 1247; 2020b). His slogan *Hapa Kazi Tu* (There is only work here) stressed productivity and honesty, and he showed up unannounced at government offices to see if people were working. Over ten thousand civil servants lost their jobs – some, on the spot. The regime curtailed political space by restricting opposition party rallies and meetings, detaining and prosecuting opposition leaders,

---

[7] Felicitas Becker (2021) points out that this decade of relative freedom was an historical anomaly, since a paternalistic, controlling state has dominated most of Tanzania's postcolonial history.

expanding laws to control NGOs, disqualifying most opposition candidates for the 2019 local elections, detaining journalists, and closing media sites (Paget 2021). A 2017 assassination attempt against CHADEMA leader Tundu Lissu led many opposition leaders to go into hiding or to defect to the CCM.[8] The 2020 national elections witnessed "unprecedented" manipulation and repression, leading Magufuli to win 84 percent of the vote (Paget 2021, 61). In 2018, the prevailing atmosphere of fear and silence colored our discussions with many youth, but when one author returned to Tanzania in mid-2021, the political environment was beginning to change. Magufuli's sudden death in March 2021 brought his vice president Samia Suluhu Hassan to power, creating opportunities for some political liberalization (see Chapter 6).

1.3.3 Uganda: Military Autocracy

Uganda's political situation reflects political crises that date to before independence. Tensions over religion and traditional authority emerged in the mid-1800s, when Islam and Christianity, and then Protestants (the Church Mission Society) and Catholics, vied for the support of the Buganda king (*kabaka*). Sectarian conflict led to several massacres, but the Protestants emerged triumphant in 1892, when Britain declared a protectorate and collaborated with the *kabaka*, thereby giving Buganda chiefs significant political and economic power (Downie 2015). Before the 1962 pre-independence election, the *kabaka* sided with the Protestant-dominated Uganda People's Congress (UPC), led by Milton Obote, against the Catholic-dominated Democratic Party (DP). Upon election, Obote established a semi-federal state that honored traditional authority. But in 1966, his military stormed the palace, dissolved all Ugandan kingdoms, established a unitary state, banned the DP, and began a radical nationalization effort (Cheeseman, Lynch, and Willis 2020, 77–78). A coup d'état in 1971 brought Idi Amin's repressive and corrupt regime to power. A Tanzanian invasion toppled Amin in 1979 and brought Obote and his exiled supporters back to power. Voters enthusiastically participated in the 1980 election (turnout was 90 percent), but Obote's use of intimidation, vote buying,

---

[8] Lissu was shot sixteen times with an automatic weapon and spent over two years abroad receiving medical care.

and electoral tampering undermined electoral legitimacy. Yoweri Museveni, a former Obote government member and guerrilla fighter, mobilized an insurrection that marched into Kampala in 1986. The "bush war" left over four hundred thousand people dead, and, along with Amin's policies, decimated the economy and fomented massive poverty (Ottaway 1999).

When Museveni's National Resistance Movement (NRM) took control, it first needed to foster stability and unity, particularly since it was perceived to be dominated by people from the southwest (Ottaway 1999, 30). The NRM recognized traditional authorities and worked through constituent assemblies to write a constitution that established a "no-party" system in which political parties could exist but not campaign. In the 1996 and 2001 elections, many candidates competed, though Museveni and the NRM won large majorities. Museveni continuously raised the specter of the country's violent past and the insurrection of the Lord's Resistance Army in northwest Uganda to gain votes. He also pointed to the country's growing economy – an annual growth rate of 6.7 percent between 1986 and 1999 and a poverty rate that declined from 56 percent in 1990 to 38 percent in 2002 (Patterson 2006, 32). Despite the no-party competition, donors funded half of the budget in the 1990s (Hauser 1999), enabling Museveni to build strong patronage ties to rural constituencies (Oloka-Onyango 2004). By the time Museveni agreed to the 2005 referendum to allow multiparty elections and remove presidential term limits, he had established a broad base of support (Keating 2011).

Despite multipartyism, the state's known capacity for violence means that even *threats* of violence ensure that many Ugandans vote for the NRM, and party rivals do not emerge (Vokes and Wilkins 2016). In the 2006, 2011, 2016, and 2021 elections, the regime harassed and arrested opposition leaders and used its massive patronage machine to deter other opposition leaders (Beardsworth 2016; Mwenda 2007). Significant NRM campaign spending makes elections "only about the money" (UG Interview 18), and NRM candidates often make it clear to voters that access to basic services is dependent on voting for the NRM (Cheeseman, Lynch, and Willis 2020, 85).

Aili Tripp (2010, 31) has described Uganda as a hybrid regime, one in which, paradoxically, there are some freedoms but "power rests with the security forces." Since the early 2010s, freedoms for civil society organizations and the media have declined. A 2016 law required NGOs to endure stringent registration rules and governmental approval for activities, and a social media tax in 2018 curtailed access to private media sources for millions (Selnes and Orgeret 2020). In this "military autocracy" (Oloka-Onyango and Ahikire 2017), the president has put military officers in key political posts, parliamentary seats, and cabinet ministries. Economic growth and generous foreign aid (over USD 2 billion in 2019) enable the president to give these ministries sizable budgets and business deals in return for loyalty (Bareebe 2020; World Bank 2021). With his son heading the elite Special Forces Command, Museveni has cemented control over the military and police (Abrahamson and Bareebe 2021) – a control facilitated by the over USD 300 million in US security aid Uganda received between 2011 and 2017 for the War on Terror (Congressional Research Service 2018). In addition, the president has consolidated control within the NRM, centralized economic and political power among those from the southwest (Lindemann 2011a, 2011b), and made parliamentarians dependent on his patronage (Collord 2016; Keating 2011). Parliament rarely challenges him, as is illustrated by overwhelming support for the 2017 constitutional amendment to remove the age limit for presidential candidates, a vote for which each NRM parliamentarian allegedly received USD 7,500. The change allowed Museveni to run again in 2021(Cheeseman, Lynch, and Willis 2020, 85–86).

The youth we met in 2018 hinted at several patterns that were manifest in the 2021 election. They discussed the corruption, political exclusion, and poverty that would be themes in the campaign of the musician-turned-politician Robert Kyagulanyi Ssentamu (a.k.a. Bobi Wine). Unlike their parents, who remember the insecurity before Museveni, many of our youth respondents had become increasingly angry about the septuagenarian president's long tenure (see Chapter 7). Youth participated at high levels in the 2021 election, despite its significant violence and electoral malfeasance. Although Museveni won, his 58 percent total (the lowest ever) may hint that the elite bargain among various ethnic, regional, and religious groups is crumbling. The youth's "unrelenting" desire for change may push the regime to a pretorian move, potentially dividing the party and military and "raising the specter of civil strife" (Abrahamsen and Bareebe 2021, 102).

1.4 A Methodology That Centers Youth Voices

While many citizenship studies focus on surveys (Bleck and van de Walle 2018; Bratton 2013) or on country or local case studies (Bodewes 2010; Hern 2019; Paller 2019), we use a broadly comparative and inductive approach and incorporate multiple methodologies. Our actor-oriented focus takes youth voices seriously and strives to understand how youth view and act on citizenship (Long 1990). We rely primarily on interviews and focus group discussions with youth that we conducted in 2018, and case studies conducted in 2011, 2019, and 2021. We pair this qualitative data with quantitative survey data from Afrobarometer Round 7 (2016/2018) on political behavior and attitudes. This pairing allows us to nuance Afrobarometer survey results completed at roughly the time of our fieldwork and to explore how youth understand citizenship conceptually and practically.

1.4.1 Focus Group Discussions

Although political scientists have been slow to adopt focus group discussions (Cyr 2016), we prioritized this method because it allows respondents to engage freely and spontaneously with research topics (Onwuegbuzie et al. 2009), inevitably uncovering new variables and causal processes. By driving the discussion, respondents often reveal far more interesting data than researchers might collect through more formalized processes. Researchers can gather individual and group-level data, as well as data through the interactive, iterative *discussion* of a topic (Cyr 2017). Focus group discussions allow people to grapple with complex topics collectively and, at times, to express shared, intersubjective understandings, often in a more social setting (McDonnell 2010). These exchanges and synthesizing conversations allowed us to see the nuances of everyday youth citizenship. This was apparent as conversations moved from an initial, legalistic view of citizenship ("having an identification card") to descriptions of the relational, obligatory nature of citizen belonging. The focus group discussions helped us to see what citizenship means in the everyday lives of youth (Paller 2019).

This methodology also offered us some protection against the imposition of our own understanding of, or assumptions about, citizenship (see Cyr 2017, 1038). Prioritizing emic data helped us to step back as youth responded to our opening question, "What does it mean to be a good citizen?" Although we used the term "citizen," our open-ended questions led youth to engage with citizenship-adjacent ideas and to convey unique stories of what citizenship meant in their lives. Just as Frederic Schaffer (2000) sought contextual understanding of democracy in Senegal and Nic Cheeseman, Gabrielle Lynch, and Justin Willis (2020) investigated normative views of elections, we let our respondents define citizenship through their debates. Their numerous definitions illustrated their vocabulary for citizenship, and their emotionally charged debates and vivid examples make us confident that respondents found citizenship both interesting and salient. However, as with any methodology, focus group discussions have some limitations. Researchers hear from only a small number of respondents, who may not be representative of all voices. Even when participants know each other, focus groups are an artificial setting, some individuals may dominate, groupthink is possible, and the presence of researchers may stifle conversations. To guard against these challenges, we collaborated with community members to identify respondents, thoroughly explained our project, worked with host-country national research partners, and provided significant time for conversations.

Our data collection design reflects the desire to hear from youth with various backgrounds that might shape their citizenship views. We identified neighborhoods where we could encounter youth across economic situations (in high- and low-income areas), from mainline and renewalist church backgrounds,[9] and across gender lines. We conducted a total of thirty-nine focus group discussions (sixteen in Uganda, nine in Tanzania, and fourteen in Ghana). We started with the variable of church attendance, selecting four churches in each city, two in low-income neighborhoods and two in middle- or high-income neighborhoods. We relied on local informants to identify various mainline or renewalist churches and to contact church leaders to arrange discussions with frequent churchgoing youth, whom we

---

[9] Mainline churches include colonial-era, mission-introduced churches (Protestants and Catholics). Renewalists include Pentecostal, charismatic, and evangelical churches, which have distinguishable historical and theological differences (see Sperber and Hern 2018). We use "renewalist" as an umbrella term (unless citing another study) to highlight these churches' relative singularity of political messaging, as well as similar traits like lively worship, members who profess being "born again," and lack of mission origin.

defined as attending church more than one to three times during a
three-month period (excluding weddings and funerals). (Those not
meeting this criterion were "infrequent churchgoers.") To tease out
potential gender differences in citizenship, we conducted separate
discussions with men and women when possible, though in some
churches we only conducted one mixed-gender focus group discussion.
(For the NVivo analysis, we separated out men's and women's
responses in those groups.) We then conducted a complementary set
of discussions with infrequent churchgoers. Almost every discussion
with infrequent churchgoers occurred in the same neighborhood as the
chosen churches and, again, most were segregated along gender lines.
We identified infrequent churchgoers through neighborhood leaders.
In all discussions, we asked how youth defined being a good citizen,
how (or if) citizenship differed for men and women, how youth
contributed to their community and country, their interest in public
affairs, (if applicable) how church attendance affected their views of
citizenship, and what community and/or religious leaders say about
citizenship (see Appendix 2 for questions).

Table 1.2 shows the number of focus group discussions per country
and their composition based on participants' gender, church attendance, and neighborhood. Participants met multiple criteria, such as
identifying as a woman, a frequent churchgoer, and a high-income

Table 1.2 *Number of focus group discussions by participant category and country*

Participant category	Ghana*	Tanzania**	Uganda***	Total
Women	6	2	8	16
Men	6	3	8	17
Mixed gender	2	4	0	6
High-income area residents	6	3	8	17
Low-income area residents	8	6	8	22
Frequent churchgoers	6	4	8	18
Renewalist churchgoers	3	1	4	8
Mainline churchgoers	3	3	4	10
Infrequent churchgoers	8	5	8	21

* Total Ghana groups = 14; **Total Tanzania groups = 9; ***Total Uganda groups = 16
Source: Compiled by the authors

neighborhood inhabitant. Each group discussion averaged six participants (with a few as large as ten), and country nationals assisted with introductions, question asking, and translating.

1.4.2 Interviews

We conducted thirty-three open-ended, in-depth interviews of thirty- to ninety-minute duration with youth who are engaged in politics or activism (eleven in Accra, ten in Dar es Salaam, and twelve in Kampala). The sample included eleven party leaders, four parliamentarians, one local government official, eight NGO officers, five CBO leaders, two protest movement leaders, and two student government leaders (Asante et al. 2021). Identified through news articles, local informants, and snowball sampling, respondents included sixteen women and seventeen men from various economic backgrounds. We did not interview individuals who were primarily entrepreneurs, although some of the NGOs and CBOs engaged in income-generating activities. Interview questions focused on two themes: (1) how youth activists defined good citizenship and (2) the factors that led to their public involvement. The first set of responses helped to nuance our focus group definitions of citizenship, while the second uncovered the drivers of youth engagement.

Because we were interested in how church programming relates to youth citizenship, we conducted twenty-eight key informant interviews with pastors at large mainline churches, and with officials at parachurch and ecumenical organizations (six in Accra, ten in Dar es Salaam, and twelve in Kampala). The organizations included the Christian Council of Ghana, the National Association of Charismatic and Christian Churches in Ghana, the Christian Council of Tanzania, the Tanzania Evangelical Fellowship, the Evangelical Lutheran Church in Tanzania (ELCT), the Uganda Joint Christian Council, the Inter-Religious Council of Uganda, and the National Catholic Secretariats of Uganda and Ghana. Because renewalist churches often lack governing bodies, we also conducted interviews with pastors at sizable renewalist congregations (Kalu 2008).

With permission, we audiotaped all interviews and focus group discussions from 2018, as well as those for the case studies conducted in 2011, 2019, and 2021. All respondents were promised anonymity in publications, and, with the exception of the Volmoed Youth

Leadership Training Programme (VYLTP) in South Africa, we have disguised the names of youth organizations, specific church congregations, and individuals.[10]

1.4.3 NVivo Analysis

We transcribed the audio recordings or employed native speakers to transcribe from Twi, Swahili, or Luganda. We read all documents for accuracy and then, for major themes that emerged around various questions. We hand-coded answers on questions about respondents' contributions to the community and country, the role of leaders in promoting citizenship, possible citizenship differences between men and women, and interest in public affairs. We also hand-coded the activist interviews and religious leader key informant interviews.

On the largest discussion topic – responses to the question, "What does it mean to be a good citizen?" and its follow-ups – we employed the content analysis program NVivo 11 to identify the frequency of thematic categories and to systematically compare these across youth in different strata. NVivo has been widely used in sociological, anthropological, public health, and, more recently, political science studies to generate themes from interviews, media stories, or social media posts (Kuperus and Asante 2021; Mohamed 2021; Motani et al. 2019). We first established a codebook of search terms for seven overarching citizenship themes that emerged in our reading of the transcripts: (1) communal, (2) build the nation, (3) moral, (4) legalistic, (5) participatory, (6) rights, (7) patriotic (see Appendix 1). We then searched for our codebook words to identify their frequency throughout the transcripts. To ensure NVivo's accuracy, we hand-coded roughly 10 percent of the focus group discussions. The NVivo analysis helped to identify broad patterns across the transcripts (a time-consuming task to do effectively by hand), to stratify findings by country and respondent characteristics (e.g., gender), and to discover a theme's overall weight. For example, words in the communal and build-the-nation

---

[10] The University of the South, Whitworth University, Calvin University, the Mengo Hospital Research Ethics Committee (Uganda), the University of Dar es Salaam, the Ethics Committee for the Humanities at the University of Ghana, and the University of Zambia provided ethics approval. The Uganda National Council for Science and Technology also provided ethics clearance. VYLTP committed to being identified in any research output.

categories were more prevalent than words in the participatory category. NVivo also efficiently checked our text reading and overall fieldwork perceptions, helped us determine words that youth used widely (possibly illustrating their specific concerns), and elucidated significant overlap in thematic categories. For example, ideas in the communal, build-the-nation, and moral categories often merged, as did those in the participatory and rights categories. This definitional murkiness illustrates the book's central theme: Everyday citizenship is fluid, contested, contextual, and action oriented precisely because it is tied to relationships, shared identities, obligations, and emotional attachments. To tease out these overlapping relationships, we returned to the transcripts and used the activist interviews to deepen our analysis.

1.4.4 Case Studies of Youth Programs

To gain a more nuanced picture of how everyday citizenship develops and plays out, we conducted five case studies of local organizations that strive to promote youth interests in South Africa, Ghana, Tanzania, and Zambia. We chose organizations that have action-oriented programs related to an identity that may color everyday citizenship: income level, church attendance, or gender. The case studies include data collected through focus group discussions, interviews with organizational leaders, informal conversations, observations of organizational activities, and focus groups and/or interviews with nonparticipants. We queried how participants perceived good citizenship and how group activities relate to youth views of and actions as citizens.[11] We recognize that case studies may have limited ability to demonstrate causality between independent variables and outcomes or to generalize beyond the case (Soiter 2020), and we do not claim a causal relationship between the organizations' programs and our youth's citizenship views. Rather, these programs represent thousands of other NGO-, CBO-, or FBO-administered programs in Africa, and they provide general patterns future scholars can investigate (Brass 2016; Hearn 2002; Hershey 2019).

---

[11] We did not analyze these discussions with NVivo because the data was organizationally specific and because the relatively small number of discussions and interviews made hand coding possible.

Chapter 4 uses two cases to explore how youth income generation programs may color youth citizen identities. First, the Network of Zambian People Living with HIV/AIDS (NZP+) illustrates how such programs in a context of scarcity and resource competition can shape everyday citizenship by fomenting a politics of envy. During 2011, one author conducted focus group discussions with thirty-three local chapters affiliated with NZP+ in several urban areas (each group had five to eight participants) and interviews with twenty-five NZP+ officers and AIDS NGO representatives. (Those applicable for this project are listed in Appendix 3.) Most NZP+ chapter members were lower-income women in their late twenties or early thirties. Although not initially focused on citizenship, through the fieldwork questioning and data analysis, citizenship themes of reciprocity, identity, and localized actions emerged. The second case includes entrepreneurial and job-experience programs for youth at two parishes under the ELCT in Dar es Salaam. During July 2021, one author interviewed seven ELCT program staff members, conducted six focus group discussions with youth participants, and engaged in casual conversations with youth. Because the program targets youth at different income levels, the case uncovers how entrepreneurial programs may interact with youth perceptions of income to shape everyday citizenship.

Chapter 5 includes two case studies that examine how messaging in Christian organizations relates to youth citizenship. The first is a congregation affiliated with the renewalist International Central Gospel Church (ICGC) and located in an Accra middle-class neighborhood. Established in 1984 by the influential Ghanaian theologian Mensa Otabil, the mega-church ICGC describes itself as a "socially conscious Christian Church which upholds the philosophy of Human dignity and Excellence" (ICGC n.d.). In addition to its over 450 affiliate churches in Ghana, Africa, and the West, ICGC operates Central University (~9,000 undergraduates) and provides scholarships for education (Annan 2016). The specific congregation we studied had several thousand worshippers each week and seventeen pastors (all but three were men). One author interviewed a senior pastor in 2018, and another author returned in July 2021 to conduct five focus group discussions with youth (two, all men and three, all women), five interviews with church leaders, and observations. She also conducted two focus group discussions with nonmembers (one, all men and the other, all women). The second case is the VYLTP in Hermanus, South

Africa. Fieldwork conducted in 2019 included two interviews with the organization's leaders, two focus group discussions, six weeks of participant observations, four focus group discussions with nonparticipants in two different neighborhoods, and four interviews with staff of a secular citizen organization.[12] Because the South African and Ghanaian Christian organizations approach citizenship from different theological perspectives – VYLTP is mainline Protestant while ICGC is renewalist – we discovered slight differences in the ways that their youth participants described everyday citizenship.

Chapter 6 interrogates the NGO Stand Up!, a group of ten current and former students at an Accra-area university. Founded in August 2016, Stand Up! focused on issues related to violence and extremism, especially gender-based violence (GBV), an issue that disproportionately affects women (Stites 2013).[13] One author conducted a focus group discussion with members in 2018, and then, in 2021, another author conducted five interviews with group members (four men and one woman). These included the former president (a man) and the then current president (a woman). Interviews asked about the group's establishment, its programs, and members' views on gender and citizenship. For comparison purposes, two focus group discussions were conducted with nonparticipants (one, all men and the other, all women). The case uncovered how the program shaped participants' views of gender and citizenship.

1.4.5 Analysis of Afrobarometer Data

As a pan-African, nonpartisan organization, Afrobarometer has conducted large-scale surveys on governance and the economy on a regular basis since 1999 in over thirty countries. We report results from urban youth (and in some cases, their elders) on select Round 7 questions. To assess local engagement, we examine questions on attending a community meeting and membership in a voluntary or community group (questions 20B and 21A). To explore citizens' views

---

[12] At times, we cite these nonparticipant focus group discussions and secular organizational interviews from South Africa to amplify themes we encountered in the three study countries.

[13] We use the phrase "gender-based violence" (GBV) to encompass a range of abusive behaviors (verbal, physical) that may target people of any gender (Council on Europe n.d.).

of their obligations to the state, we examine questions on obeying the law and paying taxes (questions 38B and 38C). Finally, to explore citizen activities aimed at shaping government personnel or policy, we look at questions on voting, joining with others to request action from the government, and attending a demonstration or protest march (questions 22, 26A, 26E).

Afrobarometer divides youth into two age strata: eighteen to twenty-five years and twenty-six to thirty-five years. This division recognizes possible lifecycle and cohort (or generational) effects.[14] Lifecycle effects revolve around "patterns of development and maturation" and accompanying life changes that may influence social or political attitudes and behaviors (Dennis 1968; Nie, Verba, and Kim 1974). For instance, marriage or parenthood for older youth might shape their voting behavior. Cohort effects occur when a chronological age group has experienced "the same event[s] within the same time interval" (Ryder 1965, 845), potentially producing distinct political attitudes that over time may contribute to social change (Alwin and Krosnick 1991, 170–71). Robert Mattes (2012) finds a cohort effect in voting behavior in post-apartheid South Africa, with the "born free" generation (those born after apartheid's end) being less likely to vote (see also de Kadt 2017).

Lifecycle effects were not readily apparent in our qualitative and quantitative data, most likely because many respondents have not yet achieved the markers of adulthood. In terms of cohorts, youth who in 2018 were between twenty-six and thirty-five years old (those born between 1983 and 1992) may have had somewhat different formative experiences than youth born between 1992 and 2000. As the "lost generation," this older cohort directly felt the continent's economic downturn and the adoption of neoliberal policies that cut jobs, health services, and education spending in the 1980s and 1990s (Cruise O'Brien 1996), as well as the continent's political liberalization in the early 1990s (Bratton and van de Walle 1994; Cheeseman 2015). The younger cohort was socialized during a period of economic growth that expanded the middle class (Resnick 2015), yet they also experienced rising income inequalities and the stagnation (or reversal) of democratic

---

[14] We use the word "cohort" instead of "generation" because the latter may be conceptually confusing. "Generation" may refer to the time between birth and the birth of one's offspring, a genealogical level (e.g., mother and aunt), people bound by an age-group consciousness (e.g., the "Greatest Generation"), and those of the same social status (e.g., initiands) (see Clark-Kazak 2009, 1310).

transitions (Bleck and van de Walle 2019; Cheeseman and Fischer 2021). Overall, we found that both groups expressed disappointment about democracy, concerns over increased inequalities, and similar views on citizenship, thereby blurring the lines across cohorts. Because these lifecycle and cohort effects seemed to play a limited role in shaping how our respondents understood citizenship, we report a weighted average for youth eighteen to thirty-five years old for most survey data. However, we only provide voting data for the older cohort because of the sizeable percentage of the younger cohort that was too young to vote in the most recent election. We point out instances when survey data for the two age strata is noticeably different.[15]

1.5 Organization of the Book

We begin our analysis by illustrating everyday citizenship among our youth respondents at the micro level. Chapter 2 centers on citizenship as a lived experience embedded in relationships and obligations and contributing to the project of building the nation. Chapter 3 then analyzes how this lived experience spills over to shape engagement with the explicitly political realm through actions such as voting, joining with others in advocacy, or protesting. Our data illustrates that few of the youth we met engage in activities to directly hold governments accountable, such as advocating or protesting. However, when they do, it is their everyday relationships that motivate these actions. By using Afrobarometer data, Chapters 2 and 3 allow us also to compare how youth views of citizenship differ (or resemble) those of individuals above thirty-five years old.

Chapters 4, 5, and 6 drill down to examine everyday citizenship for youth along various strata. Chapter 4 investigates how youth respondents of higher- and lower-income levels negotiate and contest citizenship. The economic precarity that lower-income respondents face leads them to stress citizen actions that foster reliance on others and collective activities. In contrast, higher-income youth stress productivity and self-reliance as citizenship components. Although both groups agree with legal obligations of citizenship, higher-income youth are more concerned about legal compliance by others, while

---

[15] We follow Afrobarometer reporting guidelines and round decimals to the closest whole number, with 0.5 decimals rounded up.

lower-income youth are more concerned about being accused of legal violations. Survey data indicates more lower-income youth vote in Ghana and Uganda, but income differences on other political activities are negligible. Two case studies demonstrate that paternalism, derision, and envy within and across income groups can shape citizenship identities.

Chapter 5 affirms the important role that religion plays as our respondents negotiate citizenship. Both frequent- and infrequent-churchgoing youth highlight communal aspects of citizenship, but frequent churchgoers were more likely to emphasize citizenship as building the nation and to highlight how church communities foster citizen belonging and obligations. Frequent churchgoers used more legalistic language than infrequent churchgoers, displayed more political efficacy, and defined faith-inspired actions (e.g., prayer) as citizenship. These findings align with research and Afrobarometer data correlating religious involvement with higher political activism, but they center youth voices to show how youth may contest political messaging from religious leaders and craft their own versions of citizenship. These themes emerge in the Ghana and South Africa case studies.

In Chapter 6, we illustrate how patriarchy means everyday citizenship often reflects socially constructed gender roles that constrain women. Among our respondents, men and women emphasized gender equality when discussing legalistic elements of citizenship. However, since much of everyday citizenship revolves around daily interactions, women's biological roles as mothers and men's constructed roles as protectors and providers were central to the ways that our respondents viewed citizenship. Hewing to Afrobarometer data on women's and men's formal participation and attitudes about women in office, our youth informants nonetheless deepen that data by illustrating micro-patterns of gender relations. They also push back against gendered citizenship, particularly contextualizing citizen identities in light of their own personal experiences. The case study demonstrates how a mixed-gender student group in Ghana sought to challenge those citizenship views, while also being affected by them.

Analyzing a subset of youth respondents, Chapter 7 uncovers how disappointment, frustration, and anger may color everyday citizenship. Youth report how unmet promises, corruption, repression, and exclusive politics undermine their sense of citizen belonging and amplify tensions with elders. Such frustration may lead youth to contest citizenship in alternative ways, though most do not choose these paths. A small number exit, as indicated in Afrobarometer data and by our respondents, and some actively contest citizenship through the exclusion of others along ethnic or religious lines. Although some could choose to follow populist leaders who claim to speak for the people, when we compare youth support for such leaders in Tanzania and Uganda, on the one hand, with their support for the populist Economic Freedom Fighters in South Africa, on the other, we find inconclusive evidence that youth embrace illiberal populism. A subset channels anger into local and national mobilization, illustrating youth agency.

The Conclusion summarizes our findings, reiterating how youth citizenship plays out through lived experiences that are shaped by income levels, church attendance, gender identity, and country context. Extending the book's lessons to other marginalized populations through survey data on rural youth in Ghana, Tanzania, and Uganda, we discover that, in comparison to urban youth, significantly more rural youth attend community activities, vote, and advocate, though they are less legalistic. We urge future research on how these patterns play out in specific ways for the citizenship identities of other marginalized populations. We conclude with key takeaways: Despite political, social, and economic structures that may limit their options, youth are agentic, creative, and eager to lead their communities and countries now and in the future.

2 | Manifesting Citizenship through Local and Distinct Actions

What does it mean to be a good citizen?

- *[being] well disciplined, patient, and [someone who] loves others.* (UG FGD 8)
- *[supporting] each other if someone has lost a close relative, a child is sick.* (TZ FGD 1)
- *[looking] out for things that are needed in the community ... [T]his also will ... help the country.* (GH FGD 9)

These quotes, representative of the views of many of our respondents, present a cascade of perspectives on citizenship. The first frames citizenship as individual-level emotions and personal characteristics, while the second views citizenship as the performance of multiple, mundane "localised acts" to help others and deepen horizontal relations (Bird 2016, 264; von Lieres 2014). The third places citizenship in a web of relations and responsibilities that accumulate to foster the country's development (Manqoyi 2019, 64). These respondents' statements reflect how everyday citizenship is a "processual view of citizenship that makes visible what happens at what is usually thought of as the margins" (Clarke et al. 2014, 57). This articulation decenters the state and situates citizenship identity in the "hyper local" arenas of home, school, neighborhood, and marketplace. In this chapter, we analyze this articulation by focusing on how our youth respondents perceive emotions, personal relations, and small-scale actions as constituting everyday citizenship. We find that, through these paths, youth contest and negotiate what it means to have a citizen's sense of belonging, which may be different from that of their elders' (Isin 2009; Pailey 2016). By recognizing youth's behind-the-scenes emotions and actions as citizenship, this chapter helps us move beyond narrow views of citizenship that see youth as disengaged from community contributions.

This chapter first situates our youth respondents' views in work on affective citizenship, volunteering, and community participation (Section 2.1). Secondly, it reports the trends in respondents' perspectives on citizenship from NVivo analysis of the transcripts from the three study countries (Section 2.2). The chapter's structure then emulates the above respondents' cascading views of citizenship. Section 2.3 examines how, for some respondents, individual-level emotions of love, closeness, and gratitude, as well as concern about personal character, undergird citizenship. Section 2.4 interrogates how youth respondents perceived citizenship to entail individual acts of volunteerism performed to foster relationships with others, while Section 2.5 expands our lens to show how, for some youth, localized actions such as community-meeting attendance and communal labor were acts of citizenship. We show that, even though in surveys fewer youth than elders report meeting attendance and active membership in a volunteer or community group, our youth respondents perceive their engagement to have *unique aspects*. As Section 2.6 shows, youth strive to connect their local citizenship acts to a broader understanding of national citizenship, through their commitment to "build the nation." In the process, they continuously frame their citizenship as distinct from that of their elders, as Section 2.7 highlights. We conclude that everyday citizenship is reflected in emotionality, personal efforts to act in appropriate ways, micro-level acts of kindness and generosity, and engagement in collective problem-solving – all of which accumulate to build the nation (Section 2.8). Despite assumptions that urban environments foster isolation, individualism, anonymity, and marginalization (Manqoyi 2019, 72), our respondents were highly relational and embedded in obligations that undergird citizen belonging.

2.1 Situating a Localized Youth Citizenship

Our inductive approach leads us to touch on three key themes from the vast citizenship literature. First, emotions matter for citizen identity, with citizenship often "contingent on personal feelings and acts that extend beyond the individual self … [and are] directed towards the community" (Fortier 2010, 22; Johnson 2010). Citizenship's emotional components may be channeled and replicated through memory, history, words, and deeds (Casey 2009, 248; Zembylas 2014). As individuals negotiate citizenship, emotions can determine "who and how to love, suspect, befriend, care for, embrace, welcome" (Fortier 2008, 89). Emotions can be tied to how people perceive one another and thus shape relations between community members.

Second, citizenship may reflect an identity rooted in ideas about "moral" or "acceptable" behavior. Moral standing may foster symbolic capital that can generate material and status resources (Bourdieu 1986), a positive reputation (Putnam 1994), and trust from others (Coleman 1988). Symbolic capital then can shape one's rights and responsibilities as a citizen. Personal behavior and contributions to collective action generate and reflect reputations, emotions, and belonging.

Third, citizenship manifests in localized actions, such as meeting attendance or volunteering. Meeting attendance is not necessarily an indicator of democratic participation (see Verba, Schlozman, and Brady 1995) because people may attend meetings not just to share ideas, solve problems, or organize political action but also to impress patrons, socialize, alleviate boredom, support other attendees, gossip, and/or gain material benefits that may be dispersed in such spaces (Adams 2004; Smith 2003; UG FGDs 4, 11). Volunteering is the "free giving of an individuals' labor, time and energy to a larger cause, collective goal, or public good" (Brown and Prince 2015, 29). As a "caring citizenship" that builds on people's compassion for others, volunteering may be essential in neoliberal environments where individuals must devise their own solutions to economic and social problems (Brown and Prince 2015, 30; Gupta and Ferguson 2002). Volunteering can foster reciprocities, dependencies, and "long term ties of exchange" among friends, neighbors, community members, and multiple triangulations across generations and geographies (MacLean 2010, 17). The resulting economy of affection may then enable people to cope with the material and psychosocial uncertainties of life (Hyden 1980). Voluntary activities may take the form of individual-level actions (e.g., caring for a neighbor) and/or collective action (e.g., communal labor). "Riddled with tension," volunteering is a "multivalent, slippery, and contradictory category" (Brown and Prince 2015, 30–32). Both altruistic and self-interested, it may reinforce inequalities between the giver and the recipient (Mittermaier 2014) and perpetuate repression under the guise of tradition (Okia 2019). Acknowledging the complexities of local activities, we are interested in how youth may view emotions, moral character, volunteering, and

communal labor *to be citizenship* in their own right and how they see
these activities "provid[ing] the building blocks" for a citizen identity
that connects the individual to the public realm (Halisi, Kaiser, and
Ndegwa 1998, 342).

2.2 Common Themes among Country Respondents

To begin our investigation, we looked at common trends in the focus
group participants' responses to the question, "What does it mean to
be a good citizen?" We present the NVivo analysis from the Ghana,
Tanzania, and Uganda transcripts, and then we use the voices of
respondents to illustrate how youth believed some actions constituted
citizenship. As Figure 2.1 shows, words in the communal and build-
the-nation categories were very commonly used in the three countries.
Terms such as "community," "contribute," "responsibility," and
"neighbor" were repeated frequently, indicating how "group frame-
works are at the core of the African social fabric" (Chazan et al. 1988,
7; see Appendix 1). "Community" was used almost ten times per focus

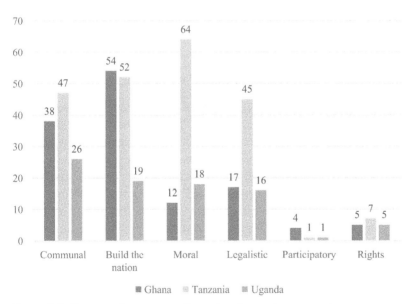

Figure 2.1 Common focus group discussion themes by country*
* Average mentions of category words per focus group
Source: The authors' NVivo data

group in Tanzania, twelve times per group in Ghana, and twenty-five times per group in Uganda. Words in the legalistic and moral categories were less common, though those in the participatory and rights categories comprised an even smaller average number of mentions. Words in the patriotic category had the smallest mentions, and thus are not included in Figure 2.1. We address the legalistic, participatory, and rights themes as they relate to citizenship in Chapter 3. There were also notable country differences, with Tanzanians' top category being morality, Ghanaians' being build-the-nation, and Ugandans' communal. (We revisit Tanzanians' focus on morality in Chapters 3 and 5.) It was apparent that youth situated their citizenship identity within their community relationships (see Bird 2016, 260–61), and it was notable that youth did not mention engagement with social media in the context of citizenship (see Chapter 3). Discussions of community obligations, engagement, and reciprocities were not divorced from broader debates about youth contributions to national development (hence the build-the-nation phrases). Echoing Peter Ekeh (1975, 92), themes of moral obligation, acceptance, belonging, and "psychological security" undergird citizenship as a normative endeavor (see also Dorman 2020, 465). We now examine how these attitudes played out in the lives of our respondents.

2.3 Citizenship as Emotions and Moral Character

Our youth respondents often imbued their ideas about citizenship activities, which we discuss in Sections 2.4–2.6, with emotional attachment or views about the moral character that citizens must possess. Many respondents were quick to note these intangible elements, particularly feelings of closeness to their community. Ugandan men who often traveled juxtaposed their physical absence from the community with their emotional closeness to it. One said, "I feel sad whenever I work outside my community, unsettled. ... When I pray from [attend] another church, I feel uncomfortable ... I start to think about who is going to sing in my place in my home church choir ... I belong here" (UG FGD 10). For a Ghanaian, closeness to the community was heightened during Homowo, an annual harvest festival of the Ga people, when those who lived far away returned: "What makes me indebted to the community is the festival season, which is Homowo. We get people coming around. That shows some kind of love. With that sometimes, it makes me love my community" (GH FGD 1). The respondent used the word "indebted" to indicate obligation and highlighted how people congregating for this event reinforced community even for those who lived far away.

Another common emotion that respondents expressed was love. As with the Ghanaian quoted above, the word was used generally to connote positive emotions toward others.[1] Another Ghanaian said, "One of the things you can see of a good citizen is when he or she behaves lovingly towards other citizens, that will also mean love or care" (GH FGD 11). For that individual, love and actions are intertwined, with both being essential for citizenship. A Ugandan man brought a different angle to the discussion, by explaining how despite the fact that his family had not loved him, the "love of his friends" had led him to be someone who helped and respected others. Love had prevented him from becoming a "dangerous person" or a bad citizen (UG FGD 2). Thus, emotional elements both fostered citizenship and were embodied in it.

Many respondents expressed that gratitude and joy were part of citizenship. These emotions often emerged when people were the recipients of kind acts during personal challenges, thereby tying emotions, relationships, and actions together in citizen identities. For example, when a Tanzanian man's sister was admitted to the hospital, he received an unexpected phone call from an acquaintance who said, "I have heard you're having a [sick person]; I'm sending you this much [money] so that it can help you" (TZ FGD 1). "Even me!" exclaimed another youth. "I have experienced that, sometime back when I felt sick. During that time, I was far from my family but people who were closer were those surrounding me. They came to visit me, see me. I was happy and felt good that even [for] me, there [are] some people who care about me and value me" (TZ FGD 1). Ghanaians expressed similar appreciation but often in the context of community members who contributed money for funeral expenses (see MacLean 2010, 79). One said, "There was a time when one of our friends passed on, and the parents were in hardship, but the community came together like

---

[1] The noun/verb *upendo/kupenda* in Swahili is generally translated as "love/to love," yet because there is no word for "like" in Swahili, *upendo/kupenda* is employed regardless of whether one's affection is slight or strong. We have translated the word as "love," yet we recognize that the strength of the emotion varies with the context.

never before ... [We asked], 'So if we want to do the funeral, who wants to buy the casket, the canopies?' Somebody devotes to buy it, and then contributions are made" (GH FGD 3; see also UG FGD 13). Sometimes, though, it was the giver – not the recipient – who expressed joy and gratitude. One Ugandan woman said how happy she was to help with the decorating and ushering at a friend's wedding, especially because she "didn't have money for a gift" (UG FGD 15). These stories demonstrate that, for our youth respondents, dependence, mutual concern, and reciprocity were all part of citizenship.

Sometimes emotions tied individuals to the state through patriotism, although only a few individuals made explicitly patriotic remarks. A few respondents articulated loyalty, pride, and devotion to their country (GH FGD 5; SA FGD 2; TZ FGD 7). A typical example came from Ghana: "You have to genuinely love your country" (GH FGD 12). Tanzanians spoke about loving their country too, and youth in both countries tied emotion to their dedication to building the nation (GH FGDs 1, 4; TZ FGD 2). A Ugandan participant combined emotional elements of citizenship with the legality that we discuss in Chapter 3. "You must love your country and, I must add, have the national ID card" (UG FGD 9). For this individual, the emotional element was insufficient without the documentary proof.

Not all respondents expressed a shared normative ideal of the harmonious collective rooted in positive emotions of love and belonging (see MacLean 2010, 79). Here some (though certainly not all) Ugandan respondents differed from those youth we encountered in Tanzania and Ghana. These Ugandans pointed out that because they moved often, they did not have the opportunity to build emotional ties through relationships: "I do not feel close to the community," one said. Another added that, as a result, he and his friends did not feel a sense of belonging because others did not know them and thought they were criminals: "People are suspicious [that] we are thieves" (UG FGD 1). A Ugandan woman said that, since the community had never helped her, she did not feel close to it, illustrating how emotions and actions intertwine in everyday citizenship (UG FGD 6). Chapter 7 explores how disappointment, frustration, and anger led some youth to contest citizenship through exit or processes that excluded others.

Another intangible element of everyday citizenship that some respondents described was moral character. We did not pursue why Tanzanians highlighted this theme (see Figure 2.1), and we can only speculate that Nyerere's framing of citizenship as African solidarity – and, more recently, the late President Magufuli's emphasis on civil servants' corruption – may have heightened this discourse (see Paget 2020b). However, some respondents in all countries argued that citizenship involved "acting rightly" in ways that were not specifically related to the law. These activities included "greeting elders," "being peaceful and not fighting," "serving as a role model," "showing others how to act," "meeting obligations," "behaving well," and "being honest" (GH FGDs 6, 10; TZ FGDs 1, 2, 9; UG FGDs 3, 5, 7, 8, 13). One Tanzanian said, "Myself, being a good citizen, I'm supposed to tell those who are yet to know how they are supposed to live and behave in order for them to become good citizens." His actions, he said, would then help others to act as good citizens "to all people and the nation" (TZ FGD 1). A Ghanaian man also stressed being a role model by teaching others, "As a good citizen ... what I can do is educate young people on how to clean the environment. Two, how to abstain from drugs, and three, how to be careful of how to use weapons" (GH FGD 1; see also UG FDG 15).[2]

Moral actions intertwined with reputational concerns in processes of citizenship contestation. On the one hand, a positive reputation could lead to citizen inclusion. A Tanzanian explained, "Nowadays there is a tendency of being accused of things you don't do. A problem might erupt and people might say, 'He was also involved,' and call the police. But people who know you will defend you by saying, 'We know this person is a good citizen [and] can't do something like that'" (TZ FGD 1). Thus, acting respectfully and considerately toward others could foster a positive reputation that, in turn, could be protective. That protection meant that one was part of the community, someone who belonged. In turn, belonging could foster collective benefits, such as "helping people to live together in peace" (GH FGD 4) or "convincing leaders to consider your village first for government programs" (UG FGD 6). Leaders might be more likely to reward communities that were not troublemakers. On the other hand, when individuals did not act in morally acceptable ways, the lost reputation could destroy trust with others (MacLean 2010), such as when someone is "always going out late at night, drinking too much, and coming home loudly and

---

[2] We did not probe the weapons remark but interpreted it to mean children's handling of knives, since injuries with such objects are common.

waking the neighbors ... leading to fights" (UG FGD 15). If everyday citizenship is partly defined through positive (or negative) relations with others, then a corrupted character influences citizen belonging. A Ugandan woman told a story of community sanctioning to illustrate how actions and their consequences affect citizen belonging:

I used to be selfish whereby I never greeted my neighbors. I always left home in the morning for work and after work I went straight home. But one day I was attacked by a thief at night and I sounded an alarm to the neighbors. ... All were watching ... through their windows and none of them came out. I sounded a strong alarm and the thief walked away, miraculously. The next morning, I didn't go to work ... Instead I started making friends with my neighbors. (UG FGD 5)

Although the woman laughed when telling the story, the seriousness was not lost on the group. They nodded in agreement: Indeed, she had not been a good citizen because of her rudeness, lack of greetings, and general unwillingness to invest in relationships with others; she had gotten her comeuppance.

As a Ugandan man summarized, echoing Alexis de Tocqueville's (2002) idea of "self-interest, rightly understood": "If I do something that hurts my neighbors or my friend I am also hurting myself" (UG FGD 4). And for a Ghanaian: "I am an individual, I am also a member of a whole community" (GH FGD 6). Being a good citizen necessitated behavior that showed consideration and respect to others.

2.4 Citizenship as Volunteering to Help Others

Many youth we encountered found volunteering to be an intrinsic element of citizenship. Volunteering conferred "identity and social value" on participants, reflected the moral and aspirational aspects of citizenship, and showed agency and a hope to "create better futures" (Brown and Prince 2015). As one respondent said, "A good citizen is a person good at volunteering to help [address] different problems ... happening in the society" (TZ FGD 6). We heard numerous examples of such individual-level actions: helping vulnerable children attend school, providing food to the hungry, transporting sick neighbors to the hospital, and feeding the elderly (GH FGDs 2, 6, 10, 11, 14; TZ FGDs 1, 2, 6, 8; UG FGDs 5, 6, 7, 12, 16). In one example, a group of Tanzanian men reported helping a "fellow youth" to rebuild his house after it was destroyed by rains and flooding (TZ FGD 6). In another case, a Ghanaian described volunteering to mentor a young girl in school (GH FGD 14). These examples illustrate a broader ethos around citizenship that several respondents pointed out: "A good citizen, first, is supposed to care about others" (TZ FGD 6).

These activities are situated in a neoliberal context in which many youth live in precarity and the state's concern for public welfare often seems lacking. Some youth need a place to sleep, money for medicine, or surrogate parents. For them, good citizens step into those gaps, and those actions deepen emotional ties that undergird one's belonging as a citizen. In urban spaces, community ties and reciprocities by necessity extend beyond kinship to friends and neighbors, complicating the idea that citizen belonging rests predominantly in primordial ties (Ekeh 1975; Geschiere 2009). People lean on others: "My friends comforted me when I was desperate" was a relatively common sentiment (UG FGD 7). A Tanzanian echoed how friends become like relations: "There was a time a big problem happened at home, to the point that I couldn't like the place ... [but] there was one of our neighbors who could help me [by letting me] stay at their home ... We became more than friends; now we are relatives" (TZ FGD 2). The tight spaces of the city – markets, informal housing, corner churches – create arenas conducive to forging, fostering, and deepening these reciprocities (Casey 2008; Lalloo 1998).

Although many respondents viewed volunteering to be one component of local citizenship, they also understood that it could be a step toward personal advancement. One Tanzanian illustrated:

[When] I'm done with my studies, I can go to any hospital and agree to be paid even [just] a transport fee, and volunteer to help people. ... Most of those who are employed [at a medical center I visited] had studied pharmacy and hold a diploma ... [and had] worked there as volunteers ... but later they were trusted and offered employment. (TZ FGD 7)

This respondent's decision to volunteer could lead to contacts and opportunities rooted in "intrinsically personal ties" (Burchardt 2013) at the same time that it allowed him to meet his citizen responsibility to use his education to benefit others. A Ugandan activist also made this point, as he recounted volunteering with one NGO and then another in hopes of eventually landing a paid position, a trajectory he linked to citizen service to others (UG Interview 19).

The youth in our study also demonstrated some ambiguities about volunteering as a citizen activity. Some felt social pressure to volunteer, despite their lack of time and energy, as well as their need to prioritize "feeding my kids" and "survival" (UG FGDs 1, 2, 4, 10). Some echoed the idea that volunteering intertwined with social exclusion when they said that they did no communal labor because they did not "feel close to my community" (UG FGD 6). Others realized that they could do little to address societal problems that demanded more than mere volunteering. As one Ugandan concluded, "Sometimes, there is nothing you can do" (UG FGD 1). Additionally, some youth volunteers exhibited a "sociology of pity" (Bochow 2018, 157): They implicitly looked down on those who needed assistance rather than seeing recipients as community members or volunteering as a way to reinforce reciprocities. This othering and paternalism were most evident among higher-income youth, as Chapter 4 highlights (GH FGDs 6, 14; UG FGD 11).

2.5 Citizenship as Working Together on Shared Problems

Everyday citizenship could take on more collective forms, moving from the individualized aspects of emotionality or voluntary aid to cooperative efforts in which people built on "sets of relations" to achieve collective goals (Pailey 2016, 822). This section first reports Afrobarometer data on attending a community meeting and active membership in a voluntary or community group for urban youth and urban elders in the three study countries (Section 2.5.1). We then examine how our respondents view these localized actions, finding that many youth believe their citizenship has distinctive elements that set it apart from their elders' citizenship (Sections 2.5.2 and 2.5.3).

2.5.1 Survey Trends

As Table 2.1 illustrates, fewer urban youth than urban elders in the three countries report attending a community meeting several times or often, and fewer urban youth than urban elders report being an active member of a voluntary or community group. Lower percentages among youth most likely reflect a lifecycle effect, as youth mobility, employment (particularly in the informal sector), and/or university enrollment may limit time to attend meetings or contribute to collective

Table 2.1 *Local actions among urban populations, by age and country*

Country	Age*	Attended community meetings (%)**	Active membership in voluntary or community group (%)	N
Ghana	Youth	20	13	733
	Elders	29	17	572
Tanzania	Youth	51	19	439
	Elders	71[a]	30	358
Uganda	Youth	34	25	209
	Elders	55	27	90

* "Youth" includes the weighted average for people eighteen to thirty-five years old, and "elders" includes the weighted average for people who are thirty-six years and above.
** Percentage answering "several times" or "often"
[a] N = 357
Source: Data from Afrobarometer (2016/2018), compiled by the authors

projects.[3] In addition, because some youth have not reached the milestones of adulthood (i.e., parenthood, full employment), they may feel they have less to contribute to public discussions than their elders do.

There are country differences. A higher percentage of Tanzanians than Ugandans or Ghanaians reports attending a community meeting. This outcome may reflect Tanzania's history of state-driven community development (see Chapter 1). Ghana has the lowest numbers for both activities; perhaps Ghanaians' overall higher-income levels make reliance on community groups that revolve around material support less necessary (see Chapter 4). More generally, Ghana has relatively low rates of informal political participation that might help explain the lower rates of community participation (Armah-Attoh and Robertson 2014). E. Gyimah-Boadi (2009) has suggested that while Ghanaians show high public interest in elections and strong popular support for democracy, a "minority engages in active forms of secular community and civic activities" due to a political culture of passivity and underdeveloped civic education. Clientelistic relationships that dominate everyday urban politics may also contribute to Ghana's underdeveloped civic culture (Paller 2019). Higher levels of poverty in Uganda

---

[3] Lifecycle effects were manifest in the fact that a higher percentage of the older youth cohort engaged in these activities.

may mean Ugandans engage in local organizations to access benefits (see Chapter 4), although, as Chapter 3 illustrates, higher percentages of urban Ugandan youth than urban Tanzanian and Ghanaian youth also engage in political advocacy and protesting.

2.5.2 Attending Meetings: Youth Voices

Most youth we met did not mention attending a community meeting as a manifestation of citizenship. However, for the participants who did, their reasons tended to focus on a desire for sociality and concerns about communal relations. Among some youth, mere *attendance* served as a citizen contribution, and they listed attendance alongside other actions, such as "engaging in general cleaning" and "community security" (UG FGD 1). A Tanzanian was more explicit: "My contribution to the society [as a youth] is to participate in different community issues, like community meetings, academic meeting[s] … political meetings, et cetera. I participate by sharing my views." A peer followed up, saying that sharing her opinions was her "contribution" (TZ FGD 1). Attendance signaled interest and investment in others, at a minimum, but the word "contribution" indicated that these individuals recognized they were giving others their time, insights, and presence.

Some youth went beyond just listing attendance as a contribution to highlighting their specific role in community discussions. A Tanzanian remarked, "[If] you're just quiet, without giving any contribution, how can others learn from you? It's important to speak out what you have from your heart" (TZ FGD 1). The respondent highlighted an embedded obligation: It would be selfish not to share so others could learn. Similarly, some Ghanaians viewed meeting attendance as a way to help their community grow. One individual said, "If we are making decisions, and I contribute my idea and by God's grace my idea is accepted and implemented and it works, then that part of the country has developed in a particular way" (GH FGD 1; see also GH FGD 14). The respondent not only stressed the value of sharing ideas for development but also the individual's *agency* in making that development possible through an idea that works. Another Tanzanian detailed how sharing his views in "community meetings for development" led to efforts to provide better security (TZ FGD 9). For these youth, it was inadequate and irresponsible to stand back as silent observers. More specifically, some pointed to the fact that *as youth* they had unique perspectives to add to community conversations (UG FGD 15). Their citizenship as manifest in meeting attendance was not the same as their elders' citizenship because they brought new views to the table.

2.5.3 Collective Action to Solve Local Problems: Youth Voices

In addition to individual acts of volunteering that embodied everyday citizenship, youth specified that citizenship encompassed engagement in more formally organized activities – often organized by youth themselves – to solve collective problems (Pailey 2016, 812–13). Respondents viewed their collective acts of citizenship – even if fewer youth than elders engaged in them (see Table 2.1) – to be distinct from their elders' citizen acts. They situated many of these activities in the particular experiences and concerns they had as youth.

These collective activities took on several guises. Some were simple routine actions: a women's group cooking food for church weddings (UG FGD 16) or neighborhood youth picking up garbage from the road or keeping rain gutters clear of silt (GH FGDs 1, 2, 4–10, 12, 14). Other actions demanded more time and energy, such as youth digging ditches or weeding open urban spaces (GH FGD 3; UG FGD 2). Many thought these activities fostered reciprocities, interdependence, and development, and met a need that the government could not or would not meet. One Ghanaian man described how contributing helped the community: "If I see my colleague working on the needs of society, because the government hasn't done it yet, I should contribute if I can. If I see him filling potholes, I can assist by providing a wheelbarrow and my effort" (GH FGD 7). Similarly, some described tutoring primary school students in overcrowded schools (TZ FGD 4; UG FGDs 2, 8, 11). These youth demonstrated agency as they sought to address the daily needs they encountered.

Although many people mentioned similar group activities, there was some variation across countries. Youth often pointed to these specific actions to demonstrate how their citizenship acts differed from those of their elders. In all three countries, several men engaged in nightly neighborhood patrols to ward off thieves (GH FGD 3; TZ FGDs 8, 9; UG FGDs 2, 3, 13). Some respondents thought patrols were necessary because "the government can't provide security to everyone" (UG FGD 3), while others emphasized that patrols were a way to show your concern for others. A Ugandan said, "If you see a suspicious person, you report to the authorities and you also alert your neighbors to find out who that person is. This helps in reducing crime" (UG FGD 5; but see Chapter 7). Daily experiences with theft led some youth to engage in these actions (UG FGD 9, 15), and many said patrolling was a unique citizenship act of youth. One Tanzanian said, "We *as youth* ... have some big responsibilities where we live to make sure that the surrounding community lives in peace ... [Some places] have participatory community security" (TZ FGD 9; emphasis added). Youth viewed providing security to be a task that youth alone could do. Another Tanzanian explained, "In our streets there is civil security and we contribute. ... Any person [who is a youth] can volunteer to take part, because that is not for the elders" (TZ FGD 8). The man alludes to the fact that youth have the energy, stamina, and good health to patrol at night or chase thieves, in contrast to elders, some of whom are "old and sick" (TZ FGD 6).

Ghanaian youth respondents were relatively unusual in their extensive focus on maintaining a clean environment, a topic they mentioned ninety-nine times compared to sixteen times in the Ugandan and Tanzanian focus groups. For Ghanaian respondents, actions to foster clean community spaces often demarcated good and bad citizens, and these actions were specific contributions that youth made to society. They weeded common areas and picked up trash, jobs that elders often lacked time and energy to do. They reminded others not to throw trash in drains and gutters. As one woman explained: "If you see someone littering or dumping trash, you ... tell the person that, 'This is not good because what you are putting there will take a long time to rot'" (GH FGD 14). These acts of citizenship preserved the environment (GH FGDs 1, 8), demonstrated commitment to the law and/or respect for state property (GH FGDs 4, 7, 9), and prevented flooding in neighborhoods (GH FGDs 2, 5, 6, 12). Ghanaian respondents' extreme focus on these activities most likely reflected the fact that improper garbage disposal and clogged gutters plague urban areas, making Ghana one of the most polluted countries in the world (Miniru 2016). Some youth connect the public service announcements and social media messages they encounter about environmental protection to citizenship expectations (see Knott 2018).

Ugandan youth also highlighted engagement on some issues of youth concern, particularly AIDS (Boyd 2015; Gusman 2009).[4] Youth participated in campaigns to educate others on HIV transmission, to urge voluntary medical circumcision for men to reduce HIV transmission, and to distribute antiretroviral medications (UG FGDs 5, 8). Youth saw HIV and AIDS as a particular issue for their age cohort, because youth aged fifteen to twenty-four years are the population segment with the fastest growing HIV prevalence (UNAIDS 2021). One activist said youth brought specific experiences to AIDS work, since living with HIV shapes their relationships with parents and their marriage prospects (UG Interview 23). These activities also illustrated how citizen acts can be situated in contested spaces because AIDS work often straddled the line between community-generated self-help and the donor-supported (and sometimes, instigated) "AIDS industry" with its accompanying professionalization of civil society (Watkins and Swidler 2012). Youth who engaged in donor AIDS projects felt obligations to their community, but they also recognized accountability to donors who paid their expenses or brought material goods (UG Interview 23). Their citizenship was situated at the intersection of donor projects, local need, and their unique youth concerns about AIDS.

Another everyday citizenship action that some Ugandan youth mentioned was collectively mobilizing to avoid police repression and corruption. These respondents described semi-organized youth gangs that warned illegal roadside sellers when the police were coming (UG FGD 5) or neighborhood groups that prevented youth arrests by convincing police to let local leaders mediate disputes (UG FGD 7). In one story, local government officials were going to destroy a water well, but a man in the community opposed them: "The police came to arrest him, but the whole community teamed up to stop the police ... because that well was being used by so many people in the community" (UG FGD 8). Although these youth actions went against the government – and thus, these individuals might be portrayed as "bad citizens" who were not law-abiding – these respondents thought the government was so repressive and corrupt that they had to mobilize to skirt its reach. These activities reflected the youth's unique experiences: They were the community members often targeted by police and those

---

[4] Uganda's HIV prevalence was 5 percent among fifteen- to forty-nine-year-olds in 2020 (UNAIDS 2021).

most physically able to mount resistance. Because the old and sick could not be expected to pick up trash, talk to youth about HIV, patrol at night, or run from the police to warn informal sellers, youth had a distinct citizenship role. Indeed, as one Ugandan said, "We are always called upon and act first" (UG FGD 5).

2.6 Local Activities Accumulate to Build the Nation

Many youth respondents stressed that local actions often moved beyond the individual or community level to "help the country develop," "ensure betterment of the country," "develop the country," "build the nation," "help the country move forward," and "improve the welfare of the country" (GH FGDs 2, 5, 8, 9, 10, 12, 14; TZ FGDs 2, 8, 9; UG FGDs 2, 7). For many, a core attribute of the good citizen was "us[ing] his gifts or talents everywhere to sacrifice and benefit the nation" (GH FGD 6). A frequent churchgoer in Tanzania explained, "As church youth, our contribution is … [helping] street children, orphans, the sick [and when we do so] properly, without being pushed, then that could be [our] contribution to the nation" (TZ FGD 8). The man emphasized the voluntary nature of these actions but also that their end goal was broader than just the individual recipient's welfare. These actions brought aggregate national benefits, such as higher literacy rates, a healthier population, or economic productivity.

For many respondents, work (both paid and unpaid) played a key role in this trajectory from individual actions to building the nation. Ghanaians said that they could teach, sell *kenkey*,[5] work in a hospital, and fix automobiles to develop the community and country (GH FGDs 3, 6, 7). One man said his job as a geographic information systems worker specifically advanced "the well-being of the people" because he mapped out the location of community centers (GH FGD 5). A Tanzanian explained, "If you're a teacher, by accomplishing your duties of teaching, then you can say you have provided a big contribution to the community and the nation, due to [the] number of those who are taught by you who are going to become leaders" (TZ FGD 8). The individual recognized the long-term benefits the nation might experience because of work done now. Some individuals included

---

[5] *Kenkey* is a staple made of fermented ground corn eaten predominantly by Ga people.

household work as citizenship acts that built the nation. One Ghanaian said, "When you say you are a good citizen, you have to do your house chores and then do your professional work" (GH FGD 9; see also TZ FGD 2; UG FGD 10).

The discourse of building the nation echoed neoliberal themes in two ways. First, it stressed how citizenship occurred via the market and private employment. One Ugandan man said that owning a business that paid taxes, created jobs, and trained workers was good citizenship because it helped individuals, contributed to the economy, and manifested a sense of national identity (UG FGD 4). Successfully embracing free market opportunities enabled youth to meet obligations and invest in relationships, two elements that mattered for everyday citizenship. Second, respondents echoed neoliberal ideas of individual responsibility, self-reliance, and diligence. A Tanzanian woman said, "Once you work hard you're helping the nation by not committing crime" (TZ FGD 8). The speaker's vision of citizenship intertwines the need to act within legal constraints, on the one hand, with the importance of working hard within those constraints, on the other. In addition, some respondents highlighted the agentic nature of citizenship actions that were freely undertaken. One Tanzanian said, "The employed, whether by government or private, once they fulfill their responsibilities properly, *without being pushed*, then that could be their contribution to the nation" (TZ FGD 8; emphasis added). For a Ghanaian, the good citizen "seeks the welfare of his nation and understands that he is crucial to the development of the nation" (GH FGD 6; see GH FGD 10). This Ghanaian believed that the actions of the individual citizen matter: They are "crucial" to development. Without citizenship acts, the nation is nothing. This statement reflects neoliberalism's focus on the individual, not the collective.

Commitment to work and to meeting one's responsibilities could both emerge from and deepen one's affinity for the nation (see Ngozwana 2014). One Ghanaian illustrated this dynamic, when he intertwined his national identity with localized responsibility:

When you say you are a citizen ... in a country, even though you are not really related to one another ... you have a shared responsibility towards one another. Some people say, "Well, what is going on with you doesn't necessarily concern me." But ... when you are a citizen you are called a Ghanaian. So at the end of the day, it's my shared responsibility or my shared concern to care for someone else in the same country. (GH FGD 4)

For this individual, citizenship was a moniker that moved beyond bloodlines – "You are called a Ghanaian." But it was not just a label; it was an identity that motivated people to care for others. These ideas echo the collective rhetoric of African nationalist leaders such as Julius Nyerere, Kwame Nkrumah, Jomo Kenyatta, Sekou Touré, and Leopold Sédar Senghor, who sought to foster a new kind of citizen who would engage in the public realm as more than just a subject (Mamdani 1996). Their vision was "imbued with a sense of community and solidarity specifically as a response to the dehumanising efforts of colonialism" (Bird 2016, 264). To promote this sense of solidarity and new citizenship, these postcolonial leaders urged youth contributions of physical labor and educational advancement (Asiedu-Acquah 2019; Burgess 1999; Kagwanja 2005; Van Gyampo and Obeng-Odom 2012). Nyerere and Nkrumah's emphasis on youth may partially explain the high use of build-the-nation words among our respondents in Tanzania and Ghana (see Figure 2.1). Indeed, one Tanzanian specifically referred to Nyerere: "Nyerere ... said that education should be integrated with work, meaning that your knowledge is supposed to help you and to help others" (TZ FGD 9). The respondent held views on citizenship that were shaped by the first president's emphasis on students' actions.

As this and Sections 2.4 and 2.5 have shown, the vast majority of youth we encountered viewed good citizenship as rooted in ties to others. People were good citizens when they helped others, treated others respectfully, worked together to solve problems, attended meetings and shared their ideas, and did activities that they believed were crucial for the future of the country. In Section 2.7, we highlight how youth views of citizenship sometimes put them in tension with elders, illustrating the very contested nature of citizenship identity.

2.7 Negotiating Citizenship: Youth and Elders

Urban youth were often in a position of "liminality" as they negotiated their citizenship in relation to their elders (Manqoyi 2019, 75; Nyamnjoh 2007, 73). This process of negotiation led to various articulations of citizen identity among the youth we encountered. First, some youth recognized elders' status and access to resources and sought material and/or mentoring ties to them (UG FGDs 9, 11, 12).

A Tanzanian woman exhorted, "[We should] see in which way we can collaborate with the leaders to build the nation" (TZ FGD 2). Two Ghanaian activists emphasized mentoring connections to elders (GH Interviews 12, 13). Several Tanzanians referred to political party leaders who helped to groom youth for "the next level" (TZ Interviews 12, 13, 16, 18–20).

Some elders acted as patrons, helping youth get jobs, national identification cards, food, access to NGO projects, and political opportunities (UG Interviews 7, 13, 20, 21). Although patronage relationships in Africa have been widely analyzed (see Gallego and Wantchekon 2020; MacLean 2010; Pitcher, Moran, and Johnston 2009; van de Walle 2007), they are neither ubiquitous nor uniform (Asante et al. 2021; Lindberg 2003; Mkandawire 2015). In the focus group discussions, Tanzanian and Ghanaian participants did not directly mention patrons, while Ugandan respondents did (but see McCauley 2012; Paller 2019; Phillips 2018). One Ugandan spoke of a local leader who "gives his community the first priority and even informs his friends first" when the government is planning to bring free items (UG FGD 2). Some youth viewed their citizenship as intricately tied to these cross-generational relations, but such ties could potentially foster dependency and undermine youth autonomy. Indeed, a group of Ugandan women described how a patron established a local feeding program for vulnerable children, an action that led these lower-income women to be dependent on him for their children's survival (UG FGD 8). Of course, some youth realized how elders might capitalize on this dependence. As one Ugandan said, "These old people only come to us at the last minute when they want us to help them, campaign for them, or mobilize votes for them" (UG FGD 5). In addition, these relational ties could foster a "differentiated citizenship" that would give some individuals unequal access to benefits and power because of those very social relations around which everyday citizenship revolved (Phillips 2018, 14; Piper and von Lieres 2015, 707). Part of youth citizenship, therefore, involved contestation and negotiation related to dependence on elders.

Second, some youth seemed to negotiate their citizenship around an ideal standard, one that their age cohort could not always meet. A few recognized that sometimes their own youthful actions led them to fall short of the good citizenship that their elders heralded. A Tanzanian man explained:

[We have] those [who] have reached a stage [where] they are old, and there are others who are small children; we are in the middle and we are tomorrow's leaders ... We should engage in issues which are beneficial for the nation so that we can be considered as [a] good example. ... Our actions should not be ... playing pool tables, betting, strikes. That will cause us [to] be called good children and not just children. (TZ FGD 7)

The speaker was ready for youth to take the mantle from those who are "old," but he also thought youth had to show maturity. At the same time, he recognized that youth remain in a junior role, when calling his cohort "good children." He illustrated how youth were stuck in a position of looking toward their future citizenship roles but also needing to gain legitimacy in the present day.

Third, some youth highlighted the distinct qualities that they believed differentiated their citizenship from that of their elders: They were adaptable and forward thinking. One Tanzanian said, "We can't just stick with things which we used to follow previously; some are outdated. With the current world, we are supposed to follow globalization ... Therefore, we are supposed to prepare the youth to be able to cope" (TZ FGD 9). This individual understood that globalization through trade and communication meant society had to adapt. A Ghanaian emphasized that, as citizens, youth were not only adaptable but also forward thinking: "A good citizen is one ... who thinks of the future of the nation, not just today ... The person is always thinking about what those coming behind will enjoy in the next years to come" (GH FGD 1; see also GH FGDs 10, 14; TZ FGD 5). A Ugandan woman portrayed the contrast between youth and elders in more confrontational terms, saying, "So the old generation, in most cases, they think we are going to walk the same way they did. Or we are going to do things the same way they did. But things are different now. ... So young people are not going to do things the way the old people did them. And that at times creates so many arguments in families" (UG Interview 23). For this individual, youth had new approaches to local and national commitments, giving them distinct roles as everyday citizens.

Fourth, some youth resented the statements from presidents, government officials, pastors, and other leaders to encourage youth to rise up as the next generation of leaders. One Pentecostal pastor in Uganda said, "The young people are actually the next leaders, the next fathers, the next parliamentarians. The next everything. So if they are not involved? Woe unto that country that doesn't care about youth!" (UG Interview 12). For some youth respondents, such exhortations seemed Janus-faced. On the one hand, they contributed to societal pressure to be and act a particular way *now*: "Everyone looks at you"; "You are watched for mistakes" (UG FGDs 1, 12). This pressure existed not just in terms of behavior (e.g., not spending time playing pool) but also in terms of the tasks of everyday citizenship. For example, Ghanaian youth said they were called to "clear weeds and gutters," while the adults in the community did not help: "For our youth, they are hard working. But for the adults, they don't support us. When something happens and you inform them, they can tell you to give them some time, but they do not mind [help] us" (GH FGD 9). Youth were expected to be responsible within their communities, but adults could opt out.

On the other hand, this "coming generation" admonition relegated youth to waithood: Their time was the *future*. A Ugandan said, "Old people don't have any plan for the youth and they don't talk about them" (UG FGD 1; see also UG FGDs 4, 7). Youth was a future issue, not a present one. Youth themselves could perpetuate the "youth-should-wait" theme, particularly when they called themselves "future leaders" or "tomorrow's generation." But this attitude shaped citizenship identity formation because it stymied belonging based on fully contributing one's skills to the community, and it prevented youth from gaining the very skills they needed as citizens who work to build the nation. One Tanzanian man explained:

You can find ... a rich old adult with some cars and shops, but since youth is not trusted, then this man can't share with [the youth] about how he runs his shops. Once he dies, those shops and cars can just perish after a very short time. This is because the youth who is left to take care [of them] has no experience on how those shops were run. (TZ FGD 5)

Finally, sometimes negotiating the meaning of citizenship led youth to turn on each other in an effort to distinguish themselves as contributing citizens. Through his nostalgic portrayal of a time before his birth, a Tanzanian man illustrated this pattern as he criticized his age cohort. He said:

The old days' youth were very good at volunteering ... But today, if you ask youth to assist in carrying stones for building a school he will say, "Aah I can't go there."... Instead, you will find them crowding at betting or playing pool. But we are told [that] in the old days you can't find a person [who if] his fellows are carrying a hoe [and] going to farm, [he is] playing pool. Also, the old days' youth were very obedient. ... But nowadays youth, once ordered to do something, they first start by questioning, "Why?" (TZ FGD 7)

The respondent seemed unaware that he had adopted the hegemonic discourse of "youth as troublemakers," thereby adding to the contestation around how youth understand their citizenship and potentially undermining the solidarity needed to address the very real problems youth face.

2.8 Conclusion

This chapter highlights that the youth we encountered viewed a host of micro-level quotidian acts as constituting everyday citizenship. These actions – and the relationships that propelled and resulted from them – aligned with youth interests and reflected a sense of agency and belonging. The youth we met envisioned a citizenship-from-below that includes emotionality, acting in morally acceptable ways, volunteering, and acting together through meeting attendance and communal labor to address local issues. Youth emphasized how these small activities, including a focus on work and neoliberal notions of responsibility, then accumulated to build the nation. Youth intertwined action with emotion, expressing how closeness, gratitude, and joy shaped the daily process of negotiating what citizenship meant to them. It was, at times, these emotional qualities that lay at the core of citizenship. As one Ugandan who was fed up with corruption and divisive politics remarked, "I love my community. I cannot work against my community. It is there where I am a citizen" (UG FGD 7). In spite of his country's problems, this man's citizen identity ultimately revolved around the people he saw and worked with on a daily basis. Identity contestation was also evident in how youth spoke of their elders, whom they both relied on and sought autonomy from. As youth emphasized their energy, vision, and forward-thinking attitudes, they also sought self-reliance and independence, stressing that, "We have no one apart from youth ourselves" (UG FGD 4).

Through actions and emotions, youth saw themselves as essential to the nation's ability to thrive. But their micro-level actions and attitudes did not promote a "disruption of the status quo" to "[undertake] a process of transformation" (Isin and Nielson 2008, 37). Instead, the vast majority viewed working, caring for the sick, picking up trash, and planning meals for funerals as sufficient acts of citizenship. These essential activities filled a gap left by a neoliberal state, but they were hardly revolutionary. In Chapter 3, we examine how, for some youth, micro-level actions informed and grew to citizenship-from-above, or youth engagement, vis-à-vis the state.

3 | Engaging the State

Being a good citizen is being law abiding, as the simplest view. . . . A good citizen does not violate the rights of the other. . . . A good citizen is that person who pays tax, that person who enjoys doing charitable things . . . but also that person who organizes for what's right, to help the marginalized . . . and who votes . . . Well, it's a complex thing.

(UG Interview 17)

In his multifaceted answer, this Ugandan youth activist clearly defines good citizenship as including actions related to the state, such as following the law, paying taxes, and voting. Unlike most of our respondents, he mentions rights protection, but, as with many youth, he does claim that the good citizen collaborates to protect the marginalized, strives to act right, and gains satisfaction through doing "charitable things." Despite his list of citizen attributes, the respondent became exasperated because he could not quite nail down the definition of a good citizen, as his final statement intimates. For him, the complexity of citizenship lay in the ways local acts that foster identity (i.e., citizenship-from-below) were inseparable from acts to engage the state (i.e., citizenship-from-above). When other respondents discussed engagement with the state, they often echoed this conceptual fuzziness. They also confirmed survey findings that youth's actions in relation to the state vary from significant engagement in low-cost citizen activities (e.g., voting) to weak engagement in high-cost activities (e.g., advocacy). Most notably, they solidly tied their duties to the state to the practicalities of their lives and their relations with others.

This chapter proceeds as we first set the stage (Section 3.1) with the literature that investigates citizenship activities in relation to the state. Section 3.2 uses Afrobarometer data from the three countries to compare how youth and their elders perceive some citizenship aspects, particularly paying taxes and obeying the law, and it then delves into how our youth respondents define such behaviors as everyday

70

citizenship. Because some respondents viewed citizenship through relational and moral lenses, following the law was not just about fear of being caught if one didn't obey but also about a desire to preserve one's reputation with peers and neighbors. In Section 3.3, we again start with the survey data to compare youth and elder engagement in voting, joining with others to request government action, and attending a demonstration or protest march. Although a greater percentage of elders than youth participate in the first two actions, only a marginally higher percentage of youth than elders report attending a protest or demonstration. The few youth respondents who engaged in these high-cost activities described how communal experiences, relationships, and the uniqueness of being youth shaped their actions. The conclusion (Section 3.4) summarizes the findings.

3.1 Investigating the Citizen–State Relationship

Although "citizenship as a relation is not necessarily restricted to the legal category" (Greenhouse 1999, 10), at its most basic, citizenship is recognition from the state that then gives individuals certain rights they may claim and obligations they must meet (Nyamnjoh 2007). This "citizenship as status" lies "at the heart of all political institutions" (Dorman 2020, 461), and it facilitates an active participation to make rights claims that complements a more passive citizen component of obeying the law and paying taxes (Westheimer and Kahne 2004, 242). Contention may arise around who can be called a citizen (Dorman 2020; Manby 2009; Marshall-Fratani 2006; Whitaker 2005) and how individuals view their role in relation to the political community (Ekeh 1975; Ndegwa 1997). Citizens may act to claim their rights, though structural factors, contextual definitions of rights, and diverging centers of authority may impede such claims (Dorman 2016; Patterson 2019; Smith 2013).

Youth may claim rights through social media engagement, and, as a "hotspot of political, social media activism," Africa outstrips the United States and United Kingdom in the number of Twitter conversations on politics (Otiono 2021). Social media facilitates information sharing, mobilization, and political discussions (Diamond 2010; Kamau 2017; Mare 2018; Nyabola 2018; Uwalaka 2022) – all factors that have led some regimes to cut internet access and/or monitor online speech (Faustine 2022). As one example, disenfranchised youth on social media helped expose the corrupt, repressive practices of former presidents Yahya Jammeh in The Gambia and Robert Mugabe in Zimbabwe, thereby building global support for the coups d'état that eventually toppled them (Otiono 2021). However, social media's ability to facilitate democratic participation may be audience and message dependent (Mutsvairo and Sirks 2015), and its thin but broad following may not generate the ties needed to sustain political interest (Gladwell 2010). Pejoratively referred to as "slacktivism," "clicktivism," and "armchair activism," political mobilization through social media has been criticized for promoting "passive listening" (Bosch, Admire, and Ncube 2020), providing few solutions, and facilitating escapism among youth with low political interest (Keating and Melis 2017). Urban youth in Harare, Zimbabwe, for example, spend hours discussing fashion, sports, gossip, sex, and relationships, making Facebook an avenue of political apathy rather than activism (Chiweshe 2017).

Rights claims also may occur through more traditional means such as voting, though citizens may vote for reasons beyond demanding democratic accountability: to exhibit virtue (Cheeseman, Lynch, and Willis 2020), for example, or to meet communal and/or ethnic obligations (Lindberg and Morrison 2008; Ndegwa 1997). Although African politicians have mobilized youth to vote in elections (Asante 2006; Clapham 2006), youth turnout rates have remained lower than rates for elders (Bratton 1999; Resnick and Casale 2014). This may reflect youth mobility (Nie, Verba, and Kim 1974; Norris 2002), poverty and education levels (Bleck and van de Walle 2018; Verba and Nie 1972), post-materialist values that trump material reasons to vote (Abramson and Inglehart 1995), lower rates of partisan identification among youth (Dalton 2000), voter registration processes (Cheeseman and Hinfelaar 2009; Norris 2004), and youth disinterest the longer an incumbent holds power (Resnick and Casale 2014).

Youth may turn to alternative avenues of engagement, recognizing, for example, that in contexts with limited choices, a rational good citizen may not vote (Cheeseman, Lynch, and Willis 2020, 193). Citizenship is often thought to entail "popular collective action and engagement with leaders" between (not just during) elections (Bratton 2013, 4), and youth may join with others through political organizations that articulate interests, speak for the marginalized, influence policies, and potentially challenge authoritarian rule (Bratton 1989;

Ellis and van Kessel 2009; Medie 2013; VonDoepp 2020). Such civil society efforts, though, can also be co-opted by the state, remain passive in the face of injustice, and be exclusive in membership, under-resourced, low in capacity, and ethically suspect (Fatton 1995; Gyimah-Boadi 1996; Obadare 2011). Additionally, youth can choose to protest, and throughout Africa contentious politics has helped to end colonialism, push multiparty democracy in the early 1990s, and demand economic and governance improvements after 2013 (Branch and Mampilly 2015; Bratton and van de Walle 1997; Mueller 2018). In Section 3.2 we examine how youth engage these citizen acts aimed at the state.

3.2 Citizenship as Legal Requirements

We use two Afrobarometer questions to uncover legalistic understandings of citizenship among urban respondents: support for paying taxes and support for obeying the law. Table 3.1 shows that both urban youth and urban elders report high levels of support for each activity. Percentages for youth and elders are practically the same, except that 4 percent more Tanzanian youth and 5 percent more Ugandan youth

Table 3.1 *Views of legal obligations among urban populations, by age and country*

Country	Age*	The tax authorities have the right to make people pay taxes (%)**	The police always have the right to make people obey the law (%)**	N
Ghana	Youth	87	87[a]	732
	Elders	90	90[b]	572
Tanzania	Youth	86	81	439
	Elders	87[c]	77	358
Uganda	Youth	88	92	209
	Elders	88	87	90

* "Youth" includes the weighted average for people eighteen to thirty-five years old, and "elders" includes the weighted average for people thirty-six years old and above.
** Percentage answering "agree" or "strongly agree"
[a] N = 731; [b] N = 570; [c] N = 357
Source: Data from Afrobarometer (2016/2018), compiled by the authors

than elders agree or strongly agree that people must follow the law. This may reflect the fact that youth are more likely than their elders to experience police harassment. There are also small country differences, with slightly more Ghanaians and Ugandans being rule followers than Tanzanians (particularly elders). This contrasts with the NVivo analysis in which Tanzanians gave many more responses in the legalistic and moral categories than Ugandans and Ghanaians (see Figure 2.1).

Turning to our respondents, many initially began by discussing a narrow, legalistic view of citizenship.[1] Tanzanians were more likely to mention words and phrases related to legal obligations than Ugandans and Ghanaians (see Figure 2.1).[2] But, as Chapter 2 highlighted, there were fewer mentions in all three countries of legalistic terms than of terms in the communal and build-the-nation categories. The discussions shed light on the Afrobarometer data and show how youth tie together legalistic and communal requirements. The first point is not captured in the Afrobarometer data: respondents' focus on the documented nature of citizenship. That is, many equated citizenship identity with the legal processes that determine citizenship status and the documents that make citizenship legible. Particular criteria such as "being born in the country" or having gone through the naturalization process made citizenship identity legible (GH FGD 4; SA FGD 1; UG FGDs 3, 4, 11). A national identification card or a passport embodied the completion of these citizenship processes, though, as Bronwen Manby (2021) illustrates, African states have been relatively unwilling to adopt naturalization processes, despite public support. Respondents also understood that these documents empower the state to "know" its citizens, be aware of what they do, and in some cases, extract from them "like the police who want a bribe" (UG FDG 4; see Scott 1998). One youth said citizenship meant "being registered with local council authorities whereby the council retains two of your passport photos" (UG FGD 2). The necessity to produce such documents to access state

---

[1] Respondents may have emphasized the egalitarian idea that all individuals should meet their legal obligations because the research team included North Americans whom they thought might expect such an answer. However, the NVivo analysis shows significantly more mentions of words in the communal and build-the-nation categories than in the legalistic one. Even when respondents first discussed legalistic elements, they did not dwell on them.

[2] There was an average of forty-five mentions of these words per focus group discussion in Tanzania, versus an average of seventeen in Ghana and sixteen in Uganda.

services, engage in economic activities, and even, at times, occupy public spaces may have been at the forefront of some Ugandans' thinking because, since 2014, the Ugandan government has stressed the need to obtain a digital identification card to access social services (Taylor 2021).

In addition, the vast majority of our respondents said that good citizens recognize their legal obligations to obey the law and pay their taxes (GH FGDs 1–3; TZ FGDs 2, 7; UG FGD 8), and many mentioned specific illegal behaviors as exemplifying bad citizenship: theft, assault, murder, property damage, drug use, kidnapping, and prostitution (GH FGDs 5–7, 12; TZ FGD 8; UG FGDs 1, 2, 6, 7, 10, 13). A few respondents conflated laws and the constitution, as one Tanzanian explained: "A good citizen is a person who ... follows the constitution. She follows the constitution and once you focus on the constitution then it shall lead you in everything" (TZ FGD 7; see also GH FGD 1; UG FGDs 5, 11). The emphasis on the constitution was more pronounced among Tanzanian respondents – a trend we did not probe in the fieldwork, though ongoing public discussions in Tanzania over the need for a new constitution may have made this topic more salient.

While confirming the Afrobarometer results, our respondents also elucidated reasons for these attitudes. First, their own encounters with crime and concerns over safety as youth led them to discuss laws against theft, violence, and assault. Feelings of insecurity and resentment about their inability to move freely at night may have led some women in Uganda, for example, to stress that "good citizens do not kidnap and kill people!" (UG FGD 15). Second, and more specific to their position as young people, some thought being a good citizen could at times be a drag: "Sometimes what brands you as a good citizen is obedience to the laws, yet sometimes they don't favor what you would like to do as a person [like smoking ganja], but you must give up what you would like to do to be a good citizen" (UG FDG 12). For this individual (and his laughing friends), youth who might want to push the boundaries to have some fun could not be good citizens.

Third, respondents situated the legalistic elements of citizenship in a context of daily living and preserving one's reputation. One said, "Theft tarnishes your good character, [making character] automatically fade away" (TZ FGD 1). For many youth, obeying the law helped to create a harmonious society (GH FGD 6; UG FGD 13), foster peace

(GH FGD 1), and promote positive relations with others (TZ FGD 1). Because following the law had a relational aspect, some youth also brought morality into these discussions; they blurred the line between legal and illegal activities (e.g., lying, drinking, and gambling were listed with theft and assault), and framed legal citizenship with moral phrases such as "behaving well," "abiding by the rules of conduct," "observing the rules of order," "isn't sexually promiscuous," and "God-fearing" (GH FGD 6; TZ FGD 8; UG FGDs 3, 14). One Tanzanian woman summed it up this way:

> Laws are there to guide us to do what they want. If I will go against the law it means I have sinned against God and also, I have broken the law. I might go to jail, but also God is the judge, even more than the rest ... If I have love, I will care for others. I will live with them happily and peacefully and do good deeds to others. (TZ FGD 2)

The respondent ties following the law to her Christian faith (see Chapter 5), legal punishment, emotions, acts of kindness, and living with others "happily and peacefully." In the process, she indicates that citizenship has active, affective, relational, and accountability components.

Some respondents offered a nuanced and particularistic view of citizens' legal obligations, locating them in temporal and spatial contexts. For these individuals, citizenship was not bound to a sovereign state's territory. One Tanzanian said, "If I will travel from here to America, I might be told that our rules [in America are that] you should not just spit anywhere. While here at home [in Tanzania], I'm used to just open [ing] the window on the *daladala* [public transportation van] and spit[ing] out... Thus, anybody who lives by following the rules and regulations of the particular place is a good citizen" (TZ FGD 7). A woman in the same group followed up, "If I visit the USA having some weapons and stuffs which are not accepted there, then they won't accept me and they will suspect that I'm going there to destroy their peace. But if I will visit the country and abide by what the country requires, then they will accept me peacefully" (TZ FGD 7; see also UG FGD 4). For these individuals, legal citizen behavior is not necessarily tied to one's documented citizenship but to a specific territory. Although they do not frame it that way, respondents seem to believe that the legal aspect of statehood in international law enables governance over all people in the state's territory (Englebert 2009). What seems crucial to these respondents is being respectful of the people in the host country, a notion that undergirds the relational elements of everyday citizenship.

In addition to obeying the law, our respondents said that a good citizen pays taxes. Although some respondents explained why tax paying was necessary – taxes enable the government to provide public goods like roads and schools (SA FGD 3; UG FGD 6) – many more recognized that paying taxes was just something citizens had to do, and the state had a legal right to extract money from the population (Englebert 2009). Despite this perceived obligation, people did complain, with Ugandans being particularly critical about taxes: "They are levying on everything!" (UG FGD 4). Afrobarometer does not ask specifically about citizen trust of tax authorities or about corruption in the tax system, so we cannot gauge the possible reasons for the widespread nature of these complaints. Additionally, the Ugandan responses may have been notable because the fieldwork occurred just as the government instituted a highly unpopular tax on social media (Ratcliffe and Okiror 2019). The theme of tax paying came up less frequently in Tanzania, and, according to Afrobarometer (see Table 3.1), the percentage of Tanzanians (youth and elders) who support tax paying was lower than among Ugandans and Ghanaians. Although we did not probe these attitudes, one Tanzanian did link her views about taxation to the state's increasingly repressive nature: "They are using money on some things which we are not happy with. For example, today when people talked of demonstration[s], the government sent some security forces and cars in the road, which is a misuse of our taxes" (TZ FGD 8).

There was a subtle contrast in our respondents' views about obeying the law and paying taxes. Although theoretically the good citizen does both, respondents did not discuss how tax evasion undermined citizenship, compared to other illegal activities such as theft or murder. It appeared that the citizenship requirement to follow the state's authority matters most when the state has a tangible (and potentially ominous) presence in people's lives, indicating that citizenship revolves around the "degree and realness of people's affiliation to the state" (Bezabeh 2011, 588). The police are a proximate, physical embodiment of the state evident in public spaces; hence, one must avoid illegal behaviors such as theft. But the tax collector is much less threatening or visible. For everyday citizens, daily, real concerns urge some citizenship actions (not stealing), while also potentially facilitating others (tax avoidance). This may explain the high number of Afrobarometer survey respondents who believe their cocitizens avoid paying taxes. For example, 72 percent of all youth and elders in Ghana say that tax avoidance is common (Isbell and Olan'g 2021). The lack of everyday concerns about the tax authority, as well as weak state capacity for enforcement, may make it possible to shirk this citizenship obligation – a fact many people recognize about others, and maybe even themselves.

3.3 Citizenship as Acts Aimed at the State

Citizens may make claims to the state via voting or advocacy, but doing so typically requires some basic interest in politics (see Resnick and Casale 2014). Rorisang Lekalake and E. Gyimah-Boadi (2016) find that 53 percent of surveyed youth in thirty-six African countries report being "somewhat" or "very" interested in public affairs (versus 58 percent of elders). We asked our youth respondents if they were interested in public affairs and why (or why not). This question generated a robust set of responses, with the majority expressing interest. Even those who said they had "no interest"[3] actually exhibited significant knowledge about and opinions on government actions, sometimes spending the next twenty minutes debating policies and political events. Similarly, most of our respondents reported following political events in the media and discussing politics with friends and family. Respondents gave several reasons for their interest: "Government decisions affect me"; "Government is me; I am government"; "A responsible citizen cares"; "We can't impact change if we are not involved"; "The solutions lie within me"; "Government talks about issues of youth"; "Youth have to take part in politics to change the system"; and "Because it's the community around us!" (GH FGDs 1, 3, 8, 12, 13; TZ FGDs 2, 5, 8, 9; UG FGDs 7, 10, 11, 14, 16).

Strikingly, although a sizeable number of respondents said they got information on politics via social media, they did not say social media engagement constituted citizenship in its own right. This response may have reflected the fact that, despite increased internet access, at the time of our fieldwork not that many urban youth in our study countries reported daily internet use: 38 percent in Ghana, 23 percent in

---

[3] Some caustically exclaimed, "I have no interest in the government because they [politicians] have no interest in me!" (UG FGDs 2, 3, 6–8).

Tanzania, and 28 percent in Uganda. Although their use far surpassed that of their elders (at least 70 percent of whom said they never used the Internet), it was still relatively low (Afrobarometer 2016/2018). Because youth respondents did not categorize social media engagement as good citizenship, we do not investigate these activities. However, we recognize that this engagement represents a growing area of research on African youth politics.

Keeping in mind our respondents' general interest in public affairs, we now examine reported engagement in three citizen activities that may directly influence state personnel and policies: voting, joining with others to request government action, and attending a protest or demonstration. We first report the Afrobarometer data on youth and elder engagement in these actions (Section 3.3.1), and then we analyze how the youth we met describe these actions (Sections 3.3.2–3.3.4). In the process, we discover that, for many respondents, these activities revolve not around rights claims but around their local obligations, community linkages, and everyday experiences.

3.3.1 Survey Trends

As Table 3.2 demonstrates, a very high percentage of urban youth (roughly 80 percent) in the three countries report voting, particularly compared to their peers in other regions of the world. However, their overall reported turnout was 6 percent to 9 percent less than for their elders. Turnout is lower in Ghana than one might expect given its democratic context (Nathan 2019). Even though incumbent leaders and/or ruling parties have been in power for long periods in Uganda and Tanzania, urban youth turnout remains high.

The data shows that fewer urban youth than elders join with others to request government action, with the difference being as much as 15 percent in Uganda. This may be because elders have had more opportunities to gain advocacy skills over their lifetimes or because they have more experience in collaborating with others. There are also sizable country differences among youth, with only 7 percent of Ghanaian urban youth reporting that they joined with others to bring an issue to government compared to 14 percent of Ugandan urban youth and 12 percent of Tanzanian urban youth. During our discussions, Tanzanians and Ugandans reported these activities more than Ghanaians did (see Section 3.3.3).

Table 3.2 *Participatory actions among urban populations, by age and country*

Country	Age*	Voted (%)**	Joined others to request govt action (%)***	Attended a demonstration or protest (%)****	N
Ghana	Youth	79[a]	7	5	733
	Elders	85	8	4	572
Tanzania	Youth	80[b]	12	1	439
	Elders	88[c]	25	<1	358
Uganda	Youth	79[d]	14	8	209
	Elders	88	29	7	90

* "Youth" includes the weighted average for people eighteen to thirty-five years old, and "elders" includes the weighted average for people thirty-six years old and above.
** Percentage of youth aged twenty-six to thirty-five years. We report only older youth because a sizable number of the eighteen- to twenty-five-year-olds said they were unable to vote in the most recent election. Eleven percent of Ghanaian youth, 29 percent of Tanzanian youth, and 9 percent of Ugandan youth said they were too young, not registered, or their name was not on the voter registration roll.
*** Percentage answering "several times" or "often"
**** Percentage answering "once or twice"
[a] N = 388; [b] N = 244; [c] N = 354; [d] N = 115
Source: Data from Afrobarometer (2016/2018), compiled by the authors

The data on protesting also illustrates that this is not an activity for many youth (or elders). Lisa Mueller (2018, 135) finds that the average age for protesters is thirty-five years and for nonprotesters thirty-seven, illustrating that youth are only marginally more likely to protest than elders (but see Lekalake and Gyimah-Boadi 2016). The percentages in Table 3.2 reflect this trend. Ghana and Uganda also have higher percentages (for youth and elders) than Tanzania. This may reflect the fact that Ghana's democratic political space makes attending such activities less risky, though significant numbers of Ugandans report this action despite repression, arrest, and, for women, sexual assault by police (Abrahamsen and Bareebe 2016; Paget 2021; UG Interviews 13, 16).

3.3.2 Youth Voices: Voting

Although survey data may elucidate turnout and factors driving it, we were more interested in whether youth even viewed voting as foundational for citizenship. The NVivo analysis found that few youth mentioned voting as an act that good citizens did. Even for the activist quoted in this chapter's introduction, voting seems an afterthought. This inattention could reflect the notion that voting is so obvious it warranted no mention. One Ugandan casually said, as if everyone knew, "As a citizen you have to go vote" (UG FGD 11; see also GH FGD 7; SA FGD 1). There was a sense of moral expectation or "appropriateness" linked to voting (Cheeseman, Lynch, and Willis 2020, 18–19). A young man from Tanzania said, "Voting is the *responsibility* of all good citizens" (TZ FGD 1; emphasis added), while a Ugandan stressed duty regardless of the outcome: "I participate in politics although sometimes my candidates don't win" (UG FGD 12).

Voting had a collective element, with youth often using the expression "we vote" (instead of "I vote") to indicate the sociality involved (UG FGDs 5, 8). People attended campaign events together, stood in line with others, voted at the same places, and sat together to wait for election results. Social benefits urged engagement, and voting built on one's daily relationships and obligations to the community. These obligations might also include voting in ways to help the community, as some Ugandan men asserted: "We first ask ourselves what we are going to gain from the candidates we vote for" (UG FGD 3). Another group reported they only voted for Catholics because they were more likely to "help the community" (UG FGD 10). A Ghanaian woman expressed the sentiment that voting can bring collective gains: "I can vote for the person I think is capable so that we all get the benefit" (GH FGD 2). Voting could be a way of upholding one's reputation by "doing right," just as one might do right by caring for a neighbor or participating in communal labor to build the country (see Chapter 2). Voting could reinforce relationships through its social elements and the voter's intention to help the community.

Very few respondents placed voting in a broader discourse of citizen rights and democratic accountability. As Figure 2.1 illustrates, few of the youth we met mentioned rights, and, when they did, their statements could be somewhat generic. A Tanzanian illustrates: "A good citizen is a person who is responsible, but also knows his rights and is able to claim [them] anywhere, at any time" (TZ FGD 8). A Ugandan added the notion of a social contract: "If you want to be a good citizen, you have to abide by the rules and the regulations. [But] you have rights as well .... You should also be heard" (UG FGD 11). For a few, rights were not described as individualistic ("my rights") but relational ("rights of others"): "A good citizen should respect the rights of other human beings ... We shouldn't trample over the rights of others" (GH FGD 1); "The rights you have shouldn't go beyond other people's rights" (UG FGD 11).

Overall, Ghanaians discuss rights more than Ugandans or Tanzanians, and they increasingly use rights language even for demands related to social service delivery (MacLean et al. 2016). In contrast, the few Ugandans and Tanzanians who did speak about rights did not talk about their intrinsic rights but rather about how their governments had *dismissed* their rights. A Tanzanian man noted, "Citizens have freedom of speech, freedom to believe any religion, or to say anything ... but your freedom of speech will come to an end ... when you ... [have] negative statements against the government. And that is where the government might order you to go back to track" (TZ FGD 2). This man took care to disguise his criticism of the government by identifying free speech as a central right in Tanzania, even though he knew exactly how limited that right was and the possible punishment for pushing the limit (see Paget 2021). We address the frustration some Tanzanians and Ugandans expressed over rights violations in Chapter 7.

In terms of voting, a few speakers discussed elections as a means to hold the government accountable. Again, this view was more apparent among Ghanaians, perhaps because electoral competition in Ghana means that votes actually can sway outcomes. A Ghanaian man described how he and his friends realized they needed to vote because of the government's inaction: "They [government officials] are not playing their roles. We need to hold them accountable because we pay taxes and know the role of the assembly and they are not doing it!" (GH FGD 3; see also GH FGD 1). Some Ghanaians we encountered explicitly said that electoral participation was a way to make claims on the system (see also SA FGD 2). A Ghanaian woman explained:

Being a good citizen means you need to participate in governance. You need to care about the things that affect your country. So, some people say, "I don't like politics." Well, guess what? You don't like politics, but politics affects you. Politics affects the wage you earn; politics affects the taxes you pay; the kind of schools your children go to. So, I feel like if you're a good citizen, you need to care about it. (GH Interview 16)

The quoted respondent articulates a liberal democratic view of elections – voters claim rights through the act of participation. But she also puts that notion of civic virtue in the context of the everyday issues people face – taxes, children's education, wages. These are the quotidian struggles that people encounter, and it is these micro-level concerns of youth that can spiral up to shape public engagement. Finally, she infuses ideas of moral obligation – "you need to care" – a phrase many respondents used, not just about voting, but more broadly about their acts of good citizenship in relation to neighbors and friends.

3.3.3 Youth Voices: Joining Others to Bring an Issue to Government

In our fieldwork, we did not encounter many youth respondents who discussed personal experiences with collective advocacy. This was not because most youth opposed such actions; several pointed to the importance of working together to engage the government. One Tanzanian explained, "We should find … [ways to solve problems] and advise the government on some areas in which we see things are not going on well. We can present our opinions in different local government meetings, in the parliament meetings, or in any place where we are" (TZ FGD 7). Another group of women advocated for taking complaints through the proper channels: "If you see that you're not satisfied with what is done by the government, then you can maybe pass through local government so that they can send your complaints and suggestions to the central government" (TZ FGD 3). And others did believe that collective advocacy could lead political leaders to be responsive and accountable, that is to "hear what we say and bring about solutions to the problem that exists" (GH FGD 1; see also GH FDG 3; SA FGD 2; TZ FGD 5; UG FGDs 11, 12, 15).

Despite these thoughts, many respondents said that youth often did not join others in collective advocacy because youth lacked the time, political savvy, connections, and resources for such actions. In addition, some respondents believed that youth just did not recognize their own power and, thus, needed capacity building to mobilize. A Ugandan explained, "We [the community organization] come up and build their capacity so they can see that they are themselves agents for positive change and can be good citizens" (UG Interview 13). Several Tanzanian youth advocated similar approaches, with one man reflecting, "I have come to realize that still there is a need for youth to understand their participation and involvement within different levels [of government] … Many youth don't know their rights and their self-consciousness is still of a low level. ... Youths need to be educated on their rights" (TZ FGD 5). For youth to advocate collectively, they needed capacity building and political confidence. Thus, their limited advocacy was partly a reflection of age.

The youth we met who did engage in collective advocacy often reported that these acts revolved around their daily struggles with social, economic, and/or emotional challenges. At a university in Ghana, ten students formed an organization to raise awareness about GBV in schools, motivated by their everyday experiences as people who themselves experienced such violence or knew others who had (GH Stand Up! 3, 4). Their goal was not only to educate young people but also to pressure politicians and businesspeople (GH FGD 13). Although the work started as something personal, for one member it then broadened to focus on protecting human rights: "I know this [work] is contributing to me being a good citizen because I am actually helping somebody to have the full benefit of their human rights because their rights are being violated and their right to a good education is being violated by the sexual desires of another person" (GH FGD 13). Similarly, a Ugandan woman living with mental illness tapped into her own experiences of stigma and discrimination to form an organization that raises awareness, supports other youth, and advocates for government funding (UG Interview 14). In South Africa, youth engaged with the Social Justice Coalition (SJC), a mass-member social organization founded in 2008 to campaign for improved sanitation, adequate housing, and safer communities in Khayelitsha, a partially informal settlement near Cape Town. A young woman who participated in SJC's work remarked, "The reason Marikana [her neighborhood] changed is because we got involved. We fought. There was one light here and we fought and fought to put up more street lights. ... We can walk in the streets now. It used to be dark, but now we have light!" (SA VYLTP 9). Although it was not solely youth who were in danger when they walked in the dark, youth mobilized on an everyday, mundane issue that mattered for their safety and wellbeing.

3.3.4 Youth Voices: Participating in a Demonstration or Protest March

Our respondents both affirm and contradict the Afrobarometer data on participation in contentious politics. Similar to the survey data, we found Ugandans but no Tanzanians who engaged in these activities. Moreover, we only encountered one Ghanaian youth activist who protested. This result may reflect the nature and size of our Ghanaian sample, as well as the fact that our focus group participants – concerned about appearing to be "upstanding" citizens – might not have admitted such actions openly. After all, protesters may not only use disruptive tactics but may also support illiberal, dangerous, and/or reactionary causes, such as xenophobia, patriarchy, and racial nationalism (Brown 2015, 62). The lack of Ghanaians who reported this political behavior may also reflect a political culture in which many work through established political parties and clientelistic relationships (Gyimah-Boadi 2009; Nathan 2019; Osei 2018; Paller 2019), though Ghanaian youth have historically engaged in protest actions for improved service delivery and education (Asante and Helbrecht 2018; Asiedu-Acquah 2019).

Discussions with youth in Zwelihle, South Africa, illustrate how in some geographical and temporal contexts protests may be viewed as an essential element of youth politics. South Africa has a deep history of protest politics (Paret 2018; Robins 2014), and, according to Afrobarometer (2016/2018), 13 percent of all South African urban youth between eighteen and thirty-five years and 12 percent of their elders reported attending a demonstration or protest march once or twice in the past year. The youth we met began our focus group discussion by defining good citizenship as following the law, voting, paying taxes, and giving back to the community. But when they were asked about how one's voice could be heard in South Africa, they stressed engagement in protests and demonstrations: "For us to be heard in South Africa, *toyi-toying* [a dance of protest used during anti-apartheid mobilization] is good. I don't even care how we are doing it. It helps them listen to us. They hear us" (SA VYLTP 7). In these conversations, not all youth thought that protests could bring positive outcomes, since, in the case of some recent, spontaneous protests, a police station and community center had been destroyed. But there was the sense that conventional participation was insufficient. "Your voice is your vote," another man said, "but *toyi-toying* is the only thing that makes them listen to our voices. If you don't *toyi-toyi*, nothing will happen" (SA VYLTP 7).

Although protesters were few in number among our respondents, the individuals who did engage in this activity elucidate how youth tie such actions to their daily, personal struggles against economic and political marginalization. Ghanaian protesters, for example, act in response to their daily struggles over poor roads and erratic power supplies (Asante and Helbrecht 2018). Sara Dorman (2020, 468–69) describes such activists: "Their experiences of marginalization and differential citizenship contribute to the formation of counter-politics, and the politicization of everyday life." These youth seemed to operate in a space of "blurred boundaries between the social and political domains," one in which they strive for "a radical equality within the social order" (Brown 2015, 3). Many protesters expressed feeling the personal sting of injustice, which may be particularly painful when it undermines the ability to meet one's obligations to kith and kin. A Ugandan activist illustrated this point, as he linked his personal experiences to a broader campaign for economic justice:

I have that personal story where I faced the wrath of this [country's] poor leadership. . . . My dad joined the bush war in 1983. Last year, he retired at the third lowest rank in the army . . . Now you see this old man – he's now sixty-four years – saluting young people because of nepotism. . . . They just entered the army ten years ago: they are majors; they are colonels. . . . That personal story will push you; it says, "We need justice to prevail." (UG Interview 16)

This respondent's life of poverty and family humiliation catalyzed his mobilization, and his continued joblessness and precarity deepened his political conviction. For him, protest politics was inextricably tied to his daily experiences.

The youth respondents who protested also highlight how the relational ties, interdependence, and identities that embody everyday citizenship both facilitate and result from such mobilization (see McAdam 1986; Melucci 1995). The above-cited Ugandan described "sitting down with my fellow friends and saying, 'Look, guys, each of us has a personal story. That painful story. Let the public know about this painful story. Better than rotting home alone. We must act'" (UG Interview 16). These friend networks not only motivated action but also provided financial support needed to pay the activist's bail when he was arrested and to support his family when he had to leave the country. In South Africa, a youth explained that her involvement in protests facilitated new relational ties and identities. She said, "I didn't know the person next to me, but we were all protesting for land, the Skulkop and the Marikana land. The whole community came together to fight and protest for these two lands, and we ended up getting them. We sang the same songs; spoke the same language. It brought us unity" (SA VYLTP 6). People forged a collective identity that was not solely rooted in their landlessness and call for justice but also in the very act of protesting.

Youth may bring a particular creativity, energy, and vibrancy to their protest activities, reflective of their generation. For example, in 2014, participants in a Ugandan good governance association released several piglets inside the parliament chambers during a formal session. This act of "creative nonviolent protest" was in response to reports of high levels of government spending on parliamentarians' salaries, vehicles, and computers. The young activists repeated the action in 2016. Their message was obvious: The parliamentarians were greedy, "greedier than pigs" (UG Interview 16). Like the South African protesters, these youth felt they had to use unconventional actions to be heard. One said, "We had so many times reached out to those people, complaining about joblessness, the suffering of young people. Many times we had held press conferences to try to educate them. . . . Until we were like, 'No, let's just . . . shame them.' When you equate them to an animal, a pig, it's a taboo" (UG Interview 16). Through naming and shaming, the youth hoped to gain the moral upper hand as they called attention to the human right to employment, food, and shelter. The reaction of the state (and some in the public) was dismissive, critical, and violent, illustrating how such acts of citizenship are "only rarely recognized as legitimate by elites" (Brown 2015, 3; News24 2016).

The Ugandan reaction illustrates how youth citizenship can be viewed when it challenges the hegemonic notion of an undifferentiated, universal "good" citizenship that supports the status quo (Thompson, Tapscott, and De Wet 2018). The above-quoted Ugandan contrasted "positive citizens" (people who love their country and fight for it to be a more just, compassionate place) with "negative citizens" (people who vote for the ruling party, obey the law, and pay taxes). Through their acquiescence to the rules of the game, negative citizens enable state institutions such as the police to block the efforts of positive citizens (UG Interview 16). The actions of so-called good citizens can foster the exclusion of minorities, immigrants, women, and others who have never been fully "incorporated into the national fabric" (Dorman 2020, 467). It is this exclusion that led a few of our youth respondents to unconventional citizenship acts.

The youth protesters we encountered reflected an optimism that, as agents, they could make a difference and get attention. In the words of one young woman, "When people protest, their aim is to get answers now" (SA VYLTP 6). One Ugandan described how a youth organization in a low-income neighborhood organized a graffiti campaign to promote voter autonomy and communal peace during the 2016 election. These messages directly challenged the usual pattern of vote buying and intimidation that the ruling party used to mobilize support (Abrahamsen and Bareebe 2016, 2021). Party militias traditionally "preyed on" the community's hungry unemployed youth, giving them "2,000 Ugandan shillings for their vote" (UG Interview 11).[4] In the past, campaign rallies and election days had been violent because youth party leaders felt pressure to convince (i.e., intimidate) community members to support a particular candidate. To prevent such actions in 2016, the organization used "art with a message" to highlight the importance of youth responsibility. The graffiti told people, "Elections are ending; Uganda continues. Please, it's your responsibility to maintain peace" (UG Interview 13). Although the art promoted the normative good of peace, its underlying message was highly disruptive to an exclusive political system in which politicians ignore poor communities until elections; prey on the impoverished to foment violence; and then, when destruction occurs, do little to help (Abrahamsen and Bareebe 2016; Tapscott 2017). It also reflected the perhaps unwarranted optimistic view that as agents, youth could make a difference on a fundamental, daily issue of security and that they could positively contest their leaders' actions. Indeed, youth were urged to remember that they are "better than how these politicians just use you" (UG Interview 13). When the youth scored a small victory – no violence in the neighborhood on Election Day – they showed how everyday citizenship can act from below to shape, even if fleetingly, belonging and worth granted from above.

3.4 Conclusion

This chapter has examined the everyday citizenship of youth from the angle of youth's relation to the state. Legalistic notions of citizenship were the first ideas mentioned by many participants, reflecting Western, neocolonial notions of subjects who are ruled through legal

[4] This was roughly USD 0.50 in 2022.

formalities because of the legacy of colonial disempowerment (Mamdani 1996). Our respondents echoed the Afrobarometer results that show high support for tax paying and following the law. Yet while the respondents mentioned a relatively strict, legal definition when first asked about citizenship, in many cases the conversation quickly turned away from legalisms. As the previous chapter illustrated, most youth respondents understood citizenship in terms of micro-level relationships and obligations that were then embodied in actions with others. Our respondents did not speak extensively on rights, stress their role in holding the government accountable, or report joining with others to advocate or protest. Only a minority mentioned voting, although the Afrobarometer data indicates that a large number of youth in the countries participate in elections.

Our respondents demonstrate how youth may link their citizenship-from-below and their citizenship-from-above. Youth report following the law because they want to be viewed positively by others and because they realize that law following shapes their relations with neighbors and friends. They vote because it is the "right" and "moral" thing to do, with very few (mostly Ghanaians) explaining that elections are arenas in which citizens sanction officeholders. Those who formed organizations to advocate to politicians and those who engaged in protest politics were driven to do so by issues that mattered to them as youth – sexual harassment, mental health, youth unemployment, election violence in the neighborhood. Very few of our youth respondents attended demonstrations or protests, with Ugandans – who feel the constraints of a tight political space – and South Africans – with a history of protest politics – discussing such actions most often. Very few spoke of rights (again, the Ghanaians dominated this discussion), but even those who did not sometimes hinted that their everyday citizenship led them to claim rights for themselves, or even for those most marginalized in society. One Ugandan explained:

If I come across young children who are not in school, I have to find out why they are not in school. Or if I come across a burnt child, I have to find out whether it was an accident or intentional. ... You can't come across these things and not ask yourself why. ... As a good citizen, you must seek help ... help at the clinic or the school or even the police. (UG FGD 2)

He illustrated citizenship as a relationship (to the neglected child), an obligation ("You can't come across these things and not ask"), an action ("seek help"), and a rights claim to state institutions (the school, clinic, or police).

Such bleeding together of citizenship-from-above and citizenship-from-below indicates how efforts to categorize citizenship into liberal or communal boxes provide an incomplete picture. Everyday citizenship encompasses a messiness of identities, contestation over belonging, awareness that legalisms matter but are never sufficient, and actions that define or redefine one's obligations and rights. If citizenship is in the eye of the beholder, conventional, state-sponsored views of good citizenship – voting, paying taxes, and carrying one's national identification card – are only a small slice of the story.

Finally, our respondents illustrate how everyday citizenship is active and agentic, even in the tight corners of unequal socioeconomic structures and repressive political systems (Anderson and Patterson 2017a; Hershey 2019; Lonsdale 2000). The words and deeds of the youth we met illustrate creativity and intentionality, and they challenge views of African youth as politically powerless or uninterested. As Chapters 4, 5, and 6 interrogate, how our youth respondents understand, contest, and act on their everyday citizenship differs according to who those youth are. We now focus on the ways that respondents from different income levels, with different rates of church attendance, and across genders negotiate and contest everyday citizenship.

4 | Confronting Economic Marginalization

People wish to do many things, but money is everything; you might have very good ideas, but without money ... [respondent shrugs].

(TZ FGD 2)

In the low-income Dar es Salaam neighborhood of Kimara, a group of church friends decided to start an income-generating project of raising watermelons for sale. As Chapter 2 showed, such micro-level activities manifest everyday citizenship. One participant, quoted above, recalled how the members had eagerly attended seminars on entrepreneurship, raised money, and secured the support of a local district commissioner. Although they raised four hundred good-quality watermelons, the participants faced shortages and high prices for the pesticides needed to sustain production. Ultimately, the venture failed due to a lack of funds. The failure mattered economically, but, for the group's members, it also undermined the citizen belonging that manifests in collective engagement.

As the vignette illustrates, many of the youth we encountered framed their citizenship in economic terms, and the word "money" cropped up frequently despite facilitators not asking any explicit questions about economic status or employment.[1] The comments from youth are set within a broader context in which Africa's market-driven economic growth has coincided with increased income inequality – a fact that challenges the idea that inequality declines as societies do better (Mueller 2018, 55–60; see also Milanovic 2016). Inequalities play out in people's access to employment, education, health care, nutrition, and income (Fox 2015; Karinge 2013; Mueller 2018, 59; UNDP 2017). The youth we encountered spoke frequently about a lack of money (and employment), and their comments highlighted worry

---

[1] "Money" was referenced an average of almost five times per focus group in Ghana, and an average of eight times per group in Uganda and Tanzania.

about not just materiality but also how economic conditions and citizenship relate. Money fostered citizenship identity through economic responsibility, it enabled one to be generous, and it provided stability that facilitated other forms of societal engagement. In short, without resources, people could not do the "many things" that the Tanzanian youth quoted above desired.

In this chapter, we question how higher-income and lower-income youth differ in their characterization of citizenship given this focus on money and the context of income inequality. We first situate our investigation in the literature on socioeconomic position and political engagement (Section 4.1). We then turn to everyday citizenship's local actions since our youth respondents overwhelmingly emphasized those (Section 4.2). Although Afrobarometer data gives inconclusive patterns on how income level, on the one hand, and engagement in community meetings and groups, on the other, relate, our lower-income respondents stressed those communal citizenship acts. Sections 4.3 and 4.4 focus on acts of citizenship-from-above, such as paying taxes or joining with others to request government action. Using both survey and fieldwork data, we find that our higher-income respondents were more likely to emphasize paying taxes and obeying the law. But the relationship between income and other behaviors (voting, joining with others to advocate to the government, and protesting) was ambiguous. Section 4.5 illustrates how our respondents' perceptions of inequalities may be reflected in paternalism, derision, and envy within and across income groups to the detriment of everyday citizenship (Dawson 2014, 874; McClendon 2018). Section 4.6, a case study from Tanzania, explores how perceptions about economic status shape youth participation in entrepreneurship programs in ways that define everyday citizenship. The conclusion summarizes our findings (Section 4.7).

4.1 Socioeconomic Position Shapes Citizenship

Citizenship as a lived experience cannot be divorced from an individual's socioeconomic position (Pailey 2021), though other identities also matter for citizen belonging (Halisi, Kaiser, and Ndegwa 1998), and researchers' narrow focus on employment and education may hamstring how youth themselves view citizenship (King 2018). Research has illustrated how other factors, such as time and access to power, also matter for political engagement (Brady, Verba, and Scholzman 1995). With these caveats in mind, because socioeconomic position intertwines with education, living situation, social capital (Bourdieu 1986), and access to state power (Sklar 1979), it can affect citizenship at all levels and color how those inside and outside power define "appropriate citizenship" (Smith 2013). For example, the citizenship of educated elites may be viewed as "political" while that of the uneducated is "developmental" (Brisset-Foucault 2013, 246). Socioeconomic position shapes access to the material resources that enable some to maintain relational ties (MacLean 2010) and gain greater autonomy (Musinguzi 2016), while poverty may erode relationships with family and friends (Mood and Jonsson 2016). The search for resources may drive some citizenship acts: Lower-income people may participate in NGO projects to get short-term material benefits rather than to promote long-term change (Anderson and Patterson 2017b; Burchardt 2013). In turn, higher-income people may shun such engagement because they neither need material benefits nor seek relationships across income lines (Patterson 2016). These processes of contesting citizenship may generate envy or a "status motivation that is felt specifically in response to 'upward comparisons' – that is, when a person is worse off than others in her group." As an antisocial behavior, envy leads to words and actions that seek to elevate the status of the envious one while degrading the status of the other (McClendon 2018, 12–15). For the youth we encountered, status often equated to material resources.

Socioeconomic position also matters for political engagement, although not always as modernization theory would predict (Bleck and van de Walle 2018, 287–88). Africans of higher income or education levels are not the socioeconomic group most likely to vote (Kuenzi and Lambright 2007, 2011; Nathan 2019),[2] partly because politicians tend to target people with greater lived poverty through vote buying (Mares and Young 2016). In addition, wealthy Africans may not feel the need to vote to defend policies that benefit them (Bleck and van de Walle 2018), and the highly educated may be more critical of government (Mattes and Mughogho 2009). Yet, voters with some education (even informal education) are more likely to vote than those with no

---

[2] Education is not necessarily coterminous with income in Africa's context of high unemployment (MacLean 2011; Mattes and Mughogho 2009).

education at all (Kuenzi 2006), and education is associated with campaigning, contacting an official, and running for office (Bleck 2015). But context matters: Relatively few highly educated Zimbabweans contact officials or attend local meetings (Croke et al. 2016); rural Zambians are more likely to vote if they have access to public services such as roads, irrespective of their income or education (Hern 2019); and lower-income people in the West with routine contact with government officials are more likely to participate (Lawless and Fox 2001). Overall, people who protest tend to have more education (Kirwin and Cho 2009; Mueller 2018, 135–36) and perceive that their material living conditions have declined (Mueller 2018, 22). Lower-income youth may deliberately shun collective action to keep themselves "under the radar" of authorities (Thieme 2013). In Sections 4.2 through 4.6, we investigate how these patterns played out among our respondents.

4.2 Income and Local Acts of Citizenship

Socioeconomic position has been defined variously, including in terms of income (AfDB 2011), formal sector employment, and/or secondary school education (Nathan 2019). Although not quite synonymous with income, we focus on the lived experience of poverty, which closely relates to income and education, and we use Afrobarometer's Lived Poverty Index (LPI) to stratify our urban youth data. This composite measure provides a broad picture of a respondent's income and living situation, as our neighborhood focus did, and one can assume that income would be a crucial determinant for the alleviation of the various measures of poverty that LPI includes (e.g., a lack of food).[3] Afrobarometer categorizes respondents as having no, low, moderate, or high lived poverty. We analyze the responses of people in the low and moderate lived poverty categories, because we wanted categories that roughly aligned with our respondents, who were neither extremely

---

[3] To determine respondents' LPI score, Afrobarometer asks, "Over the past year, how often, if ever, have you or anyone in your family gone without: (1) enough food to eat, (2) enough clean water for home use, (3) medicine or medical treatment, (4) enough fuel to cook your food, (5) a cash income." The composite expresses the mean across these dimensions. Responses are placed into four categories: no lived poverty (composite score 0), low lived poverty (0–1), moderate lived poverty (1–2), and high lived poverty (>2) (see Mattes 2020).

Table 4.1 *Urban respondents and LPI category, by country*

LPI Category	Ghana (%)	Tanzania (%)	Uganda (%)
No lived poverty	39	15	8
Low lived poverty	47	45	46
Moderate lived poverty	11	28	31
High lived poverty	2	11	12
N	1,305	796	299

Source: Data from Afrobarometer (2016/2018), compiled by the authors

wealthy nor extremely impoverished. In addition, using the median categories somewhat minimizes the country imbalances in the no and high lived poverty categories. Table 4.1 shows that 39 percent of urban respondents in Ghana have no lived poverty compared to 8 percent of urban respondents in Uganda. If we combine the no and low lived poverty categories, the totals are 86 percent of urban Ghanaians but 54 percent of urban Ugandans. By using the two median categories of lived poverty, we also capture the majority of urban youth and their elders.

Because we recognized there was no easy way to capture income among our respondents, we used neighborhood as a proxy for overall income level for focus group participants. We conducted seventeen focus group discussions in high-income neighborhoods and twenty-two in low-income neighborhoods (see Chapter 1). We relied on our informants to guide the choice of neighborhoods, recognizing that there might have been some individuals of higher income who resided in low-income neighborhoods and vice versa. For reasons of rapport building and rapport maintenance (some research assistants worked repeatedly in these communities), we did not directly ask about income. Although data on spatial distribution of income in urban Africa is limited, some studies confirm patterns of income segregation in African cities (Fox 2015, 16; Paller 2019; UNDP 2017). As verification, we observed that youth in low-income neighborhoods tended to talk more about unemployment, lack of money, and food insecurity than youth in neighborhoods we characterized as high income. In our discussion, we refer to youth as lower income and higher income, not because we have precise measures of their income levels, but because this serves as a general approximation for their overall economic

Table 4.2 *Local actions among urban youth, by LPI and country*

Country	LPI	Attended community meetings (%)*	Active membership in voluntary or community group (%)	N
Ghana	Low	21	15	374
	Moderate	23	10	80
Tanzania	Low	48	18	212
	Moderate	52	17	123
Uganda	Low	38	31	104
	Moderate	40	23	73

* Percentage answering "several times" or "often"
Source: Data from Afrobarometer (2016/2018), compiled by the authors

position. We first report Afrobarometer data on attending a meeting and active membership in a voluntary or community group, which we cross-tabulate with respondents' LPI (Section 4.2.1). Then, in Section 4.2.2, we compare data with our respondents' views.

4.2.1 Survey Trends

Table 4.2 shows the weighted average of urban youth aged eighteen to thirty-five for both local actions.[4] Recognizing that some categories have a small number of responses, we nevertheless present trends. To begin, there is a noticeable difference in terms of meeting attendance between Tanzanians, on the one hand, and Ghanaians and Ugandans, on the other, perhaps due to Tanzania's collectivist history and focus on community projects (Phillips 2018). More people with moderate LPI attend community meetings in all three countries. In terms of active group membership, the percentages are lower for urban youth with moderate LPI than for those with low LPI. The difference is the greatest in Uganda (8 percent) but negligible in Tanzania (1 percent).

Urban youth with higher poverty levels might attend meetings because this requires less time and commitment, and people with greater poverty may spend significant time hustling for income.

---

[4] As Chapter 2 noted, older youth were more engaged in these activities, but, because our interest is in comparing across LPI categories, we use the weighted average for all youth.

Meetings also may be an arena in which material benefits are distributed (e.g., food at NGO events). Indeed, high percentages of urban youth with *high* LPI report meeting attendance, including 35 percent in Ghana, 68 percent in Tanzania, and 50 percent in Uganda (data not shown). In contrast, active group membership may require commitment, including dues, time, labor, and stability in one's living situation – all factors people with greater poverty may lack.

4.2.2 Youth Voices

The NVivo analysis showed different patterns across income levels in terms of the citizenship categories (see Figure 4.1). First, in addition to being more talkative (and thus, having more responses in all of the thematic categories), the higher-income youth spent a larger proportion of the time on the legalistic aspects of citizenship than the lower-income youth did. (Below we examine differences in how higher- and lower-income youth conceptualized these aspects.) Almost one-third of searched terms from the higher-income youth were in the legalistic category, compared to fewer than one-fifth for lower-income individuals. Second, even though youth across all neighborhoods spoke of citizenship using communal and build-the-nation words, these phrases

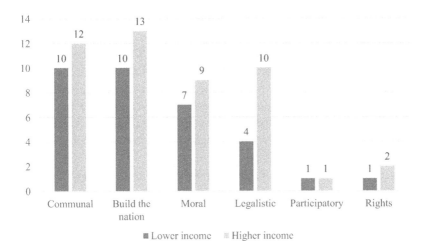

Figure 4.1 Focus group discussion themes by income level*
*Average mentions of category words per focus group
Source: The authors' NVivo data

dominated the discussions of the lower-income youth, emerging twice as often as legalistic terms. This focus on communal themes aligns with the survey result that lower-income youth attend meetings.

Focus group respondents differed across income groups in their views of local citizenship acts. Higher-income youth were keen to collaborate with others on somewhat higher-level, complex development goals, a fact that may reflect the broader policy preferences that income and education can confer (Nathan 2019, 93). They spoke about running for local office (UG FGD 11) or promoting government accountability (GH ICGC 1, 2). In contrast, lower-income youth engaged in highly specific, hands-on efforts to address immediate problems in their communities. They recounted caring for the needy, cleaning the neighborhood environment, and educating children (GH FGDs 1, 2, 7, 8; TZ FGDs 1, 2; UG FGDs 1, 2, 8, 10, 13). Both groups focused on their interests: It was just that lower-income respondents' interests were more closely tied to investing in the community.

This difference is exemplified by Ghanaian respondents' discussion of sanitation and environmental issues. All Ghanaians regardless of income level discussed the need for a clean environment, yet higher-income Ghanaians were one step removed from the communal implications. They focused on the "dos and don'ts" related to littering, picking up trash, and keeping gutters free of rubbish (GH FGDs 12, 14). In contrast, lower-income youth discussed in more detail how an unclean environment contributed to health-related problems in their communities (GH FGDs 3, 4, 7). A woman said, "When it comes to my area … we help clean choked gutters, weed around, because a lot of kids are around, maybe for them not to contract certain diseases, and not to get snakebites and other things" (GH FGD 4). A man talked at length about the need for people to act to prevent cholera and malaria in his community: "In keeping everywhere clean, we can be able to cut down the disease" (GH FGD 3). And while lower-income Ghanaians regularly and repeatedly worked together to clean their neighborhood, higher-income Ghanaians tended to focus their discussions on single organized events, such as a particular clean-up day in a specific neighborhood. When they discussed communal labor for such activities, it was described as what people in low-income neighborhoods did (GH FGD 5).

Many respondents of both income levels viewed work as a key element of everyday citizenship because it enabled them to meet financial and familial obligations and maintain reciprocities (see Chapter 2). Yet, there were subtle differences between the two income groups. First, higher-income youth often focused on their economic productivity as the ultimate example of good citizenship. One member of a university student business club explained, "Youth are vibrant and competitive. They are powerful, and so by that they contribute to the economy of the country" (TZ FGD 9). As the group described selling baseball caps on campus, they illustrated a confidence in their ability "to expand [our market] and even to employ others." They were almost evangelical as they sought to mentor other small business entrepreneurs and to encourage their peers to increase sales and develop new "hustles." One man said, "I'm trying to tell people what they should do; I'm also trying to give people confidence that they can do [it]" (TZ FGD 9). Another confidently expressed the idea that his citizenship was building the nation through neoliberalism: "Entrepreneurship [is] my contribution" (TZ FGD 9; see also GH FGD 5; UG FGD 4).

In contrast, lower-income youth seemed less confident about their economic ventures, often detailing the challenges they faced, such as government obstruction, poor infrastructure, and lack of capital and inputs (GH FGDs 2, 10; UG FGDs 1, 13; UG Interviews 13, 15, 19). As the Tanzanian man quoted in this chapter's beginning noted, one may have big plans, but without capital those plans will not be realized (TZ FGD 2). But it was not just about business failure: Youth without resources could not be good citizens who cared for their children and families, donated money for funeral expenses, or paid a neighbor's hospital bill (UG FGDs 13, 15). Such financial generosity contributed to the reciprocal ties that undergird everyday citizenship (MacLean 2010), and economic stability gave one a place in communal networks. As one Ugandan man said, "Being a good citizen means being financially okay, because if you are poor, people look at you as a burden" (UG FGD 10). Always relying on others – being a "burden" – undercut the interdependence at the heart of everyday citizenship.

A second difference between higher- and lower-income youth revolved around how they linked their *individual* economic activities with the *communal* goal of building the nation (UG FGDs 2, 5, 8). Both income groups thought their economic activities helped the country: "My income has some big or small percent contribution in bringing development" (TZ FGD 2). But lower-income people often went further, to reveal complex links between work and the common good:

"When I farm, [it] means I'm reducing [the] cost of food in the country. Through my farming, costs of that particular crop will go down and help many people afford life expenses. ... [This] contribute[s] in supporting the country economically and minimize[s] classes" (TZ FGD 2). This man optimistically saw his commitment to small-plot farming as a solution that could help reduce high food prices and hunger, problems that plague poor people. He also saw individual, entrepreneurial activity as a way to combat income inequality. His response no doubt reflects Tanzania's socialist history and Julius Nyerere's attention to class inequalities and large landowner exploitation (Lofchie 2014; Scott 1998; Shivji 2012). Yet, he was doing more than just parroting the late president. His statement illustrated a more collectivist vision of economic development than higher-income youth provided, with the latter focusing more on their own income. For example, a Ugandan businessman said, "As an investor ... I am taking care of a family in Uganda today [so] they have a good lifestyle. ... I have kids, parents, family to take care of and employ" (UG FGD 4). Thus, while both individuals engaged in the private economy, the lower-income Tanzanian situated his business in light of communal obligations, while the higher-income Ugandan situated his within narrow family obligations.

Finally, many lower-income respondents participated in community income-generating activities *rather than* in individual endeavors, most likely because they lacked capital, training, and inputs to "go it alone" (UG Interview 19). Several lower-income women, for example, worked through savings groups that loaned them funds for small business projects such as selling vegetables (GH FGD 8; UG FGDs 5, 8, 13). In Tanzania, youth bought and resold goods or produced food for sale (TZ FGDs 2, 3). For many lower-income respondents, productive labor was often tied to community obligations, further revealing the ways in which lower-income people situated their citizenship in networks of survival. One Ghanaian in an income-generating cooperative said that he needed to share his knowledge of soap making because, if he did not, this omission would "not only harm yourself, but the community at large" (GH FGD 7). In turn, achieving communal goals such as road construction, building offices, or farming necessitated collaboration, as a Tanzanian man explained: "[I should] make sure I collaborate with my fellow community people. ... I should make sure I cooperate with the community or my neighbors to bring development in the society where I live" (TZ FGD 2). For this lower-income

Tanzanian, communal labor would garner material outcomes that would, in turn, benefit more than the individual.

4.3 Income and the Legalistic Elements of Citizenship

As we have shown, our respondents initially discussed legalistic aspects of citizenship, such as paying taxes and following the law. This section first shows that large percentages of both higher- and lower-income youth support paying taxes and obeying the law, though higher-income youth are slightly more supportive of the latter. The qualitative data illustrates some reasons why this is the case.

4.3.1 Survey Trends

Urban youth voice strong support for tax paying and obeying the law, though there are slight differences in the two LPI categories (see Table 4.3). In terms of tax paying, higher percentages of Ghanaians and Tanzanians of low LPI than those of moderate LPI supported tax paying. The 12 percent spread in Tanzania is notable, with people with fewer resources being less likely to think tax paying is essential. The opposite is the case in Uganda, where slightly more people of greater poverty (2 percent) support tax paying. The lower percentage among more impoverished Tanzanians may reflect concern over corruption or

Table 4.3 *Views of legal obligations among urban youth, by LPI and country*

Country	LPI	The tax authorities have the right to make people pay their taxes (%)*	The police always have the right to make people obey the law (%)*	N
Ghana	Low	90	88	374
	Moderate	88	83	80
Tanzania	Low	90	83	212
	Moderate	78	76	123
Uganda	Low	87	90	104
	Moderate	89	96	73

* Percentage answering "agree" or "strongly agree"
Source: Data from Afrobarometer (2016/2018), compiled by the authors

the state's weak capacity to enforce tax laws (Kim and Kim 2018). In addition, higher percentages of urban youth with low LPI in Ghana and Tanzania than youth of moderate LPI agree or strongly agree with the statement that police have the right to enforce the law. Again, Tanzanian urban youth with moderate LPI give less support to law following. In contrast, more Ugandan urban youth with moderate LPI than those with low LPI support obeying the law, and their reported 96 percent agreement is the strongest of all strata.

4.3.2 Youth Voices

As with the Afrobarometer data, both higher- and lower-income youth respondents expressed support for tax paying and following the law. However, each group framed these issues differently. As Figure 4.1 illustrates, higher-income youth used words in the legalistic category more frequently than lower-income youth, and they often stressed terms related to crime.[5] A youth in a high-income neighborhood said, "A good citizen is the one who follows the laws of his country" (TZ FGD 8). In addition, higher-income youth viewed law-abiding actions in terms of a positive-sum game: If all followed the laws then self-interest was protected. A Ghanaian said, "I will not steal from my sister because I don't want her to steal from me" (GH FGD 6). Among individuals in high-income areas, citizenship was a utilitarian project, one that protected the rule follower. Several respondents were particularly concerned not about their *own* behavior – the "I" in the above-cited respondent's sentence – but about *others'* behavior. Obeying the law meant ensuring *others* did no physical or property damage. As one Ghanaian said, "To be a good citizen you have to make sure that state properties are being taken care of from other people trying to destroy them" (GH FGD 5; see also GH ICGC 1, 2). Higher-income Ugandans mentioned the "bad citizens" who perpetrated kidnapping, carjacking, abuse of children, murder, and fighting (UG FGDs 7, 14, 16). Some worried out loud about their property, saying, "One has to be security conscious" (UG FGD 4). Despite this expressed concern about crime among higher-income respondents, Afrobarometer (2016/

---

[5] The gaps were significant: In Ghana, there were thirty-one legalistic word mentions among higher-income youth versus only two among lower-income youth. In Tanzania, the numbers were 151 to forty-seven, and in Uganda, thirty to nineteen.

2018) reports that more urban respondents (of all ages) with low LPI than those with moderate LPI report *never* feeling *un*safe when walking in their neighborhoods. The results were 74 percent to 65 percent in Ghana, 72 percent to 67 percent in Uganda, and 85 percent to 83 percent in Tanzania. The emphasis on obeying the law among people who actually had little fear of crime was a theme among higher-income respondents in all three countries.

Higher-income youth seemed particularly concerned about people who use drugs, often portraying these individuals as irresponsible and needing guidance: "If there are some youth who are drug addicts, then you should warn them and give [them] advice that what they have been doing is not right. They are breaking the law of the country and also it is a sin!" (TZ FGD 8). This Tanzanian displayed both moralism – "it is a sin" – and a paternalistic attitude about citizenship, as did a Ghanaian who said, "I set good examples for people to follow" (GH FGD 6). A Ugandan woman asserted that part of her job as a good citizen was to be "vigilant" against bad citizens, reporting their suspicious activities to the police (UG FGD 14). Similarly, a higher-income Ghanaian man talked at length about how reporting crimes such as motorcyclists stealing from vendors made him a good citizen (GH FGD 11). Undergirding these statements was a focus on personal responsibility and citizenship as setting an example for others, but these assertions also minimized the complex experiences of youth addicts, including those who hustle for work and, despite addiction, strive to support family and friends (Hunter 2020).

In low-income neighborhoods, youth also focused on obeying the law, but they emphasized that a good citizen should never be accused of breaking the law. A woman told us that "a good citizen is the one who [has] never [been] found with criminal acts, like robbery; he has never committed any crime ... has never done any act which could injure or harm others" (TZ FGD 4). For many lower-income youth, this view illustrated the goal of protecting others, thereby situating legal compliance in a context of building the nation and fostering community (GH FGDs 3, 4, 8, 9; UG FGDs 1, 9). One said, "If you are a Ghanaian and you are a good citizen, you are supposed to obey the laws. ... Anything which is not good, when you do that, it will not help the country" (GH FGD 9).

In addition, legal compliance was rooted in self-preservation, since lower-income people disproportionately suffer from arbitrary police actions or capricious implementation of government policies (Justesen and Bjørnshov 2014). Afrobarometer (2016/2018) shows that across the study countries, a greater percentage of urban respondents with moderate LPI than those with low LPI report paying a bribe "once or twice" or "a few times" for health care (9 percent of people with moderate LPI versus 6 percent with low LPI) and for police assistance (5 percent to 2 percent).[6] Government's alleged arbitrariness could particularly hurt lower-income people: Some Ugandan men said that being "in the wrong place at the wrong time," even if one "had done nothing," could be particularly dangerous for poor people (UG FGD 2). Concern about living in peace, so as to not get in trouble, led another man to say that when someone moved into a community, it was very important for that new person to "not pick fights ... to be calm and well behaved in the new community where he has shifted ... because people don't know them" (UG FGD 2). Thus, while higher-income youth were concerned about *other* people engaging in criminal acts, lower-income youth were concerned about not being seen as criminals *themselves*.

It was not only fear of arrest that undergirded the ways lower-income youth discussed legal compliance. They also recognized how even the possibility of being labeled a criminal could undermine the character and relationships that defined good citizenship. One man conveyed this hypothetical scenario:

To understand a good citizen, [it] is like, maybe you found me here ... in a group of marijuana smokers, or drunks, [and] I'm holding marijuana, already smoking, or rolling it. So, if anyone passes nearby and sees me, [he] will obviously say, "That is not a good citizen, and at any time he might harm me." So, to be a good citizen depends on what your actions are. (TZ FGD 6)

This speaker illustrates that for many lower-income youth, following the law is important because of how actions affect one's standing in the community and the reactions of others. Youth offenders may be denied status as "fully fledged members of society" or even labeled as "lifetime delinquents who are beyond redemption" (Zoettl 2016, 242). Rule following shapes reputations that lie at the heart of the communal ties on which everyday citizenship is built.

---

[6] These weighted averages hide the fact that twice as many urban Ugandans of moderate LPI report bribe paying than their low LPI peers. Twenty-four percent of urban Ugandans with moderate LPI said they paid a bribe for health care.

4.4 Income and the Political Activities of Citizenship

We now explore how urban youth of different income levels engage the state through voting, joining with others to request government action, and attending a demonstration or protest march. Our respondents shed additional light on survey findings.

4.4.1 Survey Trends

Table 4.4 presents Afrobarometer data for urban youth of low and moderate LPI. Supporting previous research findings that higher income is not a major determinant of voting in many African countries (Bleck and van de Walle 2018), the percentage of Ugandan and Ghanaian youth with moderate LPI who voted in the most recent election was higher than the percentage of their peers with low LPI who voted. The reverse is the case in Tanzania.

When we examine the activity of joining with others to request government action, two findings stand out. First, as Table 4.4 shows, the percentages of urban youth engaging in this activity are relatively low overall, though there are slight country differences, with Ghanaians of low LPI being the least likely to join with others to

Table 4.4 *Participatory actions among urban youth, by LPI and country*

Country	LPI	Voted (%)[*]	Joined others to request govt action (%)[**]	Attended a demonstration or protest (%)[***]	N
Ghana	Low	77[a]	7	5	374
	Moderate	84[b]	11	3	80
Tanzania	Low	80[c]	13	<1	212
	Moderate	73[d]	11	2	123
Uganda	Low	79[e]	13	6	104
	Moderate	86[f]	12	5	73

[*] Percentage of youth aged twenty-six to thirty-five. The other columns are the weighted average of all youth.
[**] Percentage answering "several times" or "often"
[***] Percentage answering "once or twice"
[a] N = 192; [b]N = 43; [c]N = 105; [d]N = 70; [e]N = 62; [f]N = 35
Source: Data from Afrobarometer (2016/2018), compiled by the authors

advocate. The data only somewhat confirms research that shows that people with more resources may be more likely to contact officials (see Brady, Verba, and Schlozman 1995) because only slightly more urban youth with low LPI in Tanzania and Uganda report joining others in advocacy. The two cases may partly reflect the representation of women in subnational and national legislative bodies (and youth in Uganda), with these representatives being potentially easier targets for youth advocates (UG FGD 6). The survey data also somewhat supports the finding that people of higher income and education are more likely to protest. In Uganda and Ghana, only slightly more urban youth with low LPI reported attending a demonstration or protest march than their peers with moderate LPI (5 percent to 3 percent in Ghana; 6 percent to 5 percent in Uganda). The reverse is the case in Tanzania. Because the numbers are quite low in each stratum, these percentages provide minimal insights into how income and protest behavior may intersect. They also somewhat counter our respondents' views on protests (see Section 4.4.2).

4.4.2 Youth Voices

Although in some ways it is difficult to say that our qualitative data supports or refutes survey results, our respondents from different income levels do add insights into these patterns. Among the handful of mentions of voting among all respondents, lower-income Ghanaians were the most expressive. But even they only mentioned voting six times, providing inconclusive evidence that lower-income individuals vote at high rates (see Nathan 2019). More broadly, across all income groups, voting was perceived to be an obligation rather than a means to achieve democratic accountability (see Cheeseman, Lynch, and Willis 2020). One higher-income Ugandan said, "They put across [hold] elections, and you have to go and vote. That's how you can be a good citizen. You abide by the rules of conduct that come stated in the constitution" (UG FGD 14). Similarly, a lower-income Ugandan said, "The good citizen is supposed to vote" (UG FGD 10). Despite this agreement across income groups, some *lower*-income respondents situated voting in the context of benefiting the community, just as they had emphasized communal tasks. One lower-income Ghanaian said there was little she could do to impact national politics, but, at the local level, she had some agency. She said, "What I can do is that, when it is election period, I can vote for the local assembly person I think is capable so that we all get the benefit" (GH FGD 2; see also UG FGD 10). For her, voting was done with community interests in mind.

Similarly, we found inconclusive patterns in terms of individuals joining together to bring an issue to the government. Only a few higher-income Ghanaians mentioned collective advocacy to urge policymakers' attention to GBV (GH FGD 13). In Uganda, it was lower-income individuals who reported meeting with district council members to discuss tax collection and police harassment (UG FGDs 1, 10). Some youth activists we interviewed did illustrate that people of higher income had the education, connections, and resources to engage in collective advocacy. One Ugandan spoke of working with friends to lobby parliament for youth employment, and another discussed working through a CBO to advocate to district officials for street children's needs (UG Interviews 16, 17).

It was also the case that few respondents discussed protesting, making the link between this behavior and income unclear. Youth across income levels in Tanzania expressed disapproval: A higher-income youth described demonstrations as "poisons which we have been planting in each other" (TZ FGD 8), and a lower-income youth brought his Christian identity into his displeasure, saying, "Once politics is in the form of causing a riot, that's when it clashes with faith" (TZ FGD 2). Income and education did seem to give one Ugandan activist the skills needed for contentious politics, but it was his concern for the community, not his personal economic interests, that drove him to act (see Mueller 2018, 122). He explained, "As a student leader I was always involved in organizing demonstrations, strikes, sit-ins. ... I think it came naturally that after completing school I'd already been identified by like-minded, like-thinking organizations" (UG Interview 22; see also Asante et al. 2021). In contrast, in the informal settlements of Marikana (within Khayelitsha, South Africa) and Zwelihle (outside Hermanus, South Africa), it was lower-income respondents who protested poor social service delivery and lack of housing (SA VYLTP 6, 7, 9).[7] One remarked, "I like being an activist. ... I was part of the marches. ... We try to elevate the

---

[7] Afrobarometer data supports this pattern in South Africa: 15 percent of all youth with moderate LPI aged eighteen to thirty-five report protesting, compared to 12 percent with low LPI (Afrobarometer 2016/2018).

government to fast track the service delivery in our area" (SA VYLTP 9). Then another illustrated a point from Chapter 3, namely, that participation in protests and marches amplified relational ties. The respondent said, "When we are fighting for one goal, to have electricity and water, it is when I feel really, really close in Marikana. When we are connecting in a peaceful march ... Leaders, young people, and elders ... we are talking in one voice" (SA VYLTP 9). Protest by lower-income people was a way to manifest and act on concern for others, a value of everyday citizenship.

In summary, higher- and lower-income youth respondents expressed slightly different views of citizenship. Higher-income youth emphasized legalistic elements more than lower-income youth. Yet when it comes to comparing our youth participants to survey respondents on voting, joining with others to request government action, and attending a demonstration or protest, the results are inconclusive. This may reflect the fact that we let our respondents define citizenship unencumbered by questions regarding particular behaviors. Through this inductive approach, we discovered that participatory actions are not at the heart of everyday citizenship, no matter one's income level.

4.5 Citizenship and the "Other" Income Group

Sections 4.2 through 4.4 used our qualitative material to provide nuance to survey data on citizenship activities for lower- and higher-income people. We now analyze respondents' perceptions about their fellow citizens both across and within income strata. These perceptions have the potential to shape the reciprocities, obligations, and shared identities that undergird everyday citizenship.

4.5.1 Higher-Income Youth: Self-Reliance, Paternalism, and Derision

Higher-income youth stressed several distinct themes that juxtaposed their citizenship with the citizenship of lower-income youth. First, they emphasized neoliberal messages of individualism, hard work, and self-reliance. This discourse implied that people who received government assistance were not diligent, industrious good citizens. One Tanzanian said, "It can't be possible to accommodate and employ all [youth], thus we are supposed to be innovative." He then suggested that youth should not sit around waiting for jobs when it is possible to buy maize in one part of the country and sell it in another town for profit. He continued, "Why can't you ... employ yourself in that way? It is possible" (TZ FGD 7; see also GH FGD 5). Similarly, a Ugandan man said, "You know, most people blame the leaders, instead of remembering that if I want something good, it has to come from me" (UG FGD 11). In Ghana, a businessman used an analogy to explain how citizens should be industrious and independent of the government: "I'm not going to sit down like a baby bird waiting for my mother – the government – to go and look for food and bring it to me. Instead, I've taken to my wings and gone to get the food myself" (GH ICGC 1). For these individuals, lower-income people's alleged lack of initiative and hard work undermined their citizenship.

Second, several higher-income youth manifested paternalism toward lower-income youth. In Uganda and Ghana, some of these youth described the work they did to help poorer citizens: They passed out blankets, food, and used clothes or helped at orphanages in low-income neighborhoods (GH FGDs 6, 12, 14; GH IGCG 2; UG FGDs 11, 14). At the same time, they seemed relatively unaware of the economic obstacles that poor people face. One Ugandan volunteer described a church outreach project in an impoverished neighborhood: "These people ... the condition they were in was really very, very bad. They had bed bugs, the blankets were really threads, and the place was smelly. ... We [the outside volunteers] had to make sure we sprayed the place; it was so unclean." He did not question the economic structures that contributed to such poverty, and he explicitly said it was the "responsibility" of better-off individuals – not the government – to voluntarily help (UG FGD 11). Such episodic service projects were rarely rooted in equal partnerships and long-term engagement such as one might envision occurring through regular meetings and community group membership. Indeed, among the most well-off – Ghanaian urban youth with *no* lived poverty – only 15 percent report attending a community meeting several times or often (Afrobarometer 2016/2018).[8]

---

[8] This percentage compared to 47 percent of urban youth in Tanzania with no lived poverty and 28 percent of urban youth in Uganda with no lived poverty (Afrobarometer 2016/2018).

Third, a few higher-income youth overtly criticized lower-income people who were diligent, creative, and eager to pull themselves up by their bootstraps. For example, one Ghanaian complained that street sellers and vendors clog Ghanaian roads. He opined that political leaders should "drive them away" because when foreign visitors come to Ghana, they are put off by the hawkers, and Ghana's image is harmed. He went on to remark, "I think [if they are stopped] it will hurt the [specific] citizen, but then the citizen will be grateful if foreigners come to the country and see that there are no vendors on the street" (GH FGD 11). The man showed derision for lower-income sellers despite their efforts to embrace the same entrepreneurial spirit that many higher-income youth emphasized. While he had no evidence that "foreigners" viewed the street sellers negatively, foreigners became an excuse for his own pejorative views toward lower-income people. Such derision problematized building the reciprocities that undergird everyday citizenship.

4.5.2 Lower-Income Youth: Betrayal and Envy

Some of the lower-income youth we met also showed problematic attitudes for citizenship, particularly envy toward other lower-income youth. For some respondents, this led to charges of antisocial behavior. One Tanzanian activist said, "[Youth] can betray you in two minutes because they don't have economic opportunities, and ... [because] they just want money. They are corrupt" (TZ Interview 15). The individual recognized that, at times, youth acted in ways to ensure their own survival, even if this led to double crossing others. Some lower-income Ugandans criticized people in their communities who had "just enough" money to leave the neighborhood for one with better roads or a water tap; those who exited were portrayed as having let down the community (UG FGD 8). The possibility of being the target of others' envy led people to not call attention to themselves. One lower-income woman said, "There might be some things you do and people mistake you for a person who likes to be smarter than others ... and then no one will work with you" (UG FGD 5). A higher-income man explained that, although he wanted to invest in his former, low-income neighborhood, he had to do so "indirectly, because when you go there directly you are an enemy of the community" (UG FGD 4). Envy may lead to outcomes that, ironically, harm material interests (McClendon 2018, 44), and it may corrode the relations of everyday citizenship.

The case of NZP+ illustrates some of these dynamics (see Chapter 1 for background). NZP+ consists of local chapters that provide HIV education, psychosocial support, and income-generating projects to people living with HIV and AIDS. Zambia has received significant donor monies for AIDS,[9] leading the number of NZP+ groups to swell and competition for money to increase (Anderson and Patterson 2017a; ZA NZP+ 1, 2, 4–7). Envy over who received this funding could foment exclusion, as one chapter's experiences illustrated. In 2000, both people living with HIV and their sero-negative caregivers formed a group in a low-income urban neighborhood. According to its members and NZP+ officers, the group had several income-generating projects; distributed donor-provided food to all members; and showed love, care, and acceptance to all (ZA NZP+ 3, 8). But in 2008, the group was informed by the national officers that NZP+ was an organization for people living with HIV *only*. People living with HIV became envious of the people living without HIV who were gaining access to "their resources." One explained, "When there was all of this money from donors, everyone now wanted some of it. . . . They [people living without HIV] were benefiting" (ZA NZP+ 8). As a result, longstanding members living without HIV were no longer welcome, even though they too were impoverished and had spent years providing labor and care to people living with the virus (ZA NZP+ 3). Most group members living with HIV chose NZP+ affiliation over ties to their sero-negative friends. The ousted faction – which had financial control and "ran the books" – exited with most of the group's money. Envy and fear of losing resources led one group of impoverished people to turn on another group of impoverished people. Ironically, the sero-negative people were also envious after they left, still sure that they were missing out on donor money that remaining group members were receiving. Although they all lived in the same community, they no longer interacted, avoiding even cursory greetings in the street (ZA NZP+ 3, 8). Belonging rooted in reciprocities and obligations, a key aspect of everyday citizenship, suffered.

Envy could also drive some people to engage in illegal activities, as some Tanzanian and Ugandan respondents said. They reported

---

[9] Between 2004 and 2020, Zambia received USD 4 billion from the US President's Emergency Plan for AIDS Relief (US Embassy of Zambia 2021) and USD 650 million from the Global Fund to Fight AIDS, Tuberculosis, and Malaria (Global Fund 2021).

neighbors and friends who were "doing illegal businesses to help their families," illustrating both the economic hardships some youth face and the temptation to which disappointment can drive them (TZ Interview 14). Some mentioned the "normal life" of crime – one outcome of a political and economic system that considered lower-income people irrelevant and expendable (UG Interview 13). However, theft, violence, and drug use were the very actions that undermined citizen reputations, made people question reciprocal ties, and eroded dependence on other citizens. These also were activities that higher-income youth singled out as markers of bad citizenship, thereby further segregating themselves from lower-income youth, who disproportionately had these antisocial experiences. As one Ugandan pastor said, the country's economic inequality and poverty were the ultimate drivers of the negative actions that disqualified some from citizenship: "Poverty stands in the way of true citizenship" (UG Interview 9).

In summary, although not the majority, some youth we encountered displayed paternalism, derision, and envy toward people who were not on their income level and even toward some who were. These views may shed some light on research findings on trust from the World Values Survey. In our study countries, very low numbers of people agreed with the statement, "Most people can be trusted."[10] In Ghana, it was 5 percent in 2014 (a decline from 9 percent in 2009); in both Tanzania and Uganda it was 8 percent in 2004 (the last year for the survey). Although there are similarly low rates in some other African countries (e.g., 11 percent in Zambia in 2009), extremely low trust is not uniform across the continent. For example, despite South Africa's history of racial division, 24 percent agreed with the statement in 2014 (Ortiz-Ospina and Roser 2016). These low levels of trust, as well as the above-mentioned attitudes, exist despite participation in community groups and meetings (see Table 4.2). However, as the groups of youth we encountered indicate, those activities rarely occurred across income lines, making them unlikely arenas to build cross-income reciprocities and shared identities. In a vicious cycle, a lack of interactions and shared participation foments distrust and the

---

[10] The World Value Survey asks, "Generally speaking, would you say that most people can be trusted or that you need to be careful in dealing with people?" Answer choices include, "Most people can be trusted," "You can't be too careful," or "Don't know."

paternalism, derision, and envy that may undergird it (see Davenport 2015, 45; Fukuyama 1995).

4.6 Contesting Citizenship and Economic Mobility in Tanzania

This case study shows how youth's aspiration to earn an income, gain community respect, and ultimately hustle to leave poverty behind can shape their views of citizenship. We examine three different youth economic empowerment programs of the ELCT: (1) a media and production program that trains youth to film the worship service, autocue produced songs, manage the soundboard, and produce online content; (2) a farming project on church-owned land; and (3) a *boda-boda* (motorbike taxi) loan program. The first two occurred in a parish in a high-income suburb, while the third operated in a parish in a low-income neighborhood. The case shows how youth reactions to these programs reveal contestation over the economic activities that define everyday citizenship.

As Chapter 2 highlighted, many youth said daily work was a way to build the nation and to demonstrate worth as a citizen. Youth interest in the ELCT programs illustrates that one's economic aspiration may determine the *type* of work one does. This is best illustrated by contrasting the high-income church's successful media-training program with its thwarted farming project. Youth flocked to the media program that brought in experts from TV companies, offered several weeks of training, and culminated in exams and a certificate of completion. Participants were uniformly enthusiastic about the program, partly because they could then hire out their media services to other small businesses to earn income (TZ ELCT 1, 5). Yet this program was also attractive because it conferred visibility and status. One youth leader explained that more than two thousand people may attend a Sunday service, "so, someone carrying a camera in front of that mass [of people], everybody will see me, [see] that I'm working in the media team." The respondent then emphasized the value youth place on status: "We have that [idea that] because I live at [high-income suburb] ... because the status of the church is here [high] everybody thinks like I'm here [high], while [I'm] still struggling with this life" (TZ ELCT 7). Participation in the media project conferred a desired status.

In contrast, status aspirations undermined the farming project. One youth leader lamented, "Most youth are selective in activity; they don't want to go to the rural area to farm. They don't want to do *shamba* [farm] work" (TZ ELCT 2). Another put it even more bluntly, recounting, "They all just say, 'No.' Some will just say, 'Brother, *shamba? Hapana bwana* [No sir]!'" (TZ ELCT 8). Youth leaders gave several reasons for this disdain, including the familiar trope of laziness ("They just like [the] cheap life. . . . They don't like to toil" [TZ ELCT 13]). Yet the most substantive arguments were explicitly rooted in concerns about economic status, revealing that the fear of being perceived to be poor was so strong that it superseded the desire to participate in a potentially lucrative project. A woman youth leader elaborated, "It's youth perception of work . . . these dirty jobs, nobody want[s] them. . . . If I say I'm living in [high-income suburb], I have to look like [it]. . . . I don't want to be pointed out as I'm the one who is poor. So . . . I think it's a mindset . . . wanting to fit in a certain class, where you are not even there yet" (TZ ELCT 10). Another woman youth leader emphasized a common practice of hiding one's economic situation: "Someone is coming to the church wearing good clothes, wearing good shoes, looking good, smelling nice. How will you know that she is struggling? You won't. And most of us, we pretend much. We are very good at faking our lives" (TZ ELCT 7). Youth leaders saw the community as an incubator for class snobbery, which, in turn, prevented lower-income youth from engaging in programs that might actually have alleviated their (sometimes hidden) poverty.

At the low-income parish, youth also demonstrated an awareness about their economic situation. When he introduced the *bodaboda* program, the youth chairperson emphasized the lower-income status of participants: "[The] type of youth we have here are those with no formal employment and are not fit for office job[s]. . . . The big [percentage] of those who took *bodaboda* had not any other job or source of income" (TZ ELCT 6). Youth participants shared that the motorbike loan program had allowed those who "wished to reach somewhere" to move from their humble beginnings to gain respect in their communities (TZ ELCT 6). The opportunity to work and earn income allowed youth to engage more fully in everyday citizenship activities. One man said, "When we heard that we were assisted [with the *bodaboda* loan] . . . we felt that now . . . even disrespect from the street, we are going to end them completely . . . Because when you are just plain-plain, with nothing all the time, even the respect goes down." Another man added:

For people who believe[ed] we have no job to do, they will realize that we have job[s], and sometimes, when people see that your appearance in church is not different from that in the street, and that you shine in church and shine in the street, and if they ask you for five hundred [Tanzanian shillings], you give him one thousand five hundred ... they will be attracted to come [to the program]. (TZ ELCT 6)[11]

As the previous quote implies, earning respect through work enabled lower-income youth to become full members of the community; regular income allowed youth to manifest everyday citizenship, through tithing at church or supporting neighbors. One *bodaboda* driver explained this link: "We love the church ... That is a very big thing. But being in church and glorifying God we thought wasn't enough. ... We thought getting loan[s] could help us instead of just coming to sing and leave. Now we sing, and even if the pastor says, 'There [are] some offerings,' we are able to give; this is what attracted us most [to the loan program]" (TZ ELCT 6). Another respondent joked that if he peeked inside a friend's tithe envelope he would see that the friend "has got good progress." That is, the giver was meeting his financial obligations to the church.

This respect translated into a new status outside of church as well, as one loan recipient noted:

We have been respected even by youth outside the church as they see that we are empowering them. We have managed to provide job[s] to our fellow youth who are not in church and they are now riding *bodaboda*. ... They normally respect us and say, "Those youth from church are our bosses, have helped us, we are hustling.". ... That was also among the achievements that we got [from] building good relationships and trust in the community. (TZ ELCT 6)

This story reveals the aspirations of lower-income youth to engage as productive citizens and the ways that income enabled them to gain respect and a sense of citizen belonging. Yet this newfound respect also revolved around perceptions of one's economic worth. This was apparent when we compared youth demand for the *bodaboda* loan program in the low-income parish to a similar program in the high-income parish, in which only one man participated (TZ ELCT 4). This was

---

[11] These amounts were roughly USD 0.22 and USD 0.65 in mid-2022.

because driving a motorbike, like agricultural work, had a low-status reputation. It was beneath some youth's perceived worth.

Contestation over status could occur among people of the same income level too, as a debate between two lower-income youth illustrated. One, a street vendor, explained that many youth may think, "[If] I'm dressing smart, then to start walking around, selling milk on the street?! If ladies see me, how will it go?" (TZ ELCT 6). Another man countered, urging his peers to rise above this self-consciousness, "If we won't feel ashamed in hustling, we will be able to reach far in development even without blaming the government" (TZ ELCT 6). The exchange illustrates youth negotiating their belonging through everyday actions, particularly in a neoliberal context. The ELCT case study shows how awareness about their economic status and economic aspirations can shape the very types of everyday citizenship activities youth choose.

4.7 Conclusion

Using both Afrobarometer survey results and our qualitative data, this chapter indicates subtle differences between youth of higher- and lower-income levels regarding some acts of citizenship. At the local level, youth with lower incomes were more likely than those with higher incomes to attend community meetings but no more likely to join community groups. Our lower- and higher-income youth respondents illustrate that youth may perceive these activities differently, with lower-income youth being more likely to stress their reliance on one another through community-level activities. When we examine voting, joining with others to request government action, and attending a protest, the survey data indicates that lower-income youth are more likely to vote but less likely to engage in other more time-consuming actions. Because so few of our respondents actually discussed these activities, it was hard to discern explicit patterns based on income levels. But notably, lower- and higher-income youth perceived issues related to following the law and paying one's taxes in somewhat different ways. Higher-income youth expressed suspicion and concerns about others breaking the law, while lower-income youth were afraid of being labeled criminals. At times, the responses from higher-income youth reflected paternalism toward and even derision of lower-income youth. Similarly, in the Tanzanian case study, concerns about how others perceive one's economic status could actually undermine youth participation in the work activities that manifest everyday citizenship. Among people of the same economic situation, unequal access to resources could drive envy and erode the relational elements of everyday citizenship.

This chapter illustrates the contested nature of everyday citizenship for youth as they negotiate a citizenship identity with one another across income levels. Belonging, being accepted, and, ultimately, being able to contribute to one's community cannot be fully divorced from access to material resources (Shirazi 2012, 82). Everyday citizenship reflects one's ability to invest in relationships and meet obligations; questions of materiality – who has access to resources, the socially acceptable ways to earn income, how money enables some to invest in others – therefore undergird citizenship. In Chapter 5, we examine how religious identity colors negotiations over the meaning of everyday citizenship for youth.

5 | Contesting Citizenship through Religious Identity

Sometimes as a church ... we help someone who lacks clothes somewhere to cover up. We are helping out with the little things we do and so that is how I try to contribute to the country.

(GH FGD 6)

The Bible says, "All authority comes from God." ... So as a good citizen, I can't stand there and complain ... I must pray for those leaders and for whatever the nation is going through so that things become better.

(UG FGD 14)

These two frequent churchgoers illustrate how some youth negotiate everyday citizenship through the lens of Christian identity. Because 95 percent of Africans claim a religious identity (Afrobarometer 2016/ 2018), the intersection of faith and citizenship matters. This chapter explores how Christian youth,[1] as identified through frequent church attendance (see Chapter 1), view citizenship in the context of working with others, building the nation, and engaging politically. At times we compare this youth segment to infrequent churchgoers, but our focus is on youth who consistently act on their Christian identity. As the first respondent says, belonging that emerges through shared faith, regular religious practices, and the meeting of obligations can foster commitment to the country. The second respondent emphasizes that Christian citizens must harness spiritual power to address political matters. Sometimes spurred by political messaging from church leaders, and at other times questioning it, urban youth view everyday citizenship in faith-inspired, but generationally distinct, ways.

---

[1] We focus on Christianity because it is the dominant religious expression in the countries in this book. An exhaustive study would include traditional and Islamic religious identities.

118

This chapter proceeds as follows. First, we examine scholarship on religion, politics, and citizenship (Section 5.1). Next, we explore the ways our frequent and infrequent churchgoing respondents understand their citizenship identities and obligations at the local and national levels (Section 5.2). We use Afrobarometer data to illustrate that a greater percentage of urban youth who are active religious group members than those who are not active religious group members attends community meetings and joins community groups. We then compare the Afrobarometer data with that from our youth respondents. Section 5.3 uses Afrobarometer data to show that higher percentages of urban youth who are active religious group members as compared to those who are nonmembers report obeying the law, voting, joining with others to bring an issue to government, and, in Uganda, protesting. Section 5.4 shows that our frequent churchgoing respondents hew to this data. In Section 5.5, we elucidate how youth respondents negotiate and contest their citizenship in the face of messages they receive from church leaders. Section 5.6 uses the case studies of a congregation of the ICGC in Ghana and the VYLTP in South Africa to illustrate how youth as agents meld faith-based sociopolitical messaging with their situations to devise their own citizen identities. The conclusion summarizes the findings (Section 5.7).

5.1 Religion and Citizenship

African youth exercise their everyday citizenship in an environment where the public presence of religion is ubiquitous, and many believe that the spiritual realm can shape material realities (Ellis and Ter Haar 2007). Religious slogans identify small businesses, street pastors generate a hubbub of evangelizing, and vast numbers of churches and mosques large and small crisscross the landscape. Religious organizations are some of the most prominent nonstate actors in public life in Africa, and they wield considerable influence over citizens' everyday lives. They offer commentary on public policy or respond to governance challenges, and, at times, they have hampered democracy promotion (Gifford 1998; Haynes 1996; Kuperus 2011; Longman 2010; Van Gyampo and Asare 2017). They provide health and educational services, thereby helping to alleviate poverty, particularly in urban areas (Manglos and Weinreb 2013). And, most crucially for our project, they may shape how people understand political engagement. In many parts of the world, regular church attendance is strongly correlated with higher political activism, including voter turnout, general engagement with politics, and associational activism (Djupe and Grant 2001; Gerber, Gruber, and Hungerman 2016; Norris and Inglehart 2011; Omelicheva and Ahmed 2018; Williams 2018). Church participation can build civic skills such as planning or organizing events that contribute to political engagement outside of church (Djupe and Gilbert 2009; Dowd and Sarkissian 2017). Set within communities, churches are ready-made channels of political information, recruitment, or mobilization that congregants can use for political advocacy (Jones-Correa and Leal 2001).

The two dominant Christian traditions in Africa both urge their followers to be politically engaged. Renewalist messaging focuses on individual agency, the duty to elect ethical people, and obedience to authority (Burgess 2015; Freston 2001; Gifford 2004; McClendon and Riedl 2015a). In contrast, mainline churches – spurred on by more prophetic theological traditions – press Christians to hold governments accountable to the norms of justice, to invest in the common good, and to display tolerance toward other religious traditions (Kuperus 2018; Lonsdale 2009). Political messaging from these different churches can shape political interest and participation. Gwendolyn McClendon and Rachel Riedl (2019, 24; 2021) find that people exposed to Pentecostal political messaging feel empowered to lead by example in response to sociopolitical challenges, while audiences of mainline Christian messaging are more willing to hold the government accountable and challenge the status quo. As one example, Pentecostal messaging led followers to challenge the powerful elites perpetuating corruption and inequality in some Nigerian communities (Marshall 2009).

Our findings echo studies that show how congregational life provides numerous opportunities to structure civic engagement and social contributions (Djupe and Gilbert 2009; Wuthnow 2002) and how religious identity and church attendance correlate with greater interest and engagement in politics (Mangos and Weinreb 2013). Yet our analysis brings insights to these studies through its focus on youth, its attention to how faith-empowered behaviors link to citizen identity, and its concern over how youth themselves contest their everyday citizenship in light of their religious faith.

5.2 Church Attendance and Local Acts of Citizenship

Table 5.1 presents data on religious group membership among urban youth and their elders. Afrobarometer asks respondents if they are members of a religious group that meets outside of regular worship services. We analyze the responses of people who selected "not a member" and "active member" because they roughly align with our infrequent- and frequent-churchgoing respondents. They also capture the majority of survey respondents. (The other roughly 15 to 20 percent of urban respondents are either inactive or leaders.) Active religious group membership is higher for urban Ghanaians and Tanzanians than urban Ugandans, most likely reflecting the historic rivalry and violence between Catholics and Anglicans during Uganda's early independence period and the politicization of religious identity under President Idi Amin (Dowd 2015; Freston 2001). Religious commitments and formal participation are tightly bound to markers of adulthood, particularly marriage and parenthood (Stolzenberg, Blair-Loy, and Wait 1995), leading us to anticipate lower numbers of urban youth reporting active religious group membership. This is the case in Uganda (11 percent of urban youth versus 17 percent of urban elders). But in Ghana and Tanzania, roughly 33 percent of both urban youth and urban elders report active religious group membership (data not shown).

We anticipate that frequent and infrequent churchgoers will differ in their understanding of citizenship because research (discussed above) shows a correlation between religious organizational membership and associational life/political activism. This section first uses

Table 5.1 *Religious group membership among urban respondents, by country*

Category	Ghana (%)	Tanzania (%)	Uganda (%)
Not a member	46	54	69
Inactive member	12	5	10
Active member	35	33	22
Official leader	7	7	7
N	1,305	796	299

Source: Data from Afrobarometer (2016/2018), compiled by the authors

Afrobarometer data to support this assumption (Section 5.2.1). We then dive into the qualitative data (Section 5.2.2) to show that frequent churchgoers discuss local citizenship acts by explicitly relating them to faith and concerns about building the nation.

5.2.1 Survey Trends

As in Chapter 4, we consider the Afrobarometer data for urban youth on two community-level actions – attending a community meeting and being an active member of a voluntary or community group – and we cross-tabulate those results with religious group membership (see Table 5.2). Although some responses were low in number, we can still gather general patterns from the results. We realize that some survey respondents may have thought a community meeting was synonymous with a church meeting or that membership in a voluntary or community group equated with religious group membership. Nevertheless, we retain these questions because religious identity can shape communal and civic engagement through, for example, clergy who urge members to aid their communities or institutions that teach transferable leadership skills (Djupe and Gilbert 2009; Lundåsen 2022). However, because Afrobarometer only measures a specific communal activity rather than the identities associated with it, we rely on the focus group material to elucidate how religious identity informs our youth's everyday citizenship.

Table 5.2 *Local actions among urban youth, by religious group membership and country*

Country	Member of religious group	Attended community meetings (%)*	Active membership in voluntary or community group (%)	N
Ghana	Not a member	16	10	336
	Active member	23	21	262
Tanzania	Not a member	46	17	272
	Active member	52	20	135
Uganda	Not a member	23	21	153
	Active member	65	59	29

*Percentage answering "several times" or "often"
Source: Data from Afrobarometer (2016/2018), compiled by the authors

As prior scholarship suggests, a greater percentage of active religious group members than nonmembers engages in both local acts of citizenship, and, in some countries and for some actions, the difference is quite large. For example, among urban youth, active religious group members in Uganda have much higher percentages of engagement in these two actions than nonmembers. If we compare countries, Tanzanians and Ugandans active in religious organizations have the highest engagement, though even a significant minority of nonmembers participate in meetings in Tanzania. The percentage of urban youth in Ghana is the lowest on both questions: Only 23 percent of religious group members report attending community meetings often – well below the 65 percent in Uganda and 52 percent in Tanzania. As discussed in Chapter 2, the results may partly reflect Ghana's relatively low rates of informal political participation (Armah-Attoh and Robertson 2014).

5.2.2 Youth Voices

The NVivo analysis demonstrates that both frequent and infrequent churchgoers emphasized the communal thematic category, echoing findings in earlier chapters. In some ways, this seems to contradict the Afrobarometer data that shows higher communal engagement by religious group members. Yet, this finding is more complicated for conceptual and methodological reasons. Conceptually, we used the Afrobarometer questions as two measures to define local acts of citizenship, but they are not all-encompassing indicators of the local tasks and relational attitudes that lie at the heart of everyday citizenship, as Chapter 2 illustrates. Methodologically, because we used open-ended questions to ask youth how they understood good citizenship, only some volunteered actions such as community meeting attendance. Had we asked about specific communal activities (e.g., meetings), the results might have more closely conformed to the Afrobarometer findings. Despite these limitations, when we examined our respondents' words we found that many frequent churchgoers brought unique perspectives to how they understood citizenship. As Figure 5.1 shows, on average they used more build-the-nation words than infrequent churchgoers, and they readily discussed how faith undergirds citizen identity. How they link faith, communal actions, and aspirations to build the nation appears to shape their political engagement.

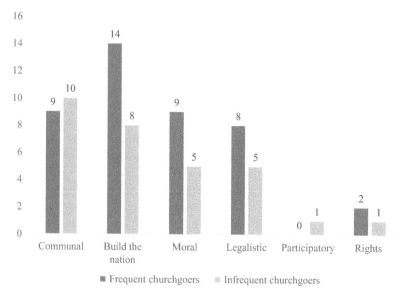

Figure 5.1 Focus group discussion themes by church attendance*
* Average mentions of category words per focus group
Source: The authors' NVivo data

At the most foundational level, many frequent churchgoers framed everyday citizenship through distinct faith-empowered lenses, and they articulated specific religious reasons for their local acts of citizenship. For example, Ugandan youth helped at an orphanage because Jesus told them to care for "the least of these" (UG FGD 11); others sought to live peacefully with others because the "Bible says we are the light of the world" (GH ICGC 2, 4; UG FGD 12); and still others provided care for non-Christian neighbors "because the Bible tells us people are made in God's image" (UG FGDs 10, 14). They also interpreted faith-empowered practices such as "praying, fasting, and examining their conscience for their nation" to be acts of citizenship (O'Neill 2009, 335). Several frequent churchgoers said that prayer was a powerful tool that citizens should channel to solve problems: "A good citizen prays. He prays for the country so that God will lift his hands on the country to avoid conflict" (GH FGD 2; see also UG FGDs 11, 14). Similarly, some frequent churchgoers believed that the Word of God could transform the country (GH FGD 3).

Second, some faith-inspired activities were done collectively, providing the opportunity for deepening identities of belonging among churchgoers. One frequent churchgoer in Uganda illustrated this collective element: "At youth group, someone will just say, 'Let us all pray for this and this in the country'" (UG FGD 16). A Tanzanian youth explained how small acts such as helping a neighbor could foster interdependence: "We live by depending on each other. You can't live like an island ... We as citizens ... should have relationships of caring for each other every day" (TZ FGD 2). A Ghanaian woman then explained how these faith identities and church-led actions spilled over into community relations: "In my church, you know that there is someone who is dying or a woman who has given birth, and so you go and console the person or bring soap to the lady who has given birth ... You make the person feel that she is part of you and you see her as a family. ... I think that it actually promotes good relations in the community" (GH FGD 4). These respondents echo scholarship indicating that church communities, like other associational groups, provide a forum for building ties, fostering belonging, and, as a result, assisting the community (Garner 2000). What made these ties unique for some youth we encountered was their inseparability from Christian faith.

For some frequent churchgoers, a shared Christian identity and its resulting relational ties then helped them to contribute to building the nation. They became a "good citizen who is a spiritual leader for the development of the community and the country" (TZ FGD 2; see Bird 2016; Fortier 2016; O'Neill 2009). Nation building also occurred through the accumulation of tasks, as two frequent churchgoers explained. Describing the aggregate benefits of local efforts to pick up trash, one Ghanaian said, "So if we are doing ... communal labor and I am part [of it], ... if it is being handled at other places and then all within there are also doing it ... in a whole, it is cleaning Ghana" (GH FGD 1). Local development efforts would incrementally build the nation. A Ugandan churchgoer metaphorically stressed that mutual dependence and acting together brought concrete outcomes: "Since we are all building the nation, we have to do it hand in hand. Lean on me as I lean on you. And together we have a better plate from where we shall get the food" (UG FGD 16). For some churchgoers, building the nation manifested in individual actions, such as being responsible, accountable, and diligent in work and school (GH ICGC 3, 4; UG FGDs 9, 16). As agents of neoliberal governmentality, churches may shape and discipline believers' behavior by fostering norms, discourses, and self-regulation (Foucault 2002). Christian "self-improvement becomes a mode of citizenship participation" (O'Neill 2009, 343) – a theme evident in the ICGC case study presented in Section 5.6.1.

5.3 Church Attendance and the Legalistic Elements of Citizenship

As Chapters 3 and 4 have shown, there was strong support among youth in all three countries for both tax paying and obeying the law. Table 5.3 shows that overall more urban active religious group members than nonmembers support meeting these legal obligations, although the differences were never more than 4 percent (in Ghana, on tax paying). Intriguingly, 2 percent *fewer* Ugandan active religious group members agreed that "the police always have the right to make people obey the law." This is a counterintuitive finding since religious messages often stress obedience to authority (Kuperus 2011). It may reflect Ugandans' significant awareness of government corruption and human rights abuses – a point some religious leaders have highlighted publicly (Dowd 2015). Overall, the survey data shows that active members of religious groups are only marginally more legalistic than nonmembers.

In the focus group discussions, as Figure 5.1 indicates, frequent churchgoers used more legalistic phrases than infrequent churchgoers

Table 5.3 *Views of legal obligations among urban youth, by religious group membership and country*

Country	Member of religious group	Tax authorities have the right to make people pay their taxes (%)*	The police always have the right to make people obey the law (%)*	N
Ghana	Not a member	86	86	336
	Active member	90	87	262
Tanzania	Not a member	86	81	272
	Active member	87	81	135
Uganda	Not a member	86	92	153
	Active member	86	90	29

*Percentage answering "agree" or "strongly agree"
Source: Data from Afrobarometer (2016/2018), compiled by the authors

did, insisting that good citizens must "protect state property," "pay their taxes," "stay away from weapons," and "report wrongdoing to police" (GH FGDs 1–6; TZ FGDs 2, 8; UG FGDs 10, 12, 13). Infrequent churchgoers mentioned these aspects of everyday citizenship as well, but their lists of permitted and prohibited activities were not as long or as prominent in our discussions. One Ugandan infrequent churchgoer even snidely said that being a good citizen meant "behav[ing] like a born again Christian and avoiding doing bad things like taking alcohol … and engaging in fights" (UG FGD 6).

In many ways, this is not surprising since religion provides a framework to guide its followers' behavior (Fox 2018, 49). As a Ugandan churchgoer said, "The principles that the Bible gives … to people help very much in shaping our lives … for our being good citizens" (UG FGD 11). Religious texts, dogmas, and practices include instructions that not only steer adherents in individual contexts (e.g., marriage, family life) but also influence believers' opinions regarding political issues and the role of government (Silberman 2005). Many religious leaders encourage their followers to be law abiding, as one pastor illustrated: "A good citizen observes the rules of that particular country. A good citizen pays his taxes, for instance … Jesus says that as Christians we must pay heed or obey our earthly authorities" (GH Interview 2).

Focus group discussions also revealed that frequent churchgoers, more than infrequent churchgoers, connected morality to being law abiding (see Figure 5.1). Some respondents explained that behaving righteously naturally carried over into following the "dos and don'ts of the country" (GH FGD 1). A Tanzanian man explained:

[A good citizen] is a good worshipper of God or God-fearing person. This is because in one way or another the bases of government regulations are very much associated in big percents with the [biblical] foundations in God's commandments, like "Thou shalt not steal"; … "Thou shalt not bear false witness against thy neighbor"; "Thou shalt not kill." You will find they relate to laws of the country, that if you steal it is an offense, but also in God's law it is a sin. (TZ FGD 2)

Another Tanzanian man emphasized, "By abiding by God's rules and regulations as a Christian this will *automatically* make you a good person in the community" (TZ FGD 8; emphasis added). For reasons we did not probe, frequent churchgoers in Tanzania had many more mentions of words in the legalistic and moral categories than church-goers in Uganda and Ghana, as these two individuals exemplify.[2]

Some frequent churchgoers went one step further, explaining how following religious rules could be crucial for building the nation, thereby linking micro- and macro-level acts of citizenship. One Ghanaian man said, "If people abide by the Word of God, they will not do the things they know they are not supposed to do. So *that alone* can cause them to live a life that will please God and at the same time lead to the development of our country" (GH FGD 5; emphasis added). A Tanzanian woman connected a lack of faith with the limited law following and nation building in her country, saying, "The major-ity of youth are not God fearing. That's why you will find even at the national level, youth are the ones who are involved in most of the evils like adultery, robbery, et cetera, while they are supposed to build the nation in one way or another" (TZ FGD 2).

These responses show these believers' singular conviction that following God is the only path ("that alone") through which develop-ment is possible, thereby potentially downplaying economic and polit-ical obstacles. The speakers highlight a certainty that following God's laws will "automatically" make one a good citizen, without question-ing the difficulty of knowing what God might want one to do in ambiguous situations. These respondents may reflect the frequent exposure churchgoing youth have to political messaging and programs that stress morality and obedience. Some churchgoing respondents, though, conveyed a more nuanced view. One Ugandan woman said, "Sometimes, I am like, 'God am I really doing the right thing? Or am I doing the wrong thing?' and I'm like, 'God, what do you really want me to do in this situation?'" (UG FGD 15). Another frequent church-goer said that being a good citizen is not just about following the rules but also about God providing another chance after mistakes: "Being a good citizen comes in a way that God gives you the grace, because there is nobody [who] is perfect. Even when you say, 'I'm a good citizen,' but then you fail. So, I think that being a good citizen is all about by the grace of God, that you can learn to be a good citizen" (UG FGD 9). Thus, even though many frequent churchgoers viewed

---

[2] Tanzanian frequent churchgoers averaged twenty-four mentions of words in the moral category (versus four each for Uganda and Ghana), and they averaged sixteen mentions of words in the legalistic category (versus five each in Uganda and Ghana).

citizenship in legalistic ways, some carried those perceptions a step further to say that citizenship is a process of learning from mistakes and that faith matters for that process.

Apart from the nuances our qualitative data unearthed, we encountered one counterintuitive finding. We expected the youth we met who attended renewalist churches would highlight the legalistic and moral themes of citizenship more than their mainline counterparts due to their exposure to political messaging stressing right living, morality, and obedience to authority (McClendon and Riedl 2019). However, renewalist churchgoers mentioned legalistic words on average four times per focus group, while mainline churchgoers mentioned them nine times. The moral theme displayed itself similarly (six average mentions for renewalists to eleven for mainliners).

There could be two explanations for these results. First, even though religious elites from the two Christian traditions may espouse *specific* political messaging in their official communiques, it is likely that mainline and renewalist churches convey *generic* Christian political messages that coalesce with legalistic and moral understandings of citizenship in daily communication (e.g., "Christians should follow authority"). Our frequent churchgoers – both renewalist and mainline – echoed such generic messaging when they suggested that good citizens needed to set good examples or pray regularly for the country (GH FGDs 2, 3, 6; UG FGDs 9, 14). Second, our youth respondents were most likely also influenced by the political messaging they receive *outside* the church or from social networks (Andolina et al. 2003; Asante 2013). Political messaging from religious organizations may be cohesive, but individuals process or embody that information differently depending on context, motivation, or status within the religious organization (Djupe and Gilbert 2009). It could be, for example, that the majority of our mainline churchgoers were higher income, even those attending churches in low-income areas, and, thus, they might have been concerned about protecting their property and following the law (see Chapter 4). Additionally, patriarchy may lead all churches to emphasize appropriate behavior for women, such as modest dress (see Chapter 6). In Uganda, both mainliners and renewalists have made public statements against homosexuality and sexual education in schools, further blurring church lines on these issues (Grossman 2015). Thus, youth negotiate and contest their citizenship understandings at times in abeyance of the religious messaging they receive.

5.4 Church Attendance, Political Activities, and Citizenship

Table 5.4 returns to the survey data for the three political activities of voting, joining with others to request government action, and participating in a demonstration or protest. It shows that urban youth active in religious groups report higher engagement in these activities than youth who are nonmembers of religious groups, with the exception of Tanzanians and Ghanaians engaged in protesting. The findings echo the above-cited scholarship that demonstrates a positive correlation between participation in congregational life and political engagement. Higher voter turnout by urban youth active in religious groups may not be surprising since these institutions may convey messages of citizen political engagement (Patterson and Kuperus 2016). The differences regarding religious group membership and political engagement are notable when it comes to joining with others to request government action. Twenty-four percent of urban youth in Uganda who were members of religious groups were engaged in advocacy versus 12 percent of nonmembers. Being a member of a religious group may provide these Ugandans the confidence and skills needed for advocacy in their repressive environment (see Sperber, Kaaba, and McClendon 2022).

Table 5.4 *Participatory actions among urban youth, by religious group membership and country*

Country	Member of religious group	Voted (%)*	Joined others to request govt action (%)**	Attended a demonstration or protest (%)***	N
Ghana	Not a member	77[a]	5	4	336
	Active member	83[b]	8	3	262
Tanzania	Not a member	77[c]	9	2	272
	Active member	80[d]	15	0	135
Uganda	Not a member	76[e]	12	6	153
	Active member	100[f]	24	7	29

* Percentage of youth aged twenty-six to thirty-five. The other columns are the weighted average of all youth.
** Percentage answering "several times" or "often"
*** Percentage answering "once or twice"
[a] N = 177; [b] N = 139; [c] N = 140; [d] N = 81; [e] N = 84; [f] N = 17
Source: Data from Afrobarometer (2016/2018), compiled by the authors

The percentages are lower in Tanzania (15 percent of religious group members to 9 percent of nonmembers) and Ghana (8 percent to 5 percent). Ghanaians again are the least likely to join with others to request government action – a finding that may be understood in light of explanations related to Ghanaians' relatively lax civil society engagement (see Chapter 2). Finally, although attending a demonstration or protest march is an uncommon activity for all respondents, only in Uganda do we find that the percentage of urban youth active in religious groups who protest is higher than the percentage of youth who are not in a religious group.

Our qualitative data shines some light on the Afrobarometer survey, though, as Chapters 3 and 4 point out, few respondents discussed voting, advocacy, or protesting as key citizenship components. Despite this fact, there were two broad discussion threads that set the frequent and infrequent churchgoers apart on these topics. First, a number of frequent churchgoers tied political engagement to the trajectory of faith, relational ties, and build-the-nation citizen components mentioned above. Some reported that church leaders urged voting for reasons that included electing wise leaders (GH FGDs 3, 5; UG FGDs 9–13); "voting for leaders who will maintain peace" (UG 13); reforming politics (GH FGD 6); and specifically electing responsible Christians who, "if you give them money to construct a road, will not corrupt everything" (UG FGD 16). Like the last speaker, several highlighted that voting to build the nation had a distinctly Christian objective. A Ghanaian man, expressing the need to vote to ensure that laws aligned with Christian values, remarked, "[I]f you don't contribute your ideas or opinions to the making of leaders, these same unbelievers will go out there to make some people who are not supposed to be leaders over us. And they will make laws which we cannot abide by" (GH FGD 1; see also UG FGD 11). A Ugandan woman said Christians could not "leave it to the world" because the result could be potentially "disastrous" (UG FGD 14). These comments demonstrate that it is not just faith driving voter motivation. Social and political interests also factor in and raise questions about how inclusively or exclusively such respondents define community.

Faith also appeared to be the impetus for the few respondents who advocated and/or protested. In Ghana, a youth activist said her Christian faith led her to engage in national politics. Although she did not specifically link faith to her protest participation, she did talk about her involvement in a march to Flagstaff House (the executive office) in 2014 to protest electricity problems and another in 2015 over electoral issues (GH Interview 16). Two Ugandan activists, in contrast, were explicit about how faith drove their actions. One found inspiration in the life of Christ – "Jesus himself was an activist. ... He couldn't sit and watch the suffering of people" – and, more broadly, in his faith – "If I didn't have faith at heart, I would become a terrorist, because of all the things they [authorities] have done to me in prison, beating you almost to death ... But I pray over and over and the anger goes away" (UG Interview 16). Another said he drew inspiration from both Christ's humility – "When he washed the feet of his disciples, it wasn't for show" – and God's desire for all people to live with dignity (UG Interview 22). These responses align with research indicating that religion has long been a motivator for political advocacy, protests, and social movement participation (Goldstein and Reed 2022; Smith 1996).

Second, more frequent churchgoers than infrequent churchgoers reported an interest in politics, with many tying this interest to their belief in the power of faith to bring about change.[3] Especially in Ghana and Uganda, frequent churchgoers expressed more interest, less cynicism, and more hope about politics than infrequent churchgoers. This occurred even in Uganda, where youth widely discussed corruption.[4] One frequent churchgoing Ghanaian said, "You must be interested in politics. It's the core Christian mandate to be interested in politics!" (GH FGD 1; see UG FGDs 9, 16). This comment was then linked to both Christian self-interest – "Because the Bible says if you fail to make laws, the unbelievers will make laws and it will go against you" – and hope for Ghana's future – "If we contribute our God-given wisdom, I think that it will help shape the country to be a better country" (GH FGD 1). Frequent churchgoers also connected their religious commitment to the need to hold an underperforming government accountable. One Ghanaian man explained, "We need to hold them accountable ...

[3] Sometimes these discussions related to rights, which frequent churchgoers discussed more than infrequent churchgoers (see Figure 5.1).
[4] In Ghana, there were fifteen mentions of interest in politics among frequent churchgoers versus seven among infrequent churchgoers. There were four mentions of no interest in politics among frequent churchgoers versus eighteen among infrequent churchgoers. In Uganda, there were eighteen mentions of interest among frequent churchgoers compared to six among infrequent churchgoers, and three mentions of no interest among frequent churchgoers versus eighteen among infrequent churchgoers.

We need to be interested and pray that we would get good people there. Because if you are less concerned it will come back to you" (GH FGD 3). And they said it was important to know what the government was doing – both "the very many bad things not worth mentioning … and the good things" – so that they could channel their faith through prayer and action to improve the country (UG FGD 12).

These responses indicate an agentic approach to politics, and they align with studies that suggest various ways that religion may motivate political action. Religious messages suggesting that political and social change can or should happen through faith-based action can inspire followers because such messages promote the efficacy, confidence, and perseverance that challenge political disillusionment (McClendon and Riedl 2015b; Preston, Salomon, and Ritter 2013; Sperber, Kaaba, and McClendon 2022). Indeed, some respondents highlighted the empowering messages they received from pastors: "They tell us that we can transform society"; "They believe in us"; "They tell us we are equipped and if we lead, others will follow" (UG FGDs 11, 13, 15). In addition, relational ties in churches, such as those described in Section 5.2.2, facilitate the information sharing and connections needed for engagement (Omelicheva and Ahmed 2018), and some decentralized church structures may create opportunities for political action (Patterson and Kuperus 2016). Yet, for many churchgoing respondents, it still boiled down to faith, as a Ugandan concluded, "I, as a Christian, can cause greater change than non-Christians because I'm having God's grace and the spirit is leading me" (UG FGD 9).

In sum, differences emerged between frequent and infrequent churchgoers along the lines of law abidance and political participation. Frequent churchgoers emphasized legalistic elements based on faith commitments that shaped their sense of right and wrong. Few of our respondents mentioned involvement in specific political actions, but, for those who did, at least among frequent churchgoers, faith seemed to be a motivating factor. Finally, frequent churchgoers exhibited greater political efficacy – a factor that could influence their political involvement.

5.5 Youth, Relations with Religious Leaders, and Citizenship

We now interrogate how youth may negotiate and contest their everyday citizenship, particularly in light of the public role of religious leaders, who are the most widely trusted leaders on the African continent (Manglos and Weinreb 2013; Uzodike and Whetho 2008). Afrobarometer (2016/2018) reports that 69 percent of all surveyed Africans trust religious leaders "somewhat" or "a lot"; trust among youth is slightly lower than it is among elders (68 percent for youth versus 71 percent for elders),[5] and the Africa-wide percentage for *urban* youth is 62 percent. Given religion's large presence in Africa, religious leaders could potentially shape youth citizenship through social networking and political messaging, and/or via patron–client relations (Boussalis, Coan, and Holman 2021; McCauley 2015; McClendon and Riedl 2015b, 2019). Because social norms urge respect for elders, youth may be particularly drawn into these processes. In addition, since everyday citizenship is rooted in relations of obligation and belonging within communities, how youth perceive these elders could matter for how they understand their citizenship identity. Yet, as Chapter 2 showed, youth may not necessarily view their relationships with elders as positive for citizenship.

Among our youth respondents, both frequent and infrequent churchgoers acknowledged the public role that religious leaders played. One Ghanaian said, "We live in a community where religious leaders are so much respected, so they can actually influence their followers" (GH FGD 13; see also GH FGD 1; TZ FGD 1). Our respondents also remarked that these leaders commented on public issues such as clean environments, homosexuality, and corruption, and that they urged citizens to pray regularly for the country and, as described above, to vote (GH FGDs 1, 3, 4, 6, 8–12, 14; TZ FGDs 2–4, 7; UG FGDs 9–12, 14, 15). Some churchgoers said their pastors discouraged them from involvement in politics because it was dirty or evil (GH FGD 2; UG FGD 16), but more pointed to religious leaders' encouragement of political engagement because it was a citizen's duty (GH FGDs 1, 6; UG FGD 15) or because believers needed to protect or advance Christian values (GH FGD 3).

Well aware of these messages, our respondents assessed religious leaders' involvement in various ways. Overall, frequent churchgoers held relatively positive opinions, quickly affirming their devotion to

---

[5] In comparison, 53 percent of all survey respondents say they trust the president somewhat or a lot. In Ghana, 69 percent of all surveyed citizens trust religious leaders; comparative figures are 90 percent in Uganda and 81 percent in Tanzania. The average for women and men across all survey countries is 69 percent.

religious leaders, expressing a willingness to listen to them, and being appreciative of their role in national development (GH FGDs 1, 5; UG FGDs 11, 15). A Tanzanian churchgoer said pastors facilitated social services, alleviated hardships, and helped congregants elect "good leaders who follow God's rules and commandments" (TZ FGD 7). Some were thankful that the church sanctioned positive political behavior and offered hope in times of despair. One of two Ugandan men explained, "When they [pastors] speak, we are relieved; ... There are many things wrong in government ... so when the church speaks about these, then we feel okay." The other added, "We may come to church angry, with a fury, but they preach and ... we see the disciples too were persecuted like us, but they were not driven into the dark. ... Even people in a rioting mindset, after church, they go back home and say, 'Let's not do this. Let's try to keep going'" (UG FGD 12). Biblical images of discipleship urged these men not to engage in contentious politics, and, in Uganda's authoritarian context, they appreciated leaders who publicly addressed political realities (Kigambo 2018).

However, there were a few frequent churchgoers who were more critical of church leaders. One implicitly denounced pastors for tainting the public's view of government: "Never should a religious leader [discuss publicly] ... any weakness of the government. Because saying that ... is like putting a blemish in the mind of the parishioners" (TZ FGD 2). Another said these leaders are not very good at remaining neutral: "We know who they voted for" (GH FGD 6). A few said they sometimes wished leaders would courageously say more. As one Ugandan woman stated, "I think talking is not enough by these church leaders. You can't say you are a Christian without action" (UG FGD 14).

While most frequent churchgoers were willing to show some under-standing of religious leaders whom they thought fell short, many more infrequent churchgoers were condemnatory. Infrequent churchgoers noted how religious leaders were or could be viewed as compromised because of their perceived political involvement. One infrequent-churchgoing Ghanaian said, "Some pastors are very political. They are NPP, NDC, CPP and others" (GH FGD 9; see also UG FGDs 1, 2, 4). Another respondent bluntly remarked, "Religious leaders claim they don't engage in politics, but they do that in secrecy" (GH FGD 7). For some of our respondents, religious actors who were politically engaged were opportunistic (GH FGD 13), untruthful (GH FGD 7), and divisive (GH FGD 7; UG Interview 13). Some thought leaders used religion for instrumental reasons. As a Ghanaian activist recounted:

These political leaders go to mosques for blessings even! The current vice president who is a Christian did this in the last election. Currently, the assemblyman from this area went to the mosque for a blessing. He's a Christian, but the imam prayed for him. ... They bring money, goats, and bags of rice. So, these politicians use religion as a tool of influence when it comes to politics. (GH Interview 11)

For this individual, prayers and material gifts given in worship spaces indicated the manipulation of religion. While these actions might be questionable, those that Ugandans recounted were even more problematic. One Ugandan infrequent churchgoer said that religious leaders were allegedly "bought off," caught in President Museveni's patronage web: "Government bribes them with gifts so they won't talk about politics" (UG FGD 2; see also UG Interviews 13, 15, 16, 20, 22). While not approving of payments, another infrequent churchgoer did say that in Uganda's authoritarian context, pastors had little choice but to remain quiet (UG FGD 7).

These perceptions of religious leaders distinctly colored the citizenship of some youth respondents. As highlighted in previous sections, feelings of belonging in the church community, relational ties, efficacy, and a desire to act to build the nation undergirded everyday citizenship for youth churchgoers, and pastors played a key role in fostering those attitudes and ties. But for youth who viewed these leaders as hypocrites or as dishonest, notions of belonging and trust were eroded. For some respondents, if renewalist pastors were believed to "prey on poor people" with the prosperity gospel (GH Interview 17), these leaders clearly had low concern for others. Other respondents wondered how religious leaders could preach biblical courage if they themselves were "cowards?" (UG FGD 7). After all, "If a religious leader will not stand up to certain things done in society, who will? An ordinary citizen is just an ordinary citizen!" (UG Interview 22). For a few respondents, if some religious leaders were so divorced from the community – "There is no pastor that lives in a ghetto and sleeps with hungry people"; "The pastor is driving a big Prado, putting on a suit daily. But these people are starving down there" (UG Interviews 15, 16) – how could they urge others to value the horizontal relationships that undergird everyday citizenship? As one Ghanaian activist explained, religion no longer influenced what he said or did politically because he had observed too many religious leaders talking about "safe topics in Ghana, like homosexuality" rather than economics or the redistribution of wealth (GH Interview 7). All of these respondents showed how disdain for, distrust of, and disgust with religious leaders could undermine key components of everyday citizenship, at least in the context of religious ties.

Gender also informs how our respondents negotiate and contest their citizenship in the context of the respect accorded to and trust placed in religious leaders. Overall, men spoke more negatively about religious leaders than women, particularly among infrequent churchgoers. Men gave two to three times as many negative comments about these leaders as women did. These results affirm what we know about women negotiating their citizenship identity in a context where they are expected to model submission and deference to men and elders, including religious elites (Boyd 2014; Gouws 2005). Yet churches are also contexts in which women may negotiate new opportunities – from support networks and spiritual sustenance in the face of social exclusion and marital disappointments (Cole 2012) to opportunities for leadership and skills development (Parsitau 2011; Sackey 2006). Thus, while concerns about bringing disgrace to themselves or garnering a reputation as a "troublemaker" may limit their criticisms of religious leaders, these women are agents who may find no pragmatic reason to complain about these leaders.

This section illustrates how respondents offered nuanced understandings of religious leadership. The youth we met acknowledged the influential, even admirable, public role many religious leaders modelled in their countries, but some were suspicious of church leaders who pursued opportunistic actions detrimental to the common good. We conclude with two case studies (Sections 5.6.1 and 5.6.2) of Christian organizations that also illustrate how context determines youth contestation of citizenship.

5.6 Negotiating Citizenship in Ghana and South Africa

The ubiquitous presence of religion in Africa leads to a multitude of religious programming, some of it aimed at youth. For example, churches support youth groups, entrepreneurship programs, mentorship, and community outreach efforts (e.g., clothing drives, dialogue programs on issues such as sanitation) (GH Interviews 1–3; UG

Interviews 1, 2, 8, 11, 12). In the following two case studies, we observe how youth contest their citizenship in the contexts of renewalist and mainline church programming. In both cases, Christian programming set the theological boundary for citizenship and/or political engagement, while youth responded in ways that both adopted and contested those messages.

5.6.1 International Central Gospel Church, Ghana

In one specific congregation of the ICGC in Ghana, church messaging led youth to construct a citizenship identity embedded in close relational ties and self-governing responsibility, although some youth molded these themes to their lived experiences to craft a citizenship identity rooted in tolerance, compromise, and humility. Both church messaging and the youth reconfigurations of that messaging emphasized building the nation.

Based in the renewalist Christian tradition, the ICGC used faith-empowered practices to promote relationships and obligations that undergird everyday citizenship with the goal of building the nation. This was most apparent when the church entrusted teams of youth to plan, organize, and execute the weekly Sunday youth service that over two hundred people attended. Youth ushered, sang in the praise band, operated the video equipment, posted items on social media, and read the biblical texts and announcements (GH ICGC 1–5). Organizing services required youth to work together, listen to others, and compromise – all attributes that deepened their ties to one another. Mentoring by elders (in their early forties) brought youth into relationships of accountability with people outside their kith and kin. Mentors (termed "facilitators") urged youth to seek their advice on spiritual practices (e.g., prayer), romantic relationships, educational challenges, and careers (GH ICGC 9, 10). Unlike some youth who reported tensions with elders (see Chapter 2), the ICGC youth valued the facilitators' knowledge: "We face many obstacles as youth and we need people to come and tell us their experiences" (GH ICGC 5). These relational ties, formed among peers and between youth and elders, mattered because they generated a sense of citizen belonging. One woman explained, "A lot of people are going through a lot of heartache. So, when we come together as believers we [can discuss] problems and then with the help of our facilitators, we are encouraged ... They make us feel like a family" (GH ICGC 1). The church became synonymous with kinship groups (the "family") as the foundation for citizenship ties (see Ekeh 1975; Mazuri 1991). In turn, these relationships contributed to building the nation. Another man explained how positive citizen actions could emerge from the relations built in church: "Just sitting at home, watching TV, on my phone – [all that] doesn't add much. But when I come here, I feel like I'm adding to building myself and society at large" (GH ICGC 4).

Church programs also promoted a citizenship of self-governance. In Bible study groups, for example, youth learned that the biblical characters David and Esther demonstrated perseverance and courage, and youth were challenged to serve as role models with similar character traits (GH ICGC 1–4, 6, 7). Church leaders told youth to set goals, work hard, strive for excellence, and recognize that they were the light of the world – all statements that promote self-governance and coalesce with renewalist political messaging. At a Sunday service, for example, a pastor admonished youth that they needed to come to church on time: "Praise and worship starts right at eight ... You must be responsible!" (GH ICGC 11). By planning youth services, youth practiced such responsibility, as well as time management, communication, and organizational skills.

Many youth said that relations of obligations and notions of responsible self-governance would then spiral up to build the nation through actions of believers outside of church. One youth said, "Yeah, we know that Jesus came to save us all. But also, to teach us how to relate as citizens in the business world outside of church" (GH ICGC 4). To help some youth build the nation as responsible citizens, the church hosted information sessions to aid their transition from secondary to tertiary education; for other youth, it brought investors, accountants, bookkeepers, marketing experts, and human resource officers to help them get started in entrepreneurship (GH ICGC 10). These actions reflected a view of building the nation situated in neoliberal governmentality through which youth with skills and a responsible mindset could look to themselves and not the state to solve problems. Diligence and the fruits of one's labor (e.g., university admission, a job) meant the state would play only a minimal role in people's lives. One youth said, "As a citizen of Ghana, we can't expect that for everything that needs to be done, we are looking up to the leaders of the country" (GH ICGC 5). The view of minimal government and maximal personal responsibility through self-directed action led many youth to define citizenship in legalistic and moral terms, while also downplaying how socioeconomic structures might hinder youth success.

As they embraced these church messages of citizenship, some ICGC youth also augmented them based on their experiences and within their own contexts, thereby adding another layer to the build-the-nation imperative. Some youth expressed how through church they had learned tolerance, compromise, and humility – values that also contributed to building the nation in a less tangible way than employment or entrepreneurship (Putnam 1994). Youth said church programming promoted humility: Pastors refer to youth participants as "workers" not "leaders"; outreach efforts required leaders to also pick up trash (GH ICGC 1, 6). A woman said that the tolerance she learned on the worship planning team spilled over into her everyday citizenship at the university: "I have to coexist. ... I'm at university now, living in the hostel, and I must live positively with my roommate" (GH ICGC 5). A man said that the tolerance he had learned at church was essential for day-to-day citizenship in Ghana, a country with economic, ethnic, and religious diversity: "As a citizen, you get with all kinds of people, from all walks of life in Ghana. And you literally have to tolerate each other ... and these are the lessons that you learn in church. How to be forgiving, how to be tolerant and patient. And these things actually constitute our day-to-day lives as citizens" (GH ICGC 4). For this individual, good citizens had to interact positively with people who were not like them (but see Chapter 7). ICGC youth programming, while primarily presenting a citizenship rooted in horizontal ties and self-governing responsibility to build the nation, did lead some youth to focus on tolerance, compromise, and humility as key citizen traits in the build-the-nation project.

5.6.2 Volmoed Youth Leadership Training Programme, South Africa

In contrast to the ICGC's day-to-day youth programming, the VYLTP is a nine-week, faith-based citizen mobilization program that accepts twelve to sixteen youth who live in residence at the Volmoed Retreat Centre in Hermanus, South Africa (VYLTP 2019). The program's political messaging encourages the construction of a citizenship identity based on participation and social justice, although some youth hone a citizenship of responsible, self-governed individuality. This tension illustrates how youth harness faith to address political matters while negotiating and contesting the meaning of faith-based citizenship based on their lived experiences.

VYLTP is modeled after the National Youth Leadership Training Programme (NYLTP), a three-month ecumenical training program based in Kwa-Zulu Natal that ran from 1967 through the early 1990s. Just as NYLTP nurtured "a new generation of ecumenical leaders by immersing them in a training program that was related to the socio-political dynamics of the country" and supported church leaders within the anti-apartheid movement (SA VYLTP 4), VYLTP's directors hope its programming will graduate young leaders who will fight for social justice in their own communities as a way to build the nation.

The VYLTP curriculum reflects mainline political messaging. Participants are exposed to seminar leaders who had tackled socio-political injustices in South Africa during the apartheid years and who continue to do so in a democratic South Africa (e.g., Edwin Arrison, John De Gruchy, the late Desmond Tutu, Father Michael Lapsley). Facilitators refer to social justice and caring for marginalized persons frequently, and they assert the expectation that young people should build their leadership skills in order to transform communities, even sometimes using unconventional political means (SA VYLTP 5).

Most of the participants identified with the program's vision of a faith-based citizenship identity oriented around participation and social justice. One woman noted, "I am going to keep up with the political issues, to advocate for things, to call out things when they are wrong, for social justice. If I don't do that activity, then I am ... just adding to existing problems" (SA VYLTP 2). Another person said, "In South Africa, when we fight for freedom, we can use the Bible!" (SA VYLTP 1). Another participant noticed that the church no longer played as active a role in South African politics and called for Christians to do so again: "People like Archbishop Tutu implemented this active relationship between religion and politics that the youth need to be a part of again!" (SA VYLTP 1). And finally, one man appreciated being able to participate in a climate march in Cape Town that was one of the active learning segments of the VYLTP curriculum. He remarked, "We went to march on climate change ... This will assist me a lot in being a good citizen!" (SA VYLTP 1).

Other participants, however, articulated a faith-empowered activism grounded in individual self-responsibility that contributed to local acts of citizenship. When asked what he hoped to get out of the program, one respondent said, "I see myself as a leader in my community and in my church. . . . I'd like to bring more young people to church. They don't have to sit around after school. There are other things out there!" (SA VYLTP 1). This person pointed out that, as an individual, he would be the person responsible for aiding his community and that church programming was the solution to larger societal issues with delinquent, unemployed youth. A woman, also highlighting the theme of self-governing responsibility and local acts of citizenship, said, "A lot of people in South Africa don't know how to be on time, but this program teaches you how to do that. . . . Learning these skills, I want to use my voice as a church leader to be a better, kinder citizen in ways that help my community" (SA VYLTP 2). For her, "better" became synonymous with self-discipline and organizational skills.

The tension between these different understandings of citizenship was displayed during an early program session. A seminar leader walked VYLTP participants through a scenario in which they were members of churches (one Catholic, one nondenominational) in a rural area of South Africa that had witnessed a number of young children dying in poorly constructed government pit latrines. Playing the roles of church pastor, youth leader, and community members, VYLTP participants discussed the actions they would take. During the report-out, a few people mentioned things like "form a Steering Committee that would push for proper toilets from the local government," "*toyi-toying*," and "getting an active religious leader to launch a campaign." But the majority of responses were localized and individualized – "pray," "fundraise for proper toilets from wealthy churches in England," or "lock the toilets at night." The seminar leader then presented the responses on a continuum of "relief – community development – advocacy/justice." When asked where most of their responses fell, participants acknowledged the narrower "relief" category. After a robust discussion, one participant exclaimed, "The church needs to do more than pray to offset the problem! . . . Prayer needs to lead us to action. We need to confront those who are exercising power in ways that harm the poor!" (SA VYLTP 5). Despite this reflection, the most common response stressed responsible self-governing actions, and this appeared to coalesce with the participants' situation: Many would be returning to their low-income communities after the program ended, and the immediate needs of their communities demanded attention. They did not have time to wait for long-term change – a point one respondent confirmed later, when he said, "A good citizen is someone who sees a challenge economically in the country, and you connect with a church or nonprofit who can help and express the view of others because they can't express it themselves" (SA VYLTP 1).

To be sure, some of the VYLTP participants gained a vision of being eager and ready to rectify injustice using active, even confrontational, political actions within a faith-based community that contributed to nation building. One participant said, "This program is teaching me that faith-based leadership will balance or impact in a political way the community and future of South Africa!" (SA VYLTP 1). This person went on to describe how grateful he was to religious leaders who modeled this kind of leadership during the apartheid years. But others admitted that they were not interested in activist politics – voting and following the law would be the extent of their political engagement (SA VYLTP 2). They were more interested in growing their faith and being responsible, self-governing citizens: "VYLTP is teaching me that I don't need to depend on anyone else. ... That is part of being a good citizen" (SA VYLTP 1). Similar to the ICGC case study above, citizenship for these young people was situated within the specific context of their experiences and reflected their lived realities.

5.7 Conclusion

This chapter has interrogated how religious identity shapes youth citizenship. Using both Afrobarometer and qualitative data, we discovered subtle yet distinct differences between frequent and infrequent churchgoers regarding their understanding of citizenship. In contrast to the Afrobarometer data, we did not find that frequent churchgoers were more committed than infrequent churchgoers to communal themes of citizenship. Yet, these relational aspects of citizenship for churchgoers were rooted in faith and intricately tied to building the nation, giving them a slightly different dimension than the views of infrequent churchgoers. In addition, expressing an understanding of citizenship-from-below based in morality and following the law was notably higher among frequent churchgoers than infrequent churchgoers. When we examined acts of citizenship aimed directly at the state – voting, bringing issues to the government's attention, or protesting – the survey data indicated that youth who are members of religious groups are more politically engaged than youth who are not. Our qualitative data demonstrated that when participants discussed political engagement, faith informed their activism, and they showed significant political efficacy – a result that is consistent with other research findings (Mangos and Weinreb 2013; Sperber, Kaaba, and McClendon 2022).

This chapter illustrates the potential of religion to shape everyday understandings of citizenship, but it also demonstrates how youth negotiate and contest their citizenship vis-à-vis religion. African youth can be inspired by religious leaders' insights regarding political engagement, but they can also regard them with suspicion and alarm. Finally, through faith-based programming, youth may accept church messaging on citizenship. But, through agentic processes, youth also take those messages and make citizenship their own. In Chapter 6, we turn to how youth across genders understand their everyday citizenship.

6 | *Affirming and Challenging Patriarchy*

Yes, you [a woman] are a citizen. Nobody will chase you out of the country. ... You're entitled to those human rights ... but things make it not equal. ... When it comes to certain opportunities, maybe I'll be denied because I'm a woman and my brother will be favored because he's male.

(UG Interview 5)

As our respondents illustrated, youth actively contest everyday citizenship in light of socially constructed gender roles. On the one hand, men and women are legally the same,[1] as our youth respondents vehemently argued. On the other hand, gender identity means that women and men face different sets of expectations about their rights and obligations in their local and national communities. Our respondents both embrace and contest those gendered norms of authority in the countries we consider, illustrating both their agency and the constraints on it. Overall, we find that the highly gendered nature of local acts of citizenship could curtail opportunities for gender equality in relation to the state. Our findings bring a youth perspective to the scholarship on gender roles in African politics, and they illustrate how youth at times challenge traditional attitudes about gender, particularly in local spaces.

This chapter proceeds in six sections. First, we examine feminist scholarship on citizenship (Section 6.1). Next, we show how a significant number of our women and men respondents viewed citizenship in terms of gendered activities (e.g., carework for women, physical labor for men) (Section 6.2). But because citizenship is a subjective and contextualized identity, some respondents held more fluid views on

---

[1] The youth we encountered generally exhibited a binary understanding of gender, which is common across Africa, and identified themselves as either men or women. Thus, we are unable to speak to the differences in citizenship experiences among LGBTQ+ youth.

gendered citizenship. Sections 6.3 and 6.4 use survey data and our respondents' voices to explore how men and women understand their citizenship identities and obligations in relation to the state. We discover that both men and women support meeting legal obligations, but they bring gendered angles to their views of voting, protesting, and running for office. However, respondents illustrate how youth continuously negotiate what it means to be a man or woman citizen, showing some maneuverability in citizen identity and activities. Section 6.5 uses the case of Stand Up! – a student-organized NGO in Ghana that educated youth about GBV – to question how citizenship-from-above revolves around localized relationships, how youth may contest gender norms as they negotiate their citizenship, and how patriarchy may condition their efforts. The conclusion (Section 6.6) summarizes the findings.

6.1 Feminist Views of Citizenship

Patriarchy – the system of structures and attitudes that assigns men more power than women in the public and private realms – undergirds gender roles and ultimately affects the gendered nature of everyday citizenship. Women are expected to be good mothers, devoted wives, and nurturing community members, while men must provide households with security, earn incomes, and serve as public decision makers (Boyd 2015; Rabe 2017; Tamale 2009; Tripp 2006). Recognizing patriarchy does not deny that some African women have challenged these roles, as queen mothers (Stoeltje 2003); as participants in anticolonial resistance, nationalist movements, and the anti-apartheid struggle (Bridger 2018; Hassim 2006; Schmidt 2005; Van Allen 1972); as war combatants (Aning 1998); as peace advocates (Mama and Okazawa-Ray 2012); as advocates against domestic violence and rape (Medie 2013); and as NGO leaders and community activists (Rosander 1997).[2] Similarly, some women we encountered were students, formal and informal sector workers, political officials, advocates, and NGO volunteers. Although some women and men respondents challenged patriarchy, the majority said that even if men and

---

[2] The literature on women in African politics and society is vast (see Bauer 2020; Johnson and Phillips 2020).

women were legally equal, gender norms still determined their citizen actions. As a Ugandan woman said, "If you're a lady, well, you can only do some things because of your sex" (UG FGD 14).

Feminists have long argued that citizenship formation is rooted in daily relations and obligations, with its contestation continuously shaped by power, relative marginality, and society's "political projects and cultural formations" (Clarke et al. 2014, 57). Citizens are not merely "atomized, passive bearers of rights" who operate as ungendered, unbodied individuals divorced from context (Lister 1997). Power and masculine hegemony mean that, even with legal equality, women may lack access to rights and substantive citizenship beyond "formal politics and law" (Mukhopadhyay 2007, 7; Oldfield et al. 2019). This lack of social, economic, health, security, and cultural rights, in turn, shapes their autonomy and ability to act as citizens in the public sphere (Gouws 2005). This means that a sole focus on the legal, public sphere ignores how private activities that women disproportionately engage in – such as household labor, parenting, and carework – shape citizenship (Lister 1997; Pateman 1989; Phillips 1991; Rabe 2017). For example, parenting may nurture social values and identities that confirm belonging, teach a sense of obligation to the community and nation (Yuval-Davis 2007), foster community development (Kershaw 2010), and ultimately lead disadvantaged people to become "subjects rather than objects" (Lister 1997; Oldfield et al. 2019). Carework promotes an ethic of trust, reciprocity, and dependency – all "undeniable aspects of the human condition" that women can weave into their citizenship identities (White 2001, 495). Yet, these activities tend to reinforce patriarchal expectations, leading women and men to filter their engagement with the state through the lens of local experiences that reinforce privilege and inequality.

6.2 Men, Women, and Local Acts of Citizenship

Feminist analysis of citizenship, research on societal promotion of gender roles (Bompani 2016; Hendriks et al. 2012), and studies of gender and citizenship in Africa (Arnot, Chege, and Wawire 2012) lead us to anticipate that our men and women youth respondents will hold different views of citizenship. We also predict this variation because citizenship is manifest in everyday activities that gender norms shape. We first present Afrobarometer data on gender and local citizenship actions (Section 6.2.1) and then explore how those patterns manifest in our respondents' lives (Section 6.2.2).

6.2.1 Survey Trends

We consider the Afrobarometer data on reported attendance at a community meeting and active membership in a community or voluntary group for urban men and women youth (see Table 6.1). By the first measure (meeting attendance), men seem to be more engaged in the community. A larger percentage of men than women reports attending meetings across all three countries, perhaps illustrating that expectations for women's household labor can restrict their time and opportunities for this public engagement. As previous chapters showed, Ghana's overall participation rates are lower on meeting attendance, for reasons related to political culture, and Tanzania's rates are higher, due in part to that country's socialist history (see Chapter 1). The men–women attendance gap is most pronounced in Uganda (19 percent), followed by Ghana (7 percent), and Tanzania (3 percent). Although we did not investigate reasons for the Ugandan gap, we anticipate that it relates to patriarchy fomented by government officials, to the fact that single mothers head one-third of Ugandan households (Uganda Bureau of Statistics 2016), and to poverty.

On active group membership, the gap between men and women tightens considerably. This may result from the traditional role that

Table 6.1 *Local actions among urban youth, by gender and country*

Country	Gender	Attended community meetings (%)*	Active membership in voluntary or community group (%)	N
Ghana	Men	23	15	364
	Women	16	12	375
Tanzania	Men	52	20	204
	Women	49	17	242
Uganda	Men	48	28	103
	Women	29	27	112

* Percentage answering "several times" or "often"
Source: Data from Afrobarometer (2016/2018), compiled by the authors

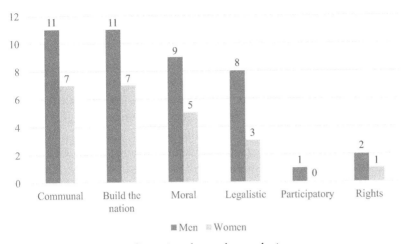

Figure 6.1 Focus group discussion themes by gender*
* Average mentions of category words per focus group
Source: The authors' NVivo data

women's associations play in providing socioeconomic and psycho-social support through shared labor, rotating credit societies, and relationship advice (see Musinguzi 2016; Patterson 1999). In addition, men's mobility due to employment may problematize their member-ship in local organizations.

6.2.2 Youth Voices

Figure 6.1 presents the NVivo analysis for men and women respond-ents. To begin, the average mention of words for all themes was higher in men-only groups than in women-only groups because the men tended to talk more and repeat ideas.[3] We asked all groups the same questions and scheduled discussions for the same duration, but many men-only discussions lasted longer. This difference may reflect societal expectations that women should be quiet (GH FGDs 12, 14), although certainly not all women held back from sharing their ideas.

Regardless of these patterns, we identify several discussion themes. First, both men and women used communal, build-the-nation, and

---

[3] In the few mixed-gender groups in Tanzania and Ghana, women were particularly quiet.

moral words and phrases most frequently and in similar proportions. This reinforces the book's theme that youth view citizenship as being manifest through everyday activities in which they work with others to build the nation. It also aligns with the Afrobarometer data showing that men and women are active in community groups, though it does not hew to the finding that higher percentages of men attend local meetings, as evidenced in Table 6.1. Second, there were slight country differences. Ugandans (both men and women) spoke in communal terms more than all Ghanaians and all Tanzanians; all Ghanaians emphasized the build-the-nation theme more than their Ugandan and Tanzanian peers. Third, the percentage of men who used legalistic terms was disproportionately higher than the percentage of women, and men emphasized legalistic concerns more frequently than Afrobarometer would lead us to expect. Fourth, although men and women respondents used moral terms in roughly the same proportions, only Ugandan respondents (mostly frequent churchgoers) stressed the morality of *women's* actions, a point we examine below.

Our qualitative data illustrates that despite agreement on basic citizenship components, the local expression of citizenship plays out in *gender-specific, country-contextualized* ways. A Ugandan man explained, "We have different roles in our society attached to our sex" (UG FGD 11), and a Ghanaian man echoed, "When you get to some communities, they say there are some things that a woman cannot do" (GH FGD 3). These views were not unique to men; some women were equally emphatic about gendered citizenship. The following sections present two sides of our respondents' perspectives: first, their assertion that everyday citizenship manifests in gendered tasks (Section 6.2.2.1), and, second, their challenges to this perspective (Section 6.2.2.2).

6.2.2.1 Affirming Gender-Defined Work as Citizenship

Although youth often identified work as a key local citizen activity, the kinds of work youth cited – and even the opportunities for such work – were segregated along gender lines. For men, everyday work activities intertwined with the "male breadwinner ideology" (Rabe 2017) in which "a man ... is obligated to look after his family ... feeding them, catering for the children's education and supporting the family" (UG FGD 2; see also TZ FGD 2; UG FGD 4). Men built the nation through work in the formal and informal sectors: They held down jobs, traveled to make money, and trained and hired others (GH FGDs 6, 7;

UG FGDs 3, 4, 10). In some cases, if a man did not play this role – or if a woman usurped him in it – his citizenship could be eroded. One informant explained, "If a man has a wife who makes more money than he does, he may not be seen as a good citizen" (UG Interview 7). This perception that men were shirking as citizens presented a particular challenge to lower-income men, who, if they could not secure the "daily bread," were viewed as "a financial burden," not a citizen (TZ FGD 2; UG FGD 1). One lower-income Ugandan man said, "We are always pressured to provide for our families. ... You can give your wife 10,000 Ugandan shillings for household expenditures and she tells you that the money is not enough. So, you ask her whether she doesn't watch the news on television!" (UG FGD 10).[4] In addition to implying that his wife was oblivious about the economy (a gendered assumption), the man described the never-ending scramble for income to feed his family – another gendered citizenship expectation.

Echoing patriarchal assumptions about masculine strength and bravery, respondents identified physically taxing and dangerous jobs as exemplifying men's nation-building commitments. One Tanzanian man noted that "by taking part in the construction of buildings like offices ... [I help bring] development in the country. ... It means I'm adding value to the country through the new building" (TZ FGD 2). Some lower-income Ghanaian men dismissed women's contributions to the community as secondary, saying that men were simply physically stronger and, therefore, could do more (GH FGDs 3, 7).

Several respondents also said that men provided security, typically through informal, neighborhood watch organizations (GH FGD 3; TZ FGDs 2, 8, 9; UG FDG 1). Even when, on occasion, women participated in these efforts, the specific actions men and women could do were clearly delineated. In an ambush, a Tanzanian man said, "The one who is expected to be in front to fight is me, but women will assist in yelling to call people for help" (TZ ELCT 6). One Ugandan woman said, "If a neighbor is attacked by thieves it's very hard for me as a woman to come out of the house and intervene" (UG FGD 6; see also UG FGDs 8, 14). Exhibiting an emotional aspect of women's perceived citizenship, another woman added, "Being a good citizen, they [men] have to contribute to security and not the women. Women have to feel protected" (UG FGD 16). Although crime was not new to Kampala, a

---

[4] This amount was roughly USD 2.50 in mid-2022.

spike in kidnappings and murders of women of diverse socioeconomic and age backgrounds in 2017 and 2018 made Ugandan respondents particularly security conscious, with men expressing worry about sisters and wives and women saying, "You don't have the ability to move at night if you are a girl or lady. … You are afraid that anytime they [will be] kidnapping me … killing me" (Sadurni 2018; UG FGD 16; USAID 2011). Men were expected to do hard jobs that directly protected women in order to show their citizenship commitment, illustrating how men's citizenship was determined in relation to women's.

While men's citizenship was expected to be manifest through physical labor and security provision, women faced different citizenship expectations regarding work. Most respondents emphasized that women have a distinct "familial citizenship" that focuses on the reproductive and nurturing roles of pregnancy, birth, childcare, and carework (Moriguchi 2019). A Ugandan woman said that "giving birth to children" was an act of citizenship, and her friend added, "Yes, because whenever we give birth to children we increase the country's population. I can give birth to the next president" (UG FGD 7; see also UG FGD 8). In addition to pregnancy and childbirth, women's citizenship included ensuring that children are well-fed, clean, and well-behaved so that they contribute to the nation's development – a theme particularly evident among higher-income Ugandan and Ghanaian women (GH FGDs 6, 10; UG FGDs 6, 7, 16). Tanzanian women emphasized that women were good citizens when they gave birth and cared for children *within the confines of marriage* (TZ FGDs 2, 4, 7). Gaku Moriguchi (2019) finds that when run-away women in Kampala return home pregnant, they may be valorized for being mothers, echoing a discourse that a woman's identity as "the mother of someone" gives her status. Carework as citizenship could extend beyond the household, such as when a woman helped another woman in childbirth, aided an elderly neighbor, or counseled children (UG FGD 4). In this carework, women of lower income were more likely than women of higher income to focus on specific citizenship acts and to lean on other women for material and social support (GH FGDs 4, 8, 10; TZ FGDs 1–6; UG FGDs 5, 8, 13). Regardless, one man made it very clear that these chores were for women only: "A man cannot go and act as a midwife. Really? No! It's disgusting! … There are some jobs that actually are specific. … It's only one gender to do that … It's not that it's in the constitution, but in real life, it's a different citizenship" (UG FGD 11).

Both socioeconomic obstacles and patriarchal attitudes may have led women to focus on these gendered roles of mothering and carework. Among African youth, women have on average fewer years of education, they own fewer assets, they have less access to digital technology, and they own less property (Gandhi 2018; Lardies, Dryding, and Logan 2019).[5] For women who work outside the home, 90 percent are employed in the informal economy, where they face unstable wages, job insecurity, and few worker protections (Woldemichael 2020). Attitudes also shape employment opportunities. In Tanzania, 69 percent of all women and 57 percent of all men agree that women should have an equal right to jobs. In Ghana, the numbers are 66 percent of all women and 58 percent of all men, and, in Uganda, 65 percent of all women and 50 percent of men (Lardies, Dryding, and Logan 2019). Thus, sizeable minorities oppose women's equality in employment, a factor that may partly explain why only a few women respondents defined citizenship as paid work.

In addition, broader societal expectations about women's behavior may have shaped the emphasis on motherhood and carework. In particular, some Ugandan respondents said that women citizens should be quiet, submissive, polite, and deferential to husbands, fathers, and elders (UG FGDs 1, 2, 5, 8). They should not dress immodestly, drink alcohol, smoke, engage in sexual relations outside of marriage, and visit nightclubs. In contrast, a man could be "a drunkard and polygamous" without it harming his citizenship (UG FGD 8; see also UG Interviews 19, 24). Women's behavior mattered not only because it could affect localized relations (see Chapter 2) but also because state officials had stressed that women's actions affect "the nation's honour, decency, and respectability" (Bompani 2016; Tamale 2016; UG FGDs 1, 8, 15). If a woman deviates from these expectations, both she and her children can face criticism, ostracism, and violence (Moriguchi 2019; Sadgrove 2014). One Ugandan man said he experienced childhood bullying after his parents divorced, his mother continued her university education, and he was sent to the village to live with his grandmother (UG Interview 19). A Tanzanian woman lamented how

---

[5] In 2019, African women's literacy rate was 13 percent lower than men's (World Bank 2020a, 2020b).

social media added to these patterns: "You will find men beating [a woman who allegedly did something bad], tearing her clothes, injuring her, and leaving her naked. There are some who instead of helping her, they take some photos and post them on social media. Then you will find them discussing and giving bad words about that victim" (TZ FGD 3). Some policymakers in Tanzania, Nigeria, Uganda, and Malawi, among other places, have deepened these messages. In 2021, for example, the Tanzanian parliament speaker ordered a woman parliamentarian to leave a formal session after her peers judged her "too tight" trousers to be inappropriate (BBC News 2021; see Bocast 2014; Brennan 2006). Such events reinforce the expectation that women build the nation through their reproductive roles and that they threaten such nation building when they challenge patriarchal expectations with independent behavior.

Many of our women respondents viewed these roles as central to their citizenship identity in a way that set them apart from men, who appeared to care less about the home. One woman explained, "You can find a woman having her office, caring for the kids and family, but you will find a man busy with luxurious things; he doesn't want to work hard or be responsible" (TZ FGD 8). Another respondent added that "[a woman] will go to school to teach, she will come back and make sure her family is doing well. They have food; children are healthy. She will stand in a church position, maybe singing in the choir. After that she will meet her community group to discuss community issues." In contrast, a man may go to work in the morning but in the evening, he will do nothing more than go out for a drink (TZ FGD 8). This commitment to the family and carework aligned with Afrobarometer data showing that, among urban youth, higher percentages of women than men believe it is best if a woman takes care of the home and children (see Figure 6.2).

Among some women respondents, an underlying message was that they had to work very hard to be viewed as good citizens, while the bar was much lower for men. One man agreed, saying: "Women are given more roles as citizens" (UG FGD 12). The man's remark also hints at another theme among some men: Women have more *opportunities* to act as good citizens because their continuous presence in the community means they know local needs and can foster positive relationships with neighbors. Men lack these relational ties because they tend to "spend little time at home" due to long work hours or travel (UG FGD 5). Thus, men who fulfill their expected citizen role as breadwinners cannot be citizens who care for neighbors.

Many men and women respondents embraced traditional gender roles in the realm of work. These expected roles reflect patriarchy, but they also illustrate how citizen identities relate to people's everyday lives, including the private sphere of family. Surveys show that large percentages of women and men see homelife as fundamentally a woman's sphere (see Figure 6.2). In fact, slightly more women than men hold this belief, indicating how many women strive to "suture together their own and their dependents' well-being in the home to the well-being of the nation" (Oldfield et al. 2019, 44). Although many youth defined women's citizenship in terms of household tasks, only a minority of men and women youth survey respondents in Tanzania and Uganda thought women's main responsibility should be in the household (Figure 6.2). The contrast between the views of our respondents and the views of those surveyed may indicate some flexibility in gendered citizenship – a pattern we now explore.

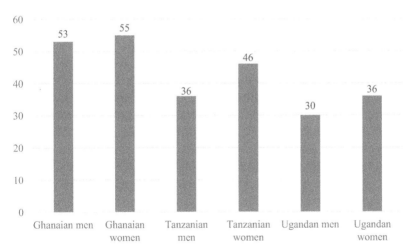

Figure 6.2 Urban youth support for women's household responsibilities*
*Percentage of urban youth who agree that it is better for a family if a woman has the main responsibility for taking care of the home and children, rather than a man
Source: Data from Afrobarometer (2016/2018), compiled by the authors

6.2.2.2 Challenging Gender-Defined Work as Citizenship

We found a significant minority of respondents who pushed back against gendered citizenship, though their reasons varied. They illustrated that youth constantly contest and reimagine core citizenship activities, as they refused to assign formal work solely to men citizens and household labor solely to women citizens. On the one hand, some exclaimed that men could do carework – a point a Ugandan man expressed in terms of midwifery. In an animated argument with others, he said, "I have seen a man help a lady to deliver a baby . . . There's no need to say that this is meant for women alone. . . . If the man is there and the lady needs help, if you're a good citizen, then you're going to do that" (UG FGD 11). For this man, helping someone in need rather than meeting particular gender expectations constituted citizenship. Another Ugandan man recounted the months he volunteered in an orphanage, holding babies and playing with children, saying these typical women's tasks constituted his citizenship (UG FDG 11). As renewalist Christians, these men exemplified scholarship highlighting a certain family focus and gender sensitivity stressed in some renewalist churches (see Chitando 2007; van Klinken 2013).

On the other hand, some respondents pointed out that women could do typical men's tasks, such as managing businesses, driving tractors, operating machinery, and selling in the marketplace: "Even a woman can go and work, even a woman can go to the army and defend her country" (UG FGD 15; see also UG FGDs 5, 7, 11). One Ghanaian man who disagreed with his peers said, "Today there is much education so that there is some work that a man can do that a woman can also do. For example, mechanic work. There are women doing that now. Spraying of cars [to clean them]? Women do that. About three days ago, a lady was learning masonry!" (GH FGD 9; see also GH FGD 10). Some respondents more broadly challenged gender roles, as a Ghanaian woman did: "In my thinking, I don't believe there is any difference . . . [W]hen there is work, if it is sweeping [a typical woman's job], men can do it. If it is weeding [a typical man's job], women can do it. It is not that men are supposed to weed and women are supposed to sweep. They all help for neatness and cleanliness of the nation" (GH FGD 2). For this woman, every Ghanaian citizen should do these routine, communal tasks to help the country.

Other respondents explained that men and women's citizenship roles had to be flexible, given changing family situations and economic contexts. The multiplicity of household patterns evident in Africa – single-parent, two-parent, multigenerational, skipped generational – led men and women to negotiate citizenship through actions outside of conventional gendered expectations (Rabe 2017). A Ugandan woman said her parents, who worked full-time, always shared housework, even though her paternal uncle criticized her father for doing such chores (UG FGD 15). Another Ugandan explained that single mothers, particularly those who are lower income, "toil, they work hard. ... [They serve] as two in one: It is a woman and also a dad" (UG FGD 9; see also UG FGD 5). For these respondents, even though citizenship sometimes played out in nontraditional ways, it was still citizenship because these individuals met obligations. In a few cases, women argued that they provided materially for the home and had little need for men who might act as a drain on the family. A Tanzanian woman recounted this scenario:

You can find a widow working hard and she manages to send her children to school to the university level. She will work several jobs until she fulfills that. But if you ... give the same responsibilities to a man, he won't even manage to send the children to the secondary school level. (TZ FGD 8)

The hypothetical woman acted as a citizen who met her obligations to work and family, but the man's inaction undermined his citizenship.

A final group of respondents understood how gender roles undermined citizen belonging for both women and men. Higher-income Ghanaians (men and women) were the most likely to describe how strict gender roles were problematic because they truncated opportunities for women to act as citizens within the household, community, and nation (GH FGDs 5, 11, 13). One activist said:

You can't [find] a home where the wife says, "Well, I have freedom of speech. I have the freedom of giving my own fair opinion, so I'll go by [opinion] A." It only happens in very rare situations ... In most cases, they [men] don't even allow women to give out their views. To me, I see men to be more advantaged as citizens because they can be given opportunities to be at the forefront, to lead in the case of any issue in the community. It's not the best. (GH Interview 11)

Another higher-income Ghanaian respondent explained that gender roles requiring women to be quiet and "relegated to the kitchen" made it impossible even to claim the right to share ideas (GH FGD 12). In contesting citizenship identity, men had an advantage.

However, gender roles could also stifle men's citizenship. Some Tanzanian men recognized how societal assumptions about women's work led men to become idle and unproductive, thereby undermining the very qualities on which men's citizenship was based. One said:

[Men] leave their homes in the morning to go out to their peers and you will find even their mothers don't tell them to help with home activities, just because at home there are some girls. The mother is expecting the girls to sweep, do the dishes, cook, et cetera, while the brother is just sitting doing nothing. That can cause some problems for youth, because they get more freedom to roam around. (TZ FGD 2)

"Roaming around," then, meant the men were not meeting their citizenship obligations as breadwinners. Similarly, when they acted violently toward women and children, men were not meeting their citizenship obligations as fathers, as a Tanzanian woman who worked to educate boys about violence and its long-term effects explained. As if speaking to one of the boys, she admonished, "In the end . . . you will become a father. What kind of father will you be?" (TZ FGD 4). Her work challenging patriarchal assumptions about violence was intended to make men into better fathers within a specific context. Thus, even efforts to push back against gendered citizenship may operate within the broader confines of patriarchy.

6.3 Men, Women, and the Legalistic Elements of Citizenship

As Table 6.2 shows, men and women urban youth value legalistic behaviors such as tax paying and obeying the police. Men were slightly more supportive than women of the state's tax-collecting role. We did not explore why, but perhaps it is because men fear tax enforcement or because their overall higher educational level makes them aware of the need for tax revenue. Similarly, most men and women agreed that the police can make people obey the law, though 8 percent fewer men than women agreed in Tanzania and Uganda. In those countries, women may be more supportive of police because they have fewer daily encounters with law enforcement officials (see below). Our qualitative findings hew to these patterns.

Most of our youth respondents initially defined citizenship using legalistic terms, leading both men and women to first state that citizenship was the same for women and men. Respondents emphasized that if a person was born in the country or possessed the necessary legal

Table 6.2 *Views of legal obligations among urban youth, by gender and country*

Country	Gender	The tax authorities have the right to make people pay their taxes (%)*	The police always have the right to make people obey the law (%)*	N
Ghana	Men	88	87	364
	Women	87	88	375
Tanzania	Men	88	77	204
	Women	86	85	242
Uganda	Men	90	88	103
	Women	85	96	112

* Percentage answering "agree" or "strongly agree"
Source: Data from Afrobarometer (2016/2018), compiled by the authors

documents, that man or woman had the legal right to vote and to receive equal legal treatment, and that individuals had the legal obligation to obey the law and pay taxes. Phrases like "we are all equal," "we are all the same," and "we are all human beings" were common (GH FGDs 3, 4, 11, 13; TZ FGDs 2, 5, 8; UG FGDs 1, 3, 5, 12, 15), as were statements such as, "The constitution does not differentiate that women and men should have different responsibilities"; "the laws are irrespective of sex"; and "when a man commits a crime [and] a woman commits the same crime, neither … can be exempted from the punishment" (GH FGD 5; TZ FGD 8; UG FGD 4). There were slight differences among women, though, with Ugandan women being much less likely to note legal aspects of citizenship and higher-income Ghanaian women being much more legalistic in their focus. Sometimes respondents' statements illustrated how legal equality could not be divorced from household dynamics, which may act as sites of "private patriarchy" that teach and reinforce domination and violence (Nyamu-Musembi 2007, 177). Such patterns juxtapose with legal equality. As one woman illustrated, "[A husband] dares touch a woman, even in the village, and she will take you to the police. And they will arrest [the husband] because it is her right not to be beaten" (UG FGD 5). For the respondent, both men and women have the legal right to physical security and police protection. The fact that she used wife beating as her example demonstrates how patriarchy infuses society to sustain the practice (Ssenkaaba 2021). Indeed, 33 percent of African women will experience interpersonal violence in their lifetime (WHO 2018), and 28 percent of survey respondents in thirty-eight African countries thought that wife beating is sometimes or always justifiable (Afrobarometer 2019).[6]

Despite their initial statements on legal equality, we found that men were generally more likely than women to reference legalistic themes (an average of eight mentions for men-only focus groups to three for women-only groups). They spent more time than women explaining that citizenship means having legal status (i.e., a national identification card), obeying the law, and paying taxes. They frequently gave examples of encounters with law enforcement officials and other state agents, and they expressed concerns about traffic stops and being arrested (GH FGD 11; TZ FGDs 1, 8; UG FGD 3). This fits with broader trends that show men are more likely than women to be harassed or beaten by the police, arrested, and imprisoned (UG FGDs 2, 10; World Prisons Brief 2020).[7]

6.4 Men, Women, and the Political Activities of Citizenship

Women and men engaged with the state as voters, advocates, and protestors, although our respondents gave these actions less focus than the legalistic, communal, and build-the-nation markers of citizenship. In addition, as Figure 6.1 shows, neither men nor women stressed rights in any country, and women mentioned rights only half as frequently as men did. This point echoes broader findings that women's organizations are only slowly beginning to adopt "rights language" to make claims on the state (see Van Allen 2015). We now consider our findings in relation to Afrobarometer data on voting, protesting, and women in elected office – a theme our respondents discussed in relation to gendered roles (Section 6.4.1). Country differences in women's representation present the opportunity to interrogate contextual factors that may affect views of women's citizenship as office holding (Section 6.4.2).

---

[6] The percentages were lower in Uganda (18 percent), Ghana (13 percent), and Tanzania (9 percent).

[7] The proportion of the population in prison in Uganda is three times that in Ghana or Tanzania (World Prisons Brief 2020).

6.4.1 Voting and Protesting: Surveys versus Youth Voices

As Table 6.3 illustrates, urban youth report voting in high numbers overall, though in Ghana and Tanzania the percentage of urban men who report voting is higher than that for urban women, with the gap being 7 percent in Tanzania. Among Ugandan youth, 2 percent more urban women vote than urban men. These national differences in women's voter turnout occur despite the fact that women's literacy rates (one driver of political participation) are roughly the same across countries (74 percent in Ghana, 73 percent in Tanzania, and 71 percent in Uganda; see World Bank 2020a). Women's higher turnout in Uganda may reflect mobilization by active women's associations (Muriaas and Wang 2012), even in the face of increasing electoral violence that deters some voters (UG Interview 16). The relatively low number of women in office may deter Ghanaian urban women voters (see below), although, by this logic, urban women in Tanzania, a country with a woman president as of 2021, might be expected to turn out at higher rates. Regardless, our youth respondents stressed that voting was a task equally open to men and women.

In contrast to voting, youth engagement in protest is limited overall – Ugandan urban women top the list, with 7 percent reporting attendance at a demonstration or protest march. In Ghana and Tanzania,

Table 6.3 *Participatory actions among urban youth, by gender and country*

Country	Gender	Voted (%)*	Attended a demonstration or protest (%)**	N
Ghana	Men	79[a]	5	364
	Women	77[b]	2	375
Tanzania	Men	83[c]	2	204
	Women	76[d]	<1	242
Uganda	Men	80[e]	5	103
	Women	82[f]	7	112

* Percentage of youth aged twenty-six to thirty-five. The other columns include the weighted average of all youth.
** Percentage answering "once or twice"
[a] N = 170; [b] N = 218; [c] N = 107; [d] N = 139; [e] N = 59; [f] N = 56
Source: Data from Afrobarometer (2016/2018), compiled by the authors

though, higher percentages of urban men than women report having attended a protest. Given these low rates of participation in protest, it is unsurprising that our respondents mentioned protest only occasionally, with most (though not all) saying that protesting was problematic for women. Challenging gender expectations, two Ghanaian women supported active participation in demonstrations, with one saying, "Now women can also demonstrate against government policies and other things. So being a good citizen, gender has no role in it" (GH FGD 14; see also GH Interview 16). However, because of the expectation that women's citizenship centered on domestic roles and that "women are not allowed to stand out and speak," for most women, citizenship was unlikely to be manifest through contentious politics (GH FGD 14; see also UG FGD 15). As a Ugandan man said, if a woman demonstrated, the people would ask, "What the hell kind of woman is this? She shouldn't be marching in the street! She should be at home, washing clothes and taking care of kids!" (UG Interview 16). Demonstrating good citizenship-from-below meant women could not fully engage in citizenship-from-above.

There was also concern that protesting could lead to sexual violence, which could bring shame and stigma to the woman and her family and diminish marriage prospects. One Ugandan man highlighted the state's vicious violence against women in the 2016 election, pointing to the intended effect of scaring women from politics. He said, "The undressing of women [by ruling party youth militias] and the way they were treated [in 2016], with squeezing their breasts—[That violation] was not just for them. It was for those who were seeing and might get ideas. To say, 'This is what happens when a woman attempts to get in the public space'" (UG Interview 22). Not unique to Uganda (Darkwa 2015; Krook 2017),[8] this physical violence – or the threat of it – curtails women's participation and contributes to "gendered geographies," or limited spaces for women's political engagement (Bridger 2018). Women globally have at times effectively used the symbolism attached to their roles as mothers, wives, and war victims to gain influence and shape public opinion (Bouvard 2002; Medie 2013). The image of the mother-citizen can be powerful, but its power also

---

[8] As one example, a 2021 news video shows a crowd of young men rushing toward Robinal Nabbanja, Uganda's first woman prime minister, and physically attacking her. After the event, she stated directly and angrily, "They wanted to kill me" (NTV Uganda 2021).

relies on women's roles as mothers who are concerned about their children (UG Interview 17). In some cases, women may maneuver as agents in the tight spaces of patriarchy.

6.4.2 *Women in Elected Office: Surveys versus Youth Voices*

In our fieldwork, we saw that the greatest contestation over gender roles revolved around women in elected office. In both the Afrobarometer data and our respondents' comments, there is a tension between, on the one hand, embracing gender norms that enable a woman to exercise good citizenship-from-below and, on the other, challenging gender norms through acts of citizenship-from-above. The objections that some youth (primarily men) raised to women in office echo themes in the African politics literature (see Bauer 2020). Yet, because their generation has witnessed an increasing number of women in politics, industry, and education, these youth's unabashedly strong opposition was surprising. The discussions also illustrated how citizenship rights and responsibilities reflect individual and community perceptions and struggles as much as legal status (Puumala and Shindo 2021).

Women's representation in elective office differed significantly in our study countries. In 2021, women comprised 37 percent of parliamentarians in Tanzania and 33 percent in Uganda, but only 15 percent in Ghana (Interparliamentary Union 2021). In addition, in March 2021, Samia Suluhu Hassan became Tanzania's first woman president after the untimely death of President John Magufuli, and, in June 2021, Uganda got its first woman prime minister. Uganda has also had two women vice presidents, including the first in Africa in 1994 (*Citizen* 2021). In contrast, in 2021, Ghanaian women did not hold such high positions, and they comprised only 20 percent of the cabinet (Ghana Web 2021).

These differences are primarily the result of quotas, which have played an even more significant role than democratic freedoms or multiparty competition in increasing women's representation in Africa since the 1990s (Bauer 2012; Kang and Tripp 2018; Stockemer 2011). In Uganda, one woman is elected from each of the 146 women-designated districts to the national parliament,[9] and in

---

[9] Over the years, the number of seats in the Ugandan parliament has increased. As of June 2021, there were 529 seats. There are also women in nonreserved seats and seats reserved for youth, people living with disabilities, workers, the elderly, and ex-officio positions.

Tanzania, 30 percent of parliamentary seats are reserved for women. In both countries, women may also compete in nonreserved seats, and they are roughly one-third of local councilors (International IDEA 2021; Interparliamentary Union 2021; Yoon 2008). Uganda's adoption of quotas reflects women's mobilization in the immediate post-civil-war years (Tripp 2000), while Tanzania's policy resulted from the historic mobilization of women within the ruling party and the country's ratification of the Declaration on Gender and Development of the Southern African Development Community (SADC) in 1997 (Geiger 1987; Yoon 2008). In contrast, and despite its status as a democracy, Ghana is one of twenty African countries that does not have gender quotas. Reasons include the destruction of civil society during military rule (Bauer 2018), divisions among women's organizations (Fallon 2008; Tsikata 2009), and limited women's involvement in drafting the democratic constitution in 1991 (Allah-Mensah 2007). Concerns about appeasing ethnic and regional voting coalitions also prevent presidents from appointing more women to the cabinet (Arriola and Johnson 2014; Bauer and Darkwah 2022).

Although quotas facilitate women's representation, attitudes about women in office matter for party recruitment, women's competitiveness for nonreserved seats, their ability to govern with support, and, in the case of Ghana, the government's adoption of quotas. Afrobarometer data shows a sharp contrast between urban men and women youth in their views about women in office. Figures 6.3 and 6.4 provide two angles on the question of women in office, with both illustrating a significant gender gap. Figure 6.3 gives the percentages of urban men and women youth who agree that men are better political leaders and should be elected over women. Sizeable minorities of men agree with this statement, with their total percentages roughly twice those of women's. Figure 6.4 presents a more positively framed statement about whether women should have the same chance as men to be elected. Majorities of men and women in all three countries agree; though, again, the gender gap is significant. Overall, women hold more positive views of their gender's representation in elected office than men do. On the second question, their agreement outpaces men's most dramatically in Tanzania, where 85 percent of women agree with the statement compared with 64 percent of men.

On both questions, Ghanaian men were the least enthusiastic about women in office. This may reflect widespread beliefs about women's

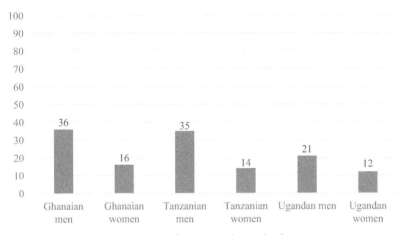

Figure 6.3 Urban youth support for men as better leaders*
* Percentage of urban youth who agree that men make better political leaders than women and should be elected rather than women
Source: Data from Afrobarometer (2016/2018), compiled by the authors

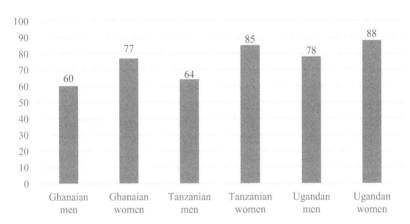

Figure 6.4 Urban youth support for women's election to office*
*Percentage of urban youth who agree that women should have the same chance of being elected to political office as men
Source: Data from Afrobarometer (2016/2018), compiled by the authors

household role (see Figure 6.2), the low number of women in office to serve as positive examples, and religious leaders who express patriarchal views. In interviews with religious leaders in the three countries, Ghanaian pastors – more often in the renewalist tradition – were those

most likely to stress that women's role was "in the home." One renew-alist pastor said, "For a good citizen, the male should be able to lead ...
Women are supposed to support. ... Women can play their God-given roles as supporters of the family" (GH Interview 3; see also Ampofo 2017; GH Interviews 4, 6).[10] In contrast, only one Ugandan religious leader made a similar comment (UG Interview 1). And, in Tanzania, church leaders expected youth to live out their role as Christian parents (TZ Interview 9), but several pastors emphasized that women's work is no longer relegated to the private sphere: "Nowadays we have women pilots; women drivers; women are in the army!" (TZ Interview 7).

Youth respondents in all three countries, particularly but not exclu-sively the men, amplified the survey data. One man said that "men are supposed to always lead" (GH FGD 3), and another added, "The reason why in Ghana only a few women participate in politics is because ... of what we call the glass ceiling. ... As a male, it is easier for me because the status quo accepts me, but a woman is different" (GH FGD 13). Some focused on women's perceived emotionality and intelligence: "A woman can't run this country, because a man has a higher IQ than a woman!" (UG FGD 1; see Adams 2016); "Women will add more sentiment [than reason] and be more emotional" (GH FGD 12). Some insisted that women candidates gained office solely because of their familial or marital ties: "A woman is defined by the man or male figures in her life. ... She is never herself, but someone's wife or daughter" (UG Interview 22). In Uganda, some criticized the quotas that they thought gave unqualified women an edge in elections (UG FGDs 9, 11). A Ugandan woman joined this complaint: "There is too much women's emancipation ... so that the guys even say, 'The ladies violate me'" (UG FGD 15). These men had appropriated the language of anti-GBV campaigns ("violate") to assert their own "vic-timhood." Even some women who supported women in office seemed to do so out of resignation and frustration with men's failure to fulfill their citizenship duties. In Tanzania, a woman said, "Men nowadays have failed to stand in their positions; therefore, women have become a big army in the families" (TZ FGD 8). These views made women who decided to run more vulnerable to attacks on their morality,

---

[10] The names of men's and women's church groups in one renewalist church illustrate this division: Mighty Men of Valor and Precious Vessels of Virtue (for women).

particularly if they were unmarried, vocal, and highly educated (Krook 2017; UG Interviews 18, 24). In response, some women shied away from contesting office, even at the local level, as one Ghanaian woman in university explained when she recalled that few women campaigned for president of her student dormitory. She assumed people would say, "The presidency is for a man; it is not for women." She ran for the post of vice president instead (GH FGD 14). An appointed Tanzanian member of parliament summed up women's lesser involvement in politics by lamenting, "I don't know what is with us [women] when it comes to politics. ... We still have patriarchy" (TZ Interview 12).

In addition, the youth we encountered discussed the structural obstacles that hamper women's entrance into politics. Patronage and connections limit women's ability to run for office. As a woman in Uganda's parliament said, "The system is so riddled with patronage ... and as a young woman, you are very vulnerable ... pitching your ideas and hoping someone will provide you support" (Beck 2003; UG Interview 21). She indicated her vulnerability and need to find someone "higher up" to support her (see also TZ FGD 5). Some Ugandans reported that women's need for a powerful patron led most women to be in the ruling party and, thus, indebted to the president (Muriaas and Wang 2012; UG FGD 7; UG Interview 22). In Tanzania, a particularly contentious political environment discouraged some women. One said, "I don't like to engage in politics because I'm afraid of the consequences. ... That might contribute to conflicts" (TZ FGD 3).

Traditional ideas about who can or should be elected to public office seemed to be shifting slightly in Tanzania with the ascendance of President Hassan, affectionately called "Mama Samia."[11] As vice president, she had taken a backseat to Magufuli's fiery leadership, and, as a result, many Tanzanians did not know what to expect when she became president. During a 2021 focus group discussion, a

---

[11] "Mama" is frequently used in Tanzania instead of "Mrs." or "Ms." as a friendly, yet respectful, title. The use of "mother" or "father" words as honorifics for African presidents is common and intended to convey warmth and respect. Examples include "papa" used for Côte d'Ivoire's first president Félix Houphouët-Boigny and Zaire's late president Mobutu sese Seko, "baba wa taifa" (father of the nation) for Tanzania's Nyerere, and "mzee" (honorific for elder) for Kenya's first president Jomo Kenyatta (see Schatzberg 2001). Although the name "Mama Samia" is clearly connected to President Hassan's gender and, thus, there was some controversy in Tanzania over using it, most Tanzanians see it as a sign of respect (see Kabogo 2021).

Tanzanian woman explained, "When Mama Samia became president, people were unsure if this president could do it. And, if she messes up, people will say, 'Isn't this what you wanted? You wanted a woman!'" (TZ ELCT 1) The speaker suggested that men were waiting for President Hassan to make a mistake that would then validate their skepticism about women in office. The president herself seemed aware of this skepticism when, at Magufuli's funeral, she said she was standing there as the president and a woman, ready to do the job (Kabogo 2021). Her presidency may be shifting attitudes within Tanzania, due to her willingness to stand up to some CCM operatives, her actions on COVID-19, her foreign policy approach, and, as she herself said, "by using my brain" (BBC Africa Daily 2022). These subtle attitude changes were evident when the above-cited respondent explained that, while citizenship "used to favor you guys more than women, people are more conscious now of how they talk because of having a woman president" (TZ ELCT 1). She suggested that, while gender assumptions may not have changed significantly, at least people are more aware of them. A pastor made this point when he referred to the country's future leadership as "Mr. President or Lady President" (TZ ELCT 9), a phrase that most likely would not have been heard before President Hassan's swearing in.

Despite these small steps, this section indicates that the efforts of urban women youth to negotiate citizenship through electoral office remain highly contested. These agentic women moved in the tight corners of patriarchy as they sought to both challenge and instrumentalize their socially acceptable citizenship-from-below. One woman illustrated this tension. She complained extensively about the money needed to run for a local governmental office in Uganda, saying that she almost did not compete because, "Politics is all about money . . . and I didn't have money" (UG Interview 18). But she solved her problem by turning to male patrons and men in her family. Her action shows both her gendered dependence on men – with their disproportionate access to income, property, and power – and her ability to instrumentalize ties to those individuals to her advantage.

6.5 Contesting Patriarchy and Citizenship in Ghana

The NGO Stand Up! illustrates how citizenship can manifest in local actions, how youth negotiate their citizenship partially by contesting gender norms, and how patriarchy shapes their efforts (see Chapter 1 for background). Working with several other NGOs, Stand Up! used social media and in-person programs at secondary schools in Accra to educate youth on "what gender-based violence is, how to spot the warning signs, how to prevent it, and how to get help" (GH Stand Up! 2). The organization illustrates how personal experiences drove these urban youth's acts of citizenship. Informants explained how they, their friends, and/or their family members had experienced GBV. The men reported a sense of realization and anger when they learned about teachers who made unwanted advances toward women students and "created a stumbling block to education" (GH Stand Up! 2, 3). In addition, relationships facilitated their local (and at one point, national) activism, as the story of the organization's founding shows. A professor urged the group's future president (a man) to compete in a campus-wide debate on the topic of extremism and violence. The man's winning team focused on GBV, because "this is something they had the experience of seeing and they could relate to it and talk about it well" (GH Stand Up! 2). After the team won, the president personally recruited a "group of influential students" from student government, residential halls, and his church to form the NGO (GH Stand Up! 1). This influential group gained the opportunity to speak at student gatherings and to deepen relational capital with one another and university faculty.

Through their efforts, members sought to contest gender norms and, in the process, redefine their own citizenship identity. They came face-to-face with the entrenched nature of patriarchy through their school-based programs. One said that if a student accuses a teacher, "the teacher will just say you are lying" (GH Stand Up! 4). They challenged patriarchy in a drawn-out social media encounter with a celebrity who "joked about rape" on Twitter. When some of the organization's members challenged him, the celebrity told them to back off, and it was only after the celebrity's financial sponsors pulled his funding that the posts came down (GH Stand Up! 5). The men in the group gained a deeper realization of the ways that gender norms – the idea that "women are to be a lower breed of human being" or women are "not supposed to talk back" – perpetuated these patterns (GH Stand Up! 2, 4). At times, they experienced small successes, such as when their Facebook posts received thousands of "likes" or the group's leader was "positively received" on talk radio (GH Stand Up! 2). They believed that, at a minimum, they had educated youth that GBV was more than "just rape" and they had "shone light on" the problem (GH Stand Up! 1, 3).

This process of contesting gender roles helped to reshape the members' citizen identity. They said combatting assumptions that violence in the home and school is "normal" was a citizenship act that helped build the nation (GH Stand Up! 2, 3, 5). They felt they had met a duty to other citizens when their work led to the removal of a principal who had "carnal knowledge" of a student (GH Stand Up! 1). In addition, they believed that their work made them more sophisticated about how gender roles shape society and undermine women's citizenship-from-above, particularly since GBV could hurt women's educational prospects. One man said, "Before I joined, I wouldn't pay attention to some issues of gender-based violence. But then I started to see below the surface. Things I thought were 'normal' because that was how you grew up ... When you do this work, it shakes you. You start to ask, 'Is this right'?" (GH Stand Up! 2). Their more astute analysis of gender norms meant that they held views unlike several Ghanaian youth we encountered (see above). They disagreed that men and women should have different citizenship roles in society, and they understood how patriarchy undermined women's ability to hold high-level government positions. They also linked gender inequality to broader issues such as societal violence in ways that other respondents did not, and they contrasted with some other men respondents who said women "just wanted to be taken care of" and that they "play the victim to get the guys to do everything" (GH Stand Up! 7).

The members also illustrated how negotiating citizenship is a process, one set within contexts that continuously shape what acts and identities are possible for the citizen. Thus, even though they challenged gender norms, some of those norms crept in to affect their work. The president made sure that the group had both men and women members, but the president and vice president (both men) were showcased on traditional media (radio, TV), while the women often did behind-the-scenes labor, such as publicity and answering questions on social media. Scheduling sometimes made it difficult for women to attend big events, most likely because those women also had to meet their citizenship-from-below obligations at home with family. Because "[the men] always think women are intellectually gifted," the women were assigned research and writing tasks (GH Stand Up! 4). However, when the women asked for more high-profile work, they got some opportunities – demonstrating the give-and-take involved in contesting citizenship identity. Similarly, some of the men found it frustrating that when they spoke to mixed-gender student groups, those who had experienced GBV were "unwilling to speak up ... fearful of trouble or stigma" (GH Stand Up! 5). The men illustrated some naïveté about the situation of people (who are predominantly women) with lived experiences of trauma. At times, though, the men did seem aware of the ways that women could be silenced because they strongly criticized Joy News when it asked an all-male panel to discuss menstruation (Byte 2020).

Finally, the organization highlights some challenges that youth face as citizen advocates. The students lacked adequate time for all of their activities, and their interests in the group changed over their university careers. Their capacity and training for some of the work was unclear since the organization's members relied on "some statistics and manuals from some of the [NGO] partners" for their school programs (GH Stand Up! 2). They had little money for programs beyond the resources of the members themselves. Even when they wanted auton-omy, they often had to depend on adult patrons, who gave them opportunities to speak at university events or introduced them to NGO officials. More broadly, because the student campaign chal-lenged traditional hierarchies, it was often dismissed. One said, "When we told the students that your mother or father shouldn't physically abuse you, the students laughed and said, 'There's no way because of tradition that I'm taking my parents to the police station'" (GH Stand Up! 2). Gerontocracy and patriarchy remained obstacles for the youth's efforts, even as they exhibited agency through actions to negotiate their citizen identities.

6.6 Conclusion

This chapter has interrogated how gender shapes youth citizenship. Our discussions with youth elucidated that men and women typically defined and understood citizenship in similar ways, emphasizing its communal and legalistic aspects and explaining how they live these out in simple, everyday ways. The vast majority of men and women agreed that everyday citizenship plays out differently for men and women, as they face various cultural and structural pressures. For example, men emphasized legalistic aspects, as they were more likely to encounter agents of the state in their everyday lives. Most women said their citizenship identity revolved around actions related to carework and family, while men reported gaining citizenship through income generation and providing protection. Our respondents made it clear that women and men engage in different kinds of work, and most appreciated how these various tasks contributed to building the nation. For most respondents, these patterns were part of the complexity of being an urban youth and navigating multiple spaces and identities.

While all youth were subject to patriarchal assumptions, a number of respondents challenged these assumptions through work that is outside the norm for their gender. Some men provided care and took up the cause of GBV in schools, and some women ran for office or joined protests for fair elections. These variations illustrate the wide range of experiences youth have as they contest everyday citizenship, but they also illustrate how the principles that undergirded everyday citizenship for many – positive relationships, reciprocity, dependence, obligation, and care for others – stretched beyond socially mandated gender roles. That is, some men helped children because they cared; some women ran for office because they felt obligations. In Chapter 7 we move from analyzing the factors that intersect with and shape citizenship – income, church attendance, and gender – to considering how youth who are disappointed, frustrated, or angry contest citizenship.

7 | *Channeling Frustration through Exit, Exclusion, and Engagement*

The youth have no jobs, and the very few jobs there are go to those who have connections to government ... They are very angry. ... They are so angry they are employing all kinds of destructive strategies to express it: crime, cross-generational sex, drugs ... We will be in trouble in years to come.

(UG Interview 10)

This book has interrogated how youth respondents negotiate citizenship at the micro and macro levels and in public and private spaces. We have queried how youth of different income levels, church attendance rates, and men's and women's identity contest their rights and obligations in a community. This chapter grapples with a core assumption about African youth that the introductory quotation exemplifies: This demographic is disappointed, frustrated, and at times angry for very justifiable reasons, and they react to their marginalization in potentially destabilizing and destructive ways (see Abbink and van Kessel 2005). Most of our respondents did not express these emotions. For most (even the angry ones), citizenship was manifest in the ways we have previously discussed, such as carework, meeting attendance, employment, communal labor, voting, and/or tax paying. However, a small number of frustrated and angry youth contested citizenship via different paths. Although few exited all of their citizenship obligations,[1] some embraced exclusionary identity-based politics, some may have found populist trends appealing, and a handful channeled their anger into activism. Examining these youth provides additional insights into how everyday citizenship is negotiated in the tight corners of economic and political marginalization.

---

[1] Youth respondents did not report exit through crime, sex, and drugs, as the interviewee suggests, though they would likely not discuss such activities.

This chapter proceeds as follows. First, we draw out some broad themes from the literatures on political exit, identity-based mobilization, populism, and social movements to speculate about how our frustrated, angry youth respondents might contest citizenship (Section 7.1). Next, we analyze how unmet government promises, corruption, repression, and political exclusion undermine youth citizenship and foment frustrations (Section 7.2). The subsequent four sections then interrogate different ways these youth might contest citizenship, which, though we separate them, need not be mutually exclusive. First, they could exit local and/or national citizenship obligations, but Afrobarometer data and our respondents provide little evidence of this path (Section 7.3). Second, they could claim their citizen identity by denying others' citizen belonging (Section 7.4). Third, they could follow a populist leader who espouses the "will of the people" while simultaneously undermining minority rights (Section 7.5). We draw lessons from the Economic Freedom Fighters (EFF) in South Africa to interrogate this possibility, but we find inconclusive evidence of such support among our respondents. Finally, frustrated youth could add to their everyday citizen obligations by channeling anger into activism (Section 7.6). The conclusion (Section 7.7) reminds us that, as actors with agency, youth continuously choose how their citizenship will play out in their daily lives.

7.1 What Paths Might Frustrated Youth Choose?

The social science literature provides insights into how our frustrated youth might contest citizenship given their political and economic constraints. First, they might choose to exit the political realm – an action intertwined with opportunities for voice, which, in turn, may foster loyalty (Hirschman 1970). Voice might take several forms, most of which we have examined in previous chapters (e.g., voting). In Africa, co-optation, repression, and corruption undermine some people's voice, leading some civil society groups to exit the public sphere (Chazan et al. 1988) and entrepreneurs to rely on informality (Rizzo 2017). Unemployment and poverty create structural impediments to voice (Resnick and Casale 2014), as do youth's higher levels of mobility, their lower rates of marriage, employment, and property ownership (Squire, Wolfinger, and Glass 1987), the lack of viable opposition parties, and weak political parties (Jennings and van Deth

1990). Despite these possibilities, few youth we encountered fully exited local or national citizen obligations.

Second, youth may define their own citizenship by instrumentalizing identities to the exclusion of others. In the African context, ethnicity – its salience heightened through colonial favoritism – may affect who rises to leadership positions (Mamdani 1996; Ndegwa 1997), how and where public goods are allocated (Franck and Ranier 2012; Lieberman 2009), who gains educational opportunities (Kramon and Posner 2016), and where people live (Paller 2019). Ethnic identities may lead people to vote for coethnics out of fear of non-coethnics (Ferree 2010; Lynch 2014), may make politicians tout ethnic identity in campaigns (Posner 2005), may drive individuals to participate in protests (Mueller 2018, 122), and may divide progressive movements (Crossouard and Dunne 2015). Ethnic favoritism may intertwine with autochthony, or the belief that, because the "people of the soil" have an indisputable link to a particular place, they should be considered citizens, while "newcomers" should not (Bøås 2009; Geschiere 2009). Religious identities may deepen ethnic mobilization or be instrumentalized in their own right for exclusive projects (Lonsdale 2009), ethnic violence (Longman 2010), votes for coreligionists (Dowd 2015), and support for policies that target sexual minorities (Grossman 2015; Ward 2015). However, the divisive potential of instrumentalized identities might be mitigated by crosscutting ties (Dowd 2015; Dunning and Harrison 2010), democratic reforms that lead politicians to court voters with public goods rather than ethnic favoritism (Harding 2020), a country's ethnic group distribution that makes ethnic claims insufficient or unnecessary for winning elections (Arriola 2013; Posner 2005; Taylor 2017), and religious leaders who speak on election peace or social justice (Kuperus 2018; Patterson 2011). Among our urban youth respondents, some contest citizenship through localized, exclusionary actions. Their experiences provide nuance to these aggregate studies of identity in African politics.

Choosing another path, some youth may support populism. With a "chameleonic nature," populism plays out differently across geography, history, and regime types (Moffitt 2017, 45; Taggart 2000).[2] Populism often shows nondemocratic tendencies, meaning that it could

---

[2] The scholarship on populism is vast and diverse (see Tuğul 2021). As a fuzzy term, populism also has been conflated with ideology (Hunger and Paxton 2022).

contribute to the growing authoritarian trend across Africa (Cheeseman and Fisher 2021). Cas Mudde and Cristobal Rovira Kaltwasser (2017) define "populism" as a "thin-centred ideology" with its core concepts being the "pure people, the corrupt elite, and the general will." The people have been variously identified as "poorer, subaltern groups" (Resnick 2010), an "amorphous, heterogeneous, largely unorganized mass" (Weyland 2022), urban-based (Weyland 2001), antiforeigner (Mudde 2007), and/or reflective of racial and class disparities (Hart 2013). The corrupt elite also takes many forms: a technocratic, bureaucratic state (Crothers 2018); establishment politicians (Essop 2015; Fraser 2017); and/or global economic powers (Tuğul 2021). Using commonplace, anti-elitist language, populist leaders portray themselves as outsiders close to the people (Canovan 1999; Moffitt 2017), and they propose swift, simple policy solutions that appeal to diverse constituencies (Laclau 2005). Though populism may have the potential to incorporate marginalized groups and challenge authoritarian rule (Mudde and Rovira Kaltwasser 2017), the belief that "popular sovereignty is the only legitimate source of power" can harm the very liberal institutions (i.e., rule of law and individual rights) that made its emergence possible (Canovan 1999; Mudde and Rovira Kaltwasser 2013; Taggart 2000). Populism's strangulation of democracy, though, depends on those very institutions' strength, particularly during crises (Weyland 2020).

In Africa, populism has tended to revolve around individual leaders because parties are usually personality driven and nonideological (Manning 2005; Resnick 2010).[3] The continent's rapid urbanization creates an arena in which populists may reach out to informal-economy workers, many of whom feel targeted by government policies (e.g., taxes) and overwhelmed by urban challenges (Resnick and Thurlow 2015). Without strong labor unions, populists take up the mantle of popular opposition to neoliberalism (Negi 2008). Their solutions to economic inequality and poverty may include redistributionist policies (e.g., jobs, food subsidies, free education).[4] In countries

---

[3] In liberal democracies, factors driving populism include the gap between institutional performance and citizen demands (Berezin 2009), weak political parties (Brubaker 2017), racial cleavages, and economic inequalities (López and Luna 2021).

[4] If they are elected, though, they often maintain neoliberal policies (see Fraser 2017; Tuğul 2021).

where ethnicity is politically salient (e.g., Kenya), populist candidates may couple urban mobilization with ethnic claims in rural areas (Cheeseman and Larmer 2015; Resnick 2010), while, in the liberationist governments of southern Africa, officials use populist rhetoric to legitimate their rule as the only alternative in a continued struggle over foreign domination (Melber 2018). Although authoritarianism and, in some cases, its populist guise have expanded across Africa, urban youth may not support these trends. Youth participation in protests against constitutional erosion and economic crises throughout Africa signal their desire for change (see Branch and Mampilly 2015; Mueller 2018), although protests are not always a "universal cry for democratic renewal" (Mueller 2020). Among our frustrated respondents, support for populism seemed muted compared to their opposition to authoritarian practices.

Finally, youth might channel their emotions into activism.[5] As Deborah Gould (2009, 443) writes, "Emotion conditions the possibilities for activism," since emotions often build on grievances (Piven and Cloward 1977) and identities of marginalization (Robins 2004). Emotions may be amplified through movement participation, helping to define the movement's symbols and language (Gamson 1992), undergirding participants' continued identification with it (Melucci 1995), and urging members' tenacity (McAdam 1986). Emotions may act as "accelerators or amplifiers" in social movements (van Stekelenburg and Klandermans 2009, 32), with people emotionally invested in a cause being unlikely to abandon it (Davenport 2015; Fenio 2011). Yet, emotions are situated within cultural, historical, and power contexts that may limit their expression and interpretation (Gould 2009). We do not find that most of the angry, frustrated urban youth we encountered became activists, but, for the small number of activists we did meet, anger motivated their actions.

7.2 The Frustrations That Urban Youth Face

In all three countries, youth had lengthy, animated discussions concerning the issues that vex them. They were particularly frustrated by unmet promises for jobs and services and by the pervasiveness of

---

[5] The social movement literature is vast, but see David Snow, Sarah Soule, and Hanspeter Kriesi (2004) as one introduction.

corruption. In Tanzania and Uganda, respondents also discussed rights infringement and authoritarian governance. Notably, urban youth believed these frustrations harmed their citizenship.

7.2.1 Unmet Promises of Jobs and Services

Some respondents detailed how their governments made empty promises. One Ghanaian woman said, "They have promised us jobs. We plead [for them to] fulfill the promises so we can get to work!" (GH FGD 2; see also GH FGDs 9, 10; UG FGDs 1, 7). A Tanzanian man pointed to the gap between government promises to promote industry and actual opportunities: "Recently [the] NHIF [National Health Insurance Fund] announced a vacancy and if you want to know the current crisis of unemployment just observe the number of those who [apply] for that position. Worse enough we are told this is the 'industrial government'" (TZ FGD 8). Some youth complained about poor social services: "They promise us gutters to help with rain and hospitals to keep us healthy, but even the attempt of providing us with the gutters, because the quality is so low, it's an insult" (GH FGD 12; see also UG FGD 4).

As a result, respondents reported feeling insulted, discouraged, and demotivated – all emotions that undermined their sense of citizen belonging. A Ghanaian said, "There is no motivation for me. They [political leaders] drive their big V8s and are concerned about their accommodations, but they don't take care of us. It's like your voice is not heard" (GH FGD 14; see also GH FGD 12). A Ugandan man made a similar point: "I'm not taken seriously when I talk about the needs of low-income earners" (UG FGD 1). Some youth expressed disappointment because these politicians were "not doing what they were supposed to do" (GH FDG 12) – a particular problem when these officials had promised patronage to party cadres, and jobs, education, and opportunities to the public (Van Gyampo and Anyidoho 2019). Government's inability or unwillingness to address their material needs meant many urban youth could not financially help others or contribute time and labor to the community, both manifestations of good citizenship (UG FGD 1). For some youth respondents, the fact that "government has let me down" made it impossible "to feel close to the community" (UG FGD 3; see also UG FGD 5). As one Ugandan questioned, "How could you call me a citizen of Uganda when

I don't feel that economy you are talking about in my pocket?" (UG Interview 10).

The urban youth we encountered who expressed these views were not atypical: Afrobarometer reports that a significant percentage of urban youth in the three study countries think that their governments are doing "very badly" or "fairly badly" in addressing the needs of youth. The numbers are higher in Uganda (64 percent) and Tanzania (58 percent) than in Ghana (36 percent), most likely because of Ghana's lower lived poverty rate.[6] This result differs slightly from our focus group discussions, in which Ghanaians' primary complaint was about the government's failure on youth unemployment.

7.2.2 Corruption

A significant number of youth respondents in all three countries pointed to forms of corruption (favoritism, bribery, embezzlement) as the reason for their frustration and anger. One Ghanaian said, "There is a lot of discrimination in the public sector. They want to punish those in lower positions and turn a blind eye on those in high positions when it comes to corruption, because they think the ones in high positions will help in their campaign and stuff" (GH FGD 4). Another Ghanaian described how local favoritism created a system of impunity for elites that undermined youth citizenship:

Recently someone eased himself [urinated] at an unauthorized place. We saw him and seized his bike and reported him to the elders. They assured us they will investigate and deal with the person. When they realized it was a leader in the community, they refused to take action and pardoned him. This discourages us from executing our rights as good citizens. (GH FGD 7)

For both Ghanaians, favoritism croded their citizenship because it discounted their interests and participation.

Two Tanzanian youth respondents discussed how favoritism and secrecy shape citizen opportunities. One man said, "[The thing] which

---

[6] The percentages for urban elders were 27 percent (Ghana), 47 percent (Tanzania), and 66 percent (Uganda). The higher Ugandan percentage may demonstrate that elders, like the religious leader quoted in the chapter's introduction, focus on youth's negative behavior and anger. They also just may be particularly aware of youth, because 70 percent of the population is under thirty years old (Population International 2010).

is considered is who knows you and not what you know" (TZ FGD 5). This problem prevented the citizenship that comes through paid work. Another said that personal connections not only undermined opportunities but also made it difficult to be an informed citizen. Emphasizing how "the Chinese industries ... steal from Tanzania," he said that citizens could not easily inquire about who benefits from foreign investment in industries such as construction materials. This is because there are "very few who are benefiting, [only] those on top" (TZ FGD 8). For this man, both the unequal access to economic benefits and the lack of transparency about state industries and foreign investment undermined citizenship.

Among respondents, Ugandan youth were the most agitated about corruption – a trend echoed in Afrobarometer (2016/2018) surveys: 55 percent of Ugandan urban youth said that "most" or "all" government officials were corrupt, compared to 38 percent in Ghana and 17 percent in Tanzania. Transparency International (2021) also reported that Uganda has a worse corruption perception score than Tanzania or Ghana.[7] One Ugandan man said, "If you go to a government hospital you have to bribe a health worker in order to treat a patient and if you don't do it, the patient dies." Corruption undermined the man's ability to act as a citizen – in this case, his ability to get needed health care for a friend or family member. As a result, he said, "I don't have any reason ... to feel like a citizen" (UG FGD 4; see also UG FGD 1). Another Ugandan took a broader view, explaining how corruption hurts everyone's citizenship. He personalized a hypothetical scenario by portraying himself ("I") and the listener ("you") as complicit, unethical players, a rhetorical device that illustrated his view that corruption is ubiquitous:

If they [the government] give you money to construct roads, you don't construct them, you just swallow it for your stomach. ... I'm just embezzling funds locally to satisfy my needs, because maybe my wife is in the hospital. ... We are all just needing to feed ourselves, and so we become like *Homo corruptus*. ... We all end up being not good citizens because how do you expect me, the person with the low status to be a good citizen, when I'm seeing the [corrupt] acts at the top? (UG FGD 9)

---

[7] In the 2021 Corruption Perception Index, Uganda received a score of twenty-seven out of one hundred, compared to thirty-nine for Tanzania and forty-three for Ghana (Transparency International 2021).

For this individual, corruption at the top filtered down, literally making citizens into a new species: *Homo corruptus*. Corruption undermined everyday citizenship because it destroyed an identity of belonging that was rooted in relationships and obligations to others. It meant people were just out for themselves, making it impossible, as one Ghanaian said, for citizens to build the country or work for the community's welfare (GH FGD 6).

7.2.3 Rights Infringement and Authoritarian Governance

With great animation, some Tanzanian and Ugandan youth described the multiple ways that rights infringement and authoritarian governance undermined their citizenship. The first way this occurred was materially, when the police harassed vendors, drivers, and informal settlement residents, many of whom were lower-income people. When the authorities confiscated merchandise, demanded bribes, or chased people for delinquent tax payments, they made supporting one's family, community, and employees – all actions defined to be citizen obligations – highly problematic (UG FGDs 1, 2). Authorities also sometimes demolished housing, thereby harming youth security and community. Tanzanians discussed the impact of these government actions, including the demolition of over six thousand houses without compensation (TZ FGD 8). One woman said, "Because they have demolished houses, people are suffering in the street." A second added, "In demolishing people's houses, for sure they didn't care. They demolished even if there still were some stuffs inside. For example, they could give the notice like today at 2 pm and by tomorrow, they come to demolish, even if you haven't removed stuffs from the house. They don't care where you are going to live, or where the family will go" (TZ FGD 3). Rapid, forced resettlement meant people had to invest time and resources into moving rather than performing income-generating work; as people scattered, they left behind friends and neighbors. These outcomes could undermine the relational aspects of everyday citizenship, and they led some to assert, "It is difficult to say ... that government has helped me" (TZ FGD 8). As these women highlight, authorities sometimes engaged in callous, destructive actions that had high costs. A Ugandan amplified this theme when she recounted: "One time a woman fell into a trench and died while being chased by the Kampala Capital City Council authorities who track down tax offenders ... [The saddest part] was she wasn't even earning that much from her business" (UG FGD 7). By destroying livelihoods, communities, and human bodies, the state harmed citizenship.

A second way some respondents thought that the state discounted their citizenship was by treating them as dehumanized or infantile subjects, not as citizens with rights. One Tanzanian man complained:

> The government has infringed very much [on rights] and they are ... granted by the constitution! ... Recently I exchanged words with the traffic police because of the fines which they have been giving, [but] sometimes you're not given the right to question ... They just say, "Give me the driving license." He [the police officer] then writes the fine. That's all. ... You can't defend yourself anywhere. (TZ FGD 2)

This individual portrays a state with little interest in its citizens, making the citizen–state relationship fraught with acrimony.

Others took up this theme, with various levels of force. Another Tanzanian described how older politicians are out of touch with youth's needs, making their citizen contributions invisible: "These elder leaders are the ones troubling us. If we had youth [representatives] it could [be] easier. [Now] the older person has to think, 'Someone came here and told me this and this and another one came here and told me this.' But youth know very well about [the] problems facing fellow youth" (TZ FGD 4). Some Ugandans went further: It was not just that leaders were clueless about youth's needs. It was that they were "incompetent"; a parliament "full of old people who do nothing but doze" (UG FGD 7); a septuagenarian president who "doesn't care" (UG FGD 3). For some Ugandans, it was not just that they had become invisible citizens (Bangura 2018) but, rather, that their citizenship had been procedurally undercut. This occurred when parliament passed the 2017 law that removed the presidential age restriction (see Chapter 1). For them, the law shut youth out and led them to feel worthless, "invalidated," "without hope," and betrayed (UG FGDs 1, 4, 7). One man angrily rejected this political exclusion: "The youth can govern too!" (UG FGD 1). Another remarked, "It is as if we are not in our own country," a statement that undercut citizenship as belonging (UG FGD 9). Despite their legal standing, these youth perceived no opportunity in politics. This was particularly striking because Uganda is one of the few African states with quotas to ensure youth representation locally and nationally (De Paredes and Desrues 2021).

Finally, youth talked about how state repression, corruption, and manipulation could create *bad* citizens, or people who did not care about their communities or others. A Tanzanian explained this transformation:

You might find a person is brought up well … and then she comes to face a hardship in life. What could cause the hardship? Maybe … bad leadership. … The leader doesn't … follow the given rules of the given country. By the leaders working against the laws [it] may cause the citizens to become bad citizens, once they start to claim their rights by force. (TZ FGD 7)

Bad citizenship, therefore, emerges because of capricious, corrupt leaders whose actions, in turn, foster hardship. Hardship pushes even the most upstanding youth to engage in violent actions. For this respondent, it is the government's fault when people choose that path.

In Uganda, some youth respondents did not explicitly say that the government created bad citizens, but the theme was evident when they spoke extensively of being suspicious of others. Suspicion was rooted in local officials' efforts to encourage "good citizens" to share information about "suspicious people," ostensibly to prevent crime and terrorism (UG FGDs 4, 10, 14, 15). In the 2016 election, local police established "nonpartisan" crime prevention units to report on local electoral crimes. However, most of the eleven million watchers supported the NRM, and their mere presence contributed to voter intimidation (Abrahamsen and Bareebe 2021). Such security efforts have led to the misidentification of criminals, physical intimidation, and violence – each of which undermines community relations (Tapscott 2017). In over half of the Ugandan focus group discussions, respondents reported that *bodaboda* drivers, community leaders, pastors, market women, and sometimes even their spouses were spying on behalf of the government. One said, "They [spies] are everywhere" (UG FGD 4). This belief affected mundane interactions among people – the foundation of everyday citizenship – and it eroded the good citizenship of some in the eyes of others.

Ultimately, many Ugandan and Tanzanian youth we encountered, particularly those of lower income, felt their governments did not really *want* good citizens, or people who could claim their rights and hold the government accountable (TZ ELCT 5). To weaken and discourage citizenship, governments took people's earnings, destroyed the physical space in which citizen acts occurred, discounted their ideas, wrote laws to keep youth out of power, and created structures that made people suspicious of one another. How do urban youth who feel this pain of an undercut citizenship strive to reclaim a citizen identity? If youth feel that conventional pathways of citizenship from below (e.g., earning income) or citizenship from above (e.g., voting) are eroded, what might they do? In Sections 7.3 through 7.6, we explore some possibilities, which are neither exhaustive nor mutually exclusive.

7.3 Contesting Citizenship through Exit

As Chapters 2 and 3 illustrate, fewer urban youth than elders engage in most citizenship acts, with the exception of attending a demonstration or protest march. We question, though, how many youth decide to exit micro- or macro-level citizenship actions. Many of our respondents complained about the government, and some of them felt distanced from their communities because of envy or distrust, but, even among the subset of frustrated and angry youth, the vast majority reported continuing to help neighbors, to do communal labor, and to obey the law.

To assess the prevalence of exit, we use Afrobarometer data on three questions: attending a community meeting, voting, and joining others to request government action. These questions allow respondents to select an answer that illustrates a *choice* to exit.[8] Respondents can reply that they "would never attend a community meeting," "would never join others to request government action," or "decided not to vote" – all phrases that connote the choice to exit. We include the percentages for elders because youth engagement is often compared to older people's participation.

Table 7.1 illustrates a few points, although the number of respondents for some categories makes the results less than definitive. The first, and most notable, is the higher rate of nonparticipation among urban Ghanaian youth and elders in the three activities. This pattern is particularly striking for actions that require collaboration: attending

---

[8] We do not use the other Afrobarometer questions from earlier chapters because respondents could select answers that indicated a lack of opportunity such as, "No, but would do if had the chance." We do not include nonparticipation in protests or demonstrations because, for many, the socially acceptable response is not to engage in such activities.

Table 7.1 *Nonparticipation in actions among urban populations, by age and country*

Country	Age*	Would never attend a community meeting (%)	Decided not to vote in most recent election (%)	Would never join others to request govt action (%)	N
Ghana	Youth	21	7[a]	30	733
	Elders	7	7	33	372
Tanzania	Youth	5	4[b]	15	439
	Elders	4	2	15	358
Uganda	Youth	4	3[c]	7	209
	Elders	3	7	6	90

* For voting, "youth" includes people aged twenty-six to thirty-five years old. For the other actions, "youth" includes the weighted average for people aged eighteen to thirty-five years old.
[a] N = 388; [b] N = 244; [c] N = 115
Source: Data from Afrobarometer (2016/2018), compiled by the authors

a meeting and joining others to request government action. We interrogate the Ghanaian pattern below, using the respondent data. Second, in Tanzania and Uganda, nonparticipation numbers are small for both youth and elders, with the exception of those Tanzanian youth and elders saying they would never join others to request government action. Third, there are some instances when more elders report nonparticipation than youth. Three percent more Ghanaian elders than youth say they would never join others to request government action, a finding we cannot further unpack with our youth respondent data. Four percent more Ugandan elders report not voting in the most recent election, perhaps because of electoral violence – a trend some youth interviewees also noted (UG Interviews 4, 15, 20, 22). Beyond these two exceptions, more youth than elders report exit-type behaviors. This point aligns with larger findings about youth engagement in politics (see Lekalake and Gyimah-Boadi 2016).

Our respondents hew to these patterns. To begin, only a small number expressed little to no interest or concern for community or political engagement. A handful were clearly apathetic: These individuals answered few questions; reported no interest in government; said, "I don't care about politics," "I don't pay attention to politics," "It doesn't really matter"; and/or admitted discussing sports, not politics, with friends (GH FGDs 5, 6, 11, 14; TZ FGDs 2–6; UG FGDs 1, 4, 9, 11). However, even these individuals reported helping with community projects, caring for others, or meeting family obligations – each of which they viewed to be an act of citizenship.

Urban youth in only two focus groups reported political exit. None of the Tanzanians did, although a few hinted that the curtailed political space under then President Magufuli cast a shadow over discussions of politics. This situation, as well as a political culture of deference to authority, may partly explain the 15 percent of Tanzanian urban youth and elders who said they would never join with others to request government action. In Ghana, one man from a higher-income neighborhood mentioned that he used to be engaged in politics, but he stopped because "the rivalry between political parties was getting too much" (GH FGD 11). For him, the alternation in power that is the hallmark of competitive democracy had not catalyzed participation. His reported behavior contrasts with work that finds that competitive elections increase voter turnout (Riker and Ordeshook 1968; but see Blais 2000). For this individual, competitive elections led to administrative turnovers and political party rivalries that undermined policy continuity. The result was many broken promises about health care, education, and development – major reasons outlined above for youth frustration.

However, his exit was not just about broken promises: It was also driven by the perception that partisanship in Ghana has become an increasingly divisive identity, one that generates contestation over who does and does not belong as a citizen. Another respondent conveyed this idea when she described her experience observing the 2016 election in Kumasi, an urban stronghold for the NPP. As an NPP supporter, she and other NPP youth viewed rival NDC supporters with suspicion when they came to vote, as if they were people who did not belong. She said, "When we saw an outsider, someone from the other party, we can see how we all look at them, and won't even sell [to] or engage with them" (GH FGD 6). The idea that citizenship – as an identity that confers belonging, rights, and responsibilities – should be tied to partisanship is evident in illiberal democracies, such as when the ruling party in Zimbabwe, the Zimbabwe African National Union-Patriotic Front (ZANU-PF), offered differential entitlements to land and jobs based on party loyalty. But parties in liberal democracies can also "confer differentiated access to resources and protection" and "attempt to moralise political loyalty as grounds for privileged treatment" (McGregor and Chatiza 2020, 18). A significant number of the Ghanaian respondents expressed frustration that each major political party engaged in promises and projects that benefitted only its supporters to the detriment of the opposing party supporters (GH FGDs 1, 5, 8, 11, 14). This differentiated access to jobs or resources excluded those without partisan citizenship.

In Uganda, most urban youth did not exit but instead animatedly reported community involvement, voting, attending meetings, and reaching out to local political leaders (UG FGDs 3, 6, 10, 11, 14). However, in one focus group discussion in a middle-income neighborhood, two women explained their decision to never vote again after the community had united to defeat the ruling NRM in 2016. The first said, "It was my first time to vote ... but what disappointed me is that the elections were rigged. From that time, I have never voted again." The other woman added, "We were sure we were going to get a new president but to our surprise, we lost the election. That is when I stopped voting" (UG FGD 7).[9] Similarly, a 2021 survey found that only 40 percent of Ugandans aged eighteen to twenty-nine trust the Electoral Commission "somewhat" or "a lot" (Krőnke 2022). These respondents illustrate how the rules of the political game (in this case, fraudulent elections) may determine political participation (Norris 2004). But fear also led to exit. As the women said, "The youth know that once you engage in Uganda's politics you are likely to be killed" (UG FGD 7). Despite their voting exit, these women still viewed their work as mothers and vendors as constituting citizenship.

The Ghanaian and Ugandan cases of reported exit only partially fit with our findings from earlier chapters on income level, church attendance, and gender. As we might predict, it was infrequent churchgoers in both countries who reported political exit (see Chapter 5), and, in keeping with the findings reported in Chapter 4, it was urban youth in Uganda and Ghana with more income who said they quit voting. Women are less likely to vote than men (see Chapter 6), making the Ghanaian man's decision to abstain outside of this pattern. However,

---

[9] We have no way of confirming if the women followed through on their threat to not vote in 2021.

because our sample is only two focus groups, it is too small for broader conclusions.

7.4 Contesting Citizenship by Excluding Others

Youth frustration and anger over their governments' poor performance, corruption, rights infringement, and authoritarianism might create conditions in which youth instrumentalize ethnic and/or religious identities to exclude others from citizen belonging (Dorman 2020; McGregory and Chatiza 2020). This possibility recognizes that the process of negotiating everyday citizenship can have both "emancipatory and exclusionary potential" (Di Gregorio and Merolli 2016, 934). This exclusion played out in the quotidian words and deeds of a minority of our urban youth respondents.

Urban youth's experiences with religious and/or ethnic discrimination vary significantly in the study countries. In Uganda, 16 percent of urban youth report several or many discriminatory experiences based on ethnicity, compared to 4 percent of their peers in Ghana, and 3 percent in Tanzania. The urban youth numbers for religious discrimination were 5 percent in Uganda, 4 percent in Ghana, and 2 percent in Tanzania (Afrobarometer 2016/2018). These patterns align with research by Nic Cheeseman and Robert Ford (2007), who placed Uganda higher than Ghana in terms of the politicization of ethnicity. In the qualitative data, Ghanaian respondents were more likely than Ugandans to bring up ethnicity, most likely because of Ugandans' fear of what many see as an ethnically exclusive regime (Lindemann 2011a). Tanzanians did not view ethnic and religious identities as salient for citizenship. These results are perhaps not surprising given the late President Nyerere's efforts to promote the common Swahili language, weaken traditional leaders, and nationalize religious educational institutions (see Chapter 1; TZ FGD 5). Not only are Ugandans and Ghanaians more likely than Tanzanians to report discrimination based on ethnic or religious identity, but Afrobarometer (2016/2018) shows that they are less tolerant of other ethnic groups: 33 percent of urban Ugandan youth said they would "somewhat" or "strongly like" having neighbors from a different ethnic group, compared to 67 percent of their peers in Ghana and 85 percent in Tanzania.

Our respondents help elucidate how these attitudes play out in localized, relational ways. First, although some youth just affirmed their ethnic identity – as one Ghanaian did when discussing the Homowo festival that the Ga people celebrate (GH FGD 7) – others saw ethnic identity as a source of division. For example, another Ghanaian boldly exclaimed, "The migrants who are in the country ... will not work hard for the progress of this country. That confirms he/she is not a good citizen" (GH FGD 7). Ethnicity, migrant status, and industriousness were conflated, and everyday citizenship – if it was defined as being a productive, contributing societal member – was not possible for outsiders. In addition, for some individuals, outsiders could undermine the livelihood needed to meet citizenship obligations (UG FGD 1). This view echoes some voices in South Africa, where anti-immigrant sentiments have acted as a proxy for xenophobia and where notions of citizenship that exclude some to the benefit of others are part of the public discourse (Solomon 2019).

Other respondents described being the target of ethnic exclusion. Some Ghanaian women said that their inability to understand and speak Ga – the predominant language spoken in their community – prevented full inclusion in neighborhood and church activities (GH FGD 2). Without this identity (and language), their citizenship was diminished because they could not forge reciprocal ties to others. Ethnicity also could erode the citizenship needed to access state services and employment, as one Ugandan man said. He complained that the Banyakole (the ethnic group from Western Uganda, the home of President Museveni) have "taken up most of the jobs in the government so we don't have the potential to help our country." Ethnically based patronage harmed his ability to perform the citizen task of building the nation through work. For him, and others in the group, "widespread tribalism" eroded their citizenship (UG FGD 10).

Some respondents moved beyond just expressing exclusive citizen attitudes to describing citizen *practices* that fostered their own belonging while downgrading the citizenship of others. In Ghana, one Christian respondent described how he felt "secure" in his community after a soccer game between a Christian team and a Muslim team because the Christians tackled the Muslims and forced them to flee (GH FGD 1). An everyday, allegedly nonpolitical event – a soccer match – became an arena in which individuals contested who did and did not belong. In Uganda, a group of frequent churchgoing women said that it was imperative they vote because otherwise they might "wake up one day and the church would be closed" because "non-

Christians" (i.e., Muslims) had power (UG FGD 16). Their perspective echoed ideas from some Christian pastors, one of whom asserted, "The Muslims are equipping their people to take on serious leadership. ... [At university] they have more law students being supported, more doctors being supported. ... Those are the most influential areas ... so we must train our church youth to be educated, to participate in politics" (UG Interview 2). Both the pastor and the youth who mimicked him focused on how the localized everyday act of attending university had long-term consequences regarding who would and would not belong in the political community. This contestation was evident when a Ugandan Christian youth parliamentarian said that, after she defeated a candidate from another religion, "they came up to fight me" (UG Interview 21).

In an extreme example, Ghanaian youth recalled several discrete events in their neighborhoods that involved land being "taken over by someone who was not native to the community" (GH FGD 1; see also GH FGD 4). It was unclear if these "outsiders" were of different ethnic or religious backgrounds, but they were not perceived by our youth participants to rightfully belong. In one case, an outsider married the only daughter of a landlord who had died. Youth telling the story asserted that the outsider's desire was blatant: He wanted to take over the landowner's land ("He came only to marry the lady ... and claim ownership of the house and even the neighboring land"). Thus, for the locals, the outsider was suspect. In response, the community rallied to kick him off the land, banish him, and reclaim the property. In the words of one man, "He [the outsider] was just wiped of this community ... [I]t puts a fear in me and it gives me that sense of *belongingness* that I am secured in a particular place. That, should anything happen to me, there are people who will defend me. So, I love my community and I am just staying there" (GH FGD 1; emphasis added). As this speaker indicated, his citizenship – or sense of belongingness – revolved around contesting the belongingness of the outsider. The result was emotion (love) and commitment. Contestation about citizenship then included the micro actions of mobilizing others (perhaps through meetings or gossip), speaking (perhaps through threats), and physically acting (perhaps by banging on the stranger's door or dragging him from the community). Although the speaker does not go into detail, we could imagine the everyday words and deeds that culminated in the exclusion of the other. The vignette illustrates how citizenship is a dynamic and "constructed norm," one not divorced from power, resources, and other identities (Dorman 2020, 267).

7.5 Contesting Citizenship by Embracing Populism

Given the frustration and anger that some respondents expressed, we might expect them to support populist leaders who portray themselves as decisive problem solvers and who may or may not have authoritarian tendencies. To interrogate this possibility, we first look at the case of the EFF in South Africa. Although situated in a democratic context with unique racial and economic structures due to the country's almost fifty years of racist apartheid policies, as a youth-led and youth-supported party, the EFF allows us to glean broader lessons about the appeal of populism (Section 7.5.1). We then explore that appeal in Tanzania and Uganda (Section 7.5.2).

7.5.1 The Economic Freedom Fighters

The EFF is centered around its founder and leader, Julius Malema, who has been described as "that angry unmannered bad boy of postapartheid politics," "dangerous," and a "demagogue and fascist" (Essop 2015; Posel 2014). Born in 1981, outside Pietersburg (now Polokwane), Limpopo Province, Malema first embraced radical politics as president of the Congress of South African Students (COSAS). In 2007, he led the African National Congress Youth League (ANCYL) to support Jacob Zuma's successful campaign for African National Congress (ANC) leadership against then President Thabo Mbeki. Malema tapped into youth frustration that Mbeki's neoliberal policies had done little to address economic inequality and high rates of Black poverty and unemployment.[10] Concerned that Malema was increasingly harming the ANC's nonracist and liberal democratic image, ANC leaders ousted him in 2012 (Heffernan 2019).[11] The police killing of thirty-four strikers at Marikana Platinum Mine in Limpopo in

---

[10] In 2022, the unemployment rate was 35 percent overall. It was 64 percent among all youth aged fifteen to twenty-four and 42 percent among youth twenty-five to thirty-four (Stats SA 2022).

[11] Malema's call for violent land seizures and his repeated performances of the political song *Dubul' Ibhunu* ("Kill the Boer! Kill the Farmer!") at ANCYL rallies heightened this concern (Gunner 2015).

2012 presented Malema a political opportunity, as he capitalized on ANC party divisions in Limpopo and the miners' sense of betrayal to form the EFF in 2013 (de Kadt, Johnson-Kanu, and Sands 2021).

The EFF exemplifies populism in style and message. Malema uses colorful, direct, antiestablishment rhetoric rooted in Black nationalism to confront the ANC, and the EFF portrays itself as a champion for the unemployed and youth (Essop 2015). The party asserts that the economic marginalization of millions of Black South Africans results from South Africa's incomplete economic transition from apartheid (Essop 2015; Posel 2014). It calls for nationalization of the mines (still predominantly a white-owned industry despite diversification efforts) and the redistribution of land (predominantly white-owned and highly salient to all South Africans) (see Holmes 2020). These proposals pit a majoritarian will against minority rights in ways that concern some racial and ethnic groups. Despite their redistributionist bent, EFF cadres have accumulated significant wealth in the post-apartheid era (Posel 2014). And, although populists claim to work against the system, EFF parliamentarians (who held 10 percent of seats in 2022) report a desire to channel citizen participation through the multiparty system (Booysen 2015). As a "kingmaker," the EFF increasingly casts decisive votes in local-level coalitions (Lieberman and Lekalake 2022).

The EFF illustrates the complexity of youth support for populism. On the one hand, the party has mobilized youth with messages that resonate in South Africa's unequal society. The party's vote total increased from 6 percent in the 2014 national election to 11 percent in 2019 because of its collaboration with the urban poor, grassroots vote drives, and recruitment of student leaders at universities (Booysen 2015; Lieberman and Lekalake 2022). According to one survey, youth constituted 60 percent of EFF support in the 2021 local elections, and the party draws heavily from the unemployed, former ANC supporters, Blacks, men, and youth protestors (Bekker and Runciman 2022; Runciman, Bekker, and Maggott 2019). On the other hand, the majority of South African youth continue to support the ANC. In 2021, 16 percent of youth said they would vote for the EFF, while 31 percent said they would vote for the ANC (Afrobarometer 2019/2021). Many ANCYL members support Malema's economic vision but want change to happen "from the inside" (Heffernan 2016), and the EFF has limited rural support (du Plessis 2021). Over time, the EFF's need to compromise ideologically in governing coalitions, its ability to navigate the space between illegality and legality while decrying ANC corruption,[12] and its limited representation in national institutions may prevent it from delivering on promises, thereby disappointing youth (Booysen 2015). There is no guarantee that the EFF's populist mobilization, while bringing youth into party politics, will keep them there in the long term.

7.5.2 Tanzania and Uganda

Respondents in Tanzania and Uganda provide a murky picture of youth support for populism. In Tanzania, the late President Magufuli demonstrated some populist attributes. He emulated the liberation themes of southern African populism when he criticized "Western imperialists" and donors, and when he promoted some key state-owned industries such as Air Tanzania (Paget 2020a). He also claimed to "protect the people" from panic and economic disaster when he downplayed the threat of COVID-19 (Patterson 2022). However, his populism did not extend to vilifying elites in the ruling CCM party or major industries. Instead, his "elitist plebeianism" portrayed those elites as protecting the people against a middle stratum of corrupt, lazy civil servants. This discourse justified widespread attacks on state officials, and it generated the image of a decisive president ("the Bulldozer"), but it left CCM leaders and their business allies unscathed (Paget 2020b). In 2017, 80 percent of urban youth reported that they approved or strongly approved of this partial populist's performance (Afrobarometer 2016/2018), and a few of our youth respondents spoke positively of him, pointing to his prioritization of infrastructure projects (TZ FGD 1), his highly publicized discipline requirements (TZ FGD 6), and his willingness to listen to the poor and "[help] the vulnerable" (TZ FGD 8). However, unlike the EFF case, youth may support the CCM because it is the ruling party, the opposition is very weak (especially after 2016), and the CCM controls patronage. In addition, the EFF relies heavily on youth, but the CCM is a catchall party (Morse 2018). Finally, the above-reported frustrations from Tanzanian youth illustrate that Magufuli as a partial populist had not won over some (or many) of our respondents. Magufuli and the

---

[12] Malema was indicted in 2013 on charges of fraud, corruption, money laundering, and racketeering, though he did not go to trial (Heffernan 2019). On corruption in the ANC, see Chutel (2022) and Lodge (2014).

CCM do not give strong evidence that youth unquestioningly follow populists (or even partial populists).

Uganda's Robert Kyagulanyi Ssentamu (a.k.a. Bobi Wine, the "ghetto president") and his National Unity Platform more clearly embody populism, though some scholars assert that an overemphasis on Kyagulanyi misunderstands how his 2021 electoral efforts continued the campaign patterns of previous opposition parties and learned from prior oppositional campaigns (Wilkins, Volkes, and Khisa 2021). Kyagulanyi has stressed his outsider status as a successful rapper (Harvard International Review 2020), called for a generational transfer of power, defined "the people" as youth, and criticized the NRM's poor record (Melchiorre 2021). Kyagulanyi's message of anticorruption resonates with some urban youth who are, as one respondent said, "fed up" with the president (UG FGD 9). Similar to the EFF, the party appeals to youth, calls for economic redistribution (e.g., jobs, food), and faces the challenge of mobilizing rural voters. Yet, unlike the EFF, the party faces extreme state repression (Human Rights Watch 2022). The timing of our fieldwork (three years before the 2021 election) and fear of the regime made it difficult to discern our respondents' support for this populist. Indeed, no one openly declared support for Kyagulanyi, even in low-income neighborhoods where, at that point, his following was growing. In a thinly veiled reference to him, one higher-income woman cautioned, "You might want to put in a leader who is from the ghetto to be president, but ... they have no political background ... You may want a charismatic leader and, in the end, he may spoil everything" (UG FGD 14). Despite her remarks, the high level of frustration with the government seemed to indicate youth as a fertile constituency. Indeed, the National Unity Platform won 35 percent of the total vote in 2021, with urban youth reportedly being a key voting block for the party (Abrahamsen and Bareebe 2021).

A broader question emerges: Are urban youth willing to support more authoritarian forms of governance, populist or otherwise? Afrobarometer (2016/2018) shows that sizeable majorities of urban youth aged eighteen to thirty-five think that "democracy is preferable" (82 percent in Ghana, 77 percent in Tanzania, 80 percent in Uganda).[13]

---

[13] For urban elders, 84 percent of Ghanaians, 86 percent of Tanzanians, and 83 percent of Ugandans said democracy was preferable. The elder–youth spread was greatest in Tanzania (9 percent fewer youth).

In addition, few urban youth approved or strongly approved of one-person rule (9 percent of Ghanaians, 3 percent of Tanzanians, and 4 percent of Ugandans). Tanzanian youth's lower support for democracy may square with their support for Magufuli, but their rejection of one-person rule does not. Similarly, Ghanaian youth's high preference for democracy and their approval of one-person rule seem at odds, though perhaps this relates to personalism in politics and the overall small number of urban youth in these surveys. The youth we met in the more authoritarian contexts of Tanzania and Uganda echoed these trends: They wanted opportunities to express their ideas, to work without fear of repression or extraction, and to fairly compete for power. For them, these illiberal democratic regimes had not delivered jobs, education, or better social services. Even the supporters of authoritarians seemed to recognize these problems, as indicated by the statement from the *only* Ugandan youth respondent who spoke positively about the president: "When people say that President Museveni should retire, I always tell them that the president has delivered. ... We have freedom and peace ... We can manage to get what [food] to eat, although some people fail to get what to eat. But there is no government which is perfect" (UG FGD 3). The speaker's apologetics are tempered by his recognition that the president has failed on a fundamental issue: access to food.[14] It is such issues that may potentially galvanize everyday citizens to demand more.

7.6 Contesting Citizenship through Activism

Many youth engaged in micro- and macro-level acts of everyday citizenship, despite their anger and frustration. But a few explicitly *used* anger to catalyze activism, and previous chapters have illustrated some of those individuals' activities. Here we use a local example from Uganda and a national example from Zambia to show how youth may channel emotion into mobilization.

A Ugandan man explained how anger led him to start a youth community organization. Life with an abusive father after his mother died pushed him to join a criminal gang. As an angry, violent man, he clashed with police and neighbors. His crucible came after he and a

---

[14] Roughly 20 percent of the population faced food insecurity in 2019 (World Bank 2019).

friend happened upon an abandoned pushcart at night during a thunderstorm. Having not eaten for days, they were overjoyed that it was filled with pancakes (sweet cakes), which they stole. He recounted:

When I ran home to eat them, I didn't have any source of light apart from the lightning . . . I started eating before the lightning hit and . . . then the lightning strikes, and we see that the pancakes are full of maggots. We had already eaten three or four! . . . We started fearing [panicking]. We didn't have even a single penny [for] medication and the government facilities are distant. I thought we would die. I was just praying, "Please God spare us." . . . And in that night, I started to think: "This world will never take you as relevant unless you consider yourself relevant. . . . Everyone thinks we are gangsters . . . We are suffering because of the perceptions that people have about us . . . Can we be something more?" From that moment on, we took our anger and focused on something productive. We started bringing youth together. (UG Interview 13)

The vignette shows how the man's emotions of anger, fear, frustration, and ultimately efficacy culminate in his starting an organization to empower youth and promote peace in politics.

In Zambia, youth – as 54 percent of all voters – helped to unseat the ruling party's Edgar Lungu in 2021 (Gondwe 2021). Youth had helped to bring the Patriotic Front (PF) to power in 2011, when Michael Sata (whom Lungu replaced in 2014) defeated the incumbent party, the Movement for Multiparty Democracy (Cheeseman and Larmer 2015). The PF promised jobs, low food prices, and housing to informal workers, who faced poverty, high unemployment, and government harassment. Yet once in office, the PF increasingly centralized power, narrowed the political space for civil society (Fraser 2017), harassed opposition leaders, and then rigged the 2016 election (Haggard and Kaufman 2021; Resnick 2022). By 2020, government cuts in education spending, scandals over stolen COVID-19 money, and austerity measures that prevented hiring in the public sector had deepened youth frustration (Sinyangwe 2021). But for many, the tipping point was a story reported on social media that the PF chairperson allegedly had told Zambians that they should just eat sweet potatoes and other local foods if they could not afford bread. Angry and emboldened, youth started to exchange jokes on TikTok about the president being "cancelled." (This action points to the possibilities of using social media to share political information and create a campaign narrative, as mentioned in Chapter 3). Registering to vote became a badge of pride

(Hara 2021), and the number of first-time voters reached a record high (Gondwe 2021). Anger over the ruling party's alleged disdain for the people led youth to vote against a party they had supported for a decade.

These cases illustrate several themes. First, youth operate in the very tight corners of poverty, hunger, and dependency – a point our respondents continuously made. But, despite being hemmed in, youth act as agents as they maneuver in these spaces. Second, youth use the assets at their disposal (i.e., social media, friendship groups), and they capitalize on specific moments to motivate positive action. Finally, youth cannot be pigeonholed: The violent Ugandan becomes a voice for peace; the disinterested Zambian registers and then votes to deepen her country's democracy.

7.7 Conclusion

This chapter has focused on a subset of youth respondents who expressed frustration and anger in relation to citizenship. We have shown that these emotions revolve around unkept promises, corruption, repression, and exclusive politics. Youth perceive that these governmental deficiencies undermine their everyday citizenship. Despite these frustrations, most youth did typical micro-level and public acts of citizenship – carework, communal labor, voting. But some choose to react in other or additional ways. Few of these youth chose to exit, and their support for populism was tepid at best. A few became activists, though most angry youth did not. The most common reaction, though adopted by a minority, was defining one's citizenship at the expense of the other. In Ghana and Uganda, we heard of incidents of identity-based exclusion that ranged from verbal slights to violent acts. Although these were definitely troublesome, in the context of youth's economic and political marginalization, perhaps it is surprising that we did not encounter more such examples. The multiple emotions and activities youth respondents manifest in light of their frustrations show the complexity and context-specific aspects of everyday citizenship.

In the face of quotidian challenges, youth were agents who acted out their citizenship. They asserted their knowledge: "We aren't foolish! We understand about taxes and roads!" (UG FGD 15). They demanded government accountability: "Youth have been more engaged, and following up on issues concerning the government" (TZ FGD 5). They saw political engagement as *the only possible means* through which they could improve their countries: "As a citizen, my contribution to my country is the leader I elect, and if I elect a corrupt leader … I have let my country down" (UG FGD 2); "We are the people and we choose our leader" (GH FGD 8). And, when nothing else worked, they used sarcasm and humor to resist the demoralization that accompanied poor governance and corruption: "I just pray to God to put me in such government positions so that I too can embezzle money" (UG FGD 2). As this respondent's friends guffawed, they illustrated both a common understanding of marginalization and a shared hope for a better future. In the end, most youth we encountered – even the frustrated, angry ones – expressed a citizenship of belonging that is embodied in their close relationships, daily activities, and basic engagement in politics.

Conclusion
Challenging Marginalization, Claiming Citizenship

Being a good citizen has a broader aspect . . . The little things that go into it are how you live every day and how worthy your everyday life is to society. This is citizenship.

(GH ICGC 4)

For our over three hundred youth respondents, citizenship was an identity daily worked out through relationships and obligations to others and the state. By defining citizenship as an identity that puts youth in relationships with others, we challenge one-dimensional views of citizenship as focused on rights claims and democratic accountability. We honor the voices of urban youth who said citizenship plays out in acts ranging from caring for a neighbor, to voting, to hustling for income. The daily acts of youth *that matter to them* and that are unique *to their experiences* constitute *their* citizenship.

Our goals in this conclusion are threefold. First, we summarize the book's lessons (C.1). Next, we question how our analysis might be applied to other marginalized populations, and we look at rural youth in our three study countries. We discuss some initial patterns from Afrobarometer surveys and raise questions for future research (C.2). Third, we conclude with a key takeaway: Despite the tight corners of economic inequality, gerontocracy, patriarchy, repression, and corruption that many African urban youth face, youth are agentic, creative, and eager to lead their communities and countries (C.3).

C.1 Citizenship Is in the Eye of the Beholder

Although citizenship is a legal classification that bestows rights and responsibilities (Greenhouse 1999), it is also much, much more. For this book's respondents, the subjectivity of the identity reached beyond kinship or ethnic ties, on the one hand, or civic identities of nationalism and liberal democratic participation, on the other. Most respondents

199

started by discussing citizens' legal obligations (e.g., obeying the law) and then focused on how citizenship was a process situated in simple acts that tied people together, that occurred in proximate places (the neighborhood, the church), and that happened at particular moments (the vote, the dispute with police, the community meeting). Picking up trash, telling someone about HIV, and patrolling the neighborhood at night constituted citizenship, as did greeting others, not being a loud drunkard, and "watching each other's backs" (GH ICGC 2). Our NVivo analysis found that – regardless of income, gender, church attendance, or country – youth stressed these local, relational elements. As Lauren MacLean (2010) writes, though, these citizenship elements are not rooted in pure altruism, and youth were not Pollyannaish about their citizenship. Their acts of everyday citizenship revolved around the confluence of reciprocities, material interests, and status concerns, as when some Christian youth admitted that they voted for the express purpose of protecting their own religious interests. In addition, youth did not always act out citizenship in ways that invested in relational ties, as when some lower-income people turned on each other in envy.

Illustrating how citizenship-from-below blurs with citizenship-from-above, our youth respondents often perceived actions such as work or nurturing children as components in building the nation. Similarly, some viewed meeting legal obligations in terms of the moral "dos and don'ts" of good behavior. And although they rarely used the term "rights," they did have a sense of how the state at times dismissed their freedoms. They often framed these restrictions in terms of lived experiences of lost income or destroyed shelter. When they discussed citizenship as voting or advocacy, they emphasized themes of moral obligation, social connections, and, at times, democratic accountability. This multilayered view means we cannot assume youth voters are merely manipulated by party leaders or swayed through clientelism (see Bob-Milliar 2014; Van Gyampo 2020).

By coupling Afrobarometer data with youth voices, we gained two new angles on youth citizenship. First, we unearthed the attitudes and identities that motivate survey responses. Afrobarometer shows that youth engagement in community meetings or community groups is relatively low, but these surveys do not measure the informal activities that our respondents considered part of citizenship, such as cooking food for a funeral or teaching others a skill. In surveys, youth report high support for legal obligations such as following the law, but our respondents indicated that fear of lost reputation (not just fear of police) drives such attitudes. Surveyed youth report high levels of voting, a topic our respondents barely discussed as exemplifying good citizenship or as part of their daily negotiations over citizen identity.

Second, we were able to tease out how youth view the differences between their citizenship and that of their elders. Much lower percentages of urban youth than elders attend community meetings, are active group members, vote, and, in Tanzania and Uganda, join others to request government action. Although lifecycle effects partly elucidate these differences, our discussions with youth add another layer of understanding. Youth negotiate citizenship around multiple messages. Elders tell them "to wait," as they are the "next generation." Elders remind them of their generation's problems (drug use, teenage pregnancy, crime, joblessness) – messages that can be deflating. Laws, party structures, and unspoken rules about age hierarchies can explicitly and implicitly exclude them from opportunities. Youth respond by creating their own citizen spaces and identities. They embrace local tasks that their physical energy and knowledge enable them to do, and they claim those as citizenship. They build on their own experiences to mobilize others around issues of economic and social marginalization. They lean on friendships and shared experiences to fuel citizen acts, from picking up trash to throwing piglets into parliament.

Income level, church attendance, gender identity, and country context further shaped how youth viewed and acted on their citizenship. Our higher-income youth respondents stressed legal obligations over communal tasks, perhaps indicating their relative material independence. In contrast, lower-income youth tended to view citizenship as interdependence, and they sometimes felt shut out of citizen belonging because they had no money to meet citizen obligations. Christian identity led some believers to equate citizenship acts with Christian practices such as prayer; many frequent churchgoers also explicitly situated political activities such as voting and protesting in the tenets of their faith. Regardless of the political messaging they received from religious elites, Christian youth often merged self-discipline, responsibility, and local obligations to devise a citizenship of their own that stressed building the nation. Despite legal equality, many youth respondents stressed women's citizen acts as carework and men's citizen acts as physical labor and security provision. At times, youth showed flexibility in gendered citizen roles (e.g., women who constructed roads), as they situated those in particular economic or familial contexts. Citizen malleability also led many youth to support women in office, though Ghanaians were the least likely to do so.

In addition, we find that country context matters for how our youth respondents view citizenship. Although urban youth in all three countries stressed communal and build-the-nation themes, Ghanaian respondents spoke more of rights and democratic accountability, and less of morality and legality. Tanzanians placed significant emphasis on morality, a theme that seemed to undergird their attention to building the nation and meeting communal obligations. Indeed, surveyed Tanzanians reported very high rates of attendance at meetings and voting. Their moral lens, with its accompanying concern about reputation, may partly explain their reported low protest participation. Yet, not all Tanzanians were quiet obedient citizens: Some voiced anger and disappointment over rights violations (see Chapter 7). Ugandan youth provided another angle on urban youth citizenship, one rooted in extreme economic and political struggle. Unlike Tanzanians, they did not stress morality (except in reference to women's behavior), and, unlike Ghanaians, they spoke little of rights. They reported more communal engagement than Ghanaians (though less than Tanzanians), sometimes sharing stories of citizen confrontation with state agents on behalf of communal interests. Their stories of corruption, repression, and poverty were the most extreme, and their anger, the most notable.

C.2 Extending the Analysis: Rural Youth Citizens

Urban youth are a rapidly growing demographic who face challenges including unemployment, poor service delivery, and political marginalization. Yet, they are not the only marginalized group in African society. Investigating everyday citizenship in populations such as ethnic minority youth, youth living with disabilities, youth migrants, or rural youth could generate new insights about how individuals maneuver to forge identities of citizen belonging in other tight spaces. To extend our analysis, we look at Afrobarometer data (2016/2018) regarding one of these marginalized groups: rural youth in Ghana, Tanzania, and Uganda. Rural people do not exist in bounded, enclosed enclaves, and they experience contestation over power and voice, just as urban youth do. Rural youth face economic, social, geographic, and political marginalization, rooted in historic processes of dispossession and discrimination (Hodgson 2017, 39). Health outcomes are worse in rural areas, poverty is higher, and, in many rural areas, agricultural productivity remains low (Mueller and Thurlow 2019). In such contexts, what might everyday citizenship look like among rural youth?

As Table C.1 illustrates, rural youth in all three countries are more communally engaged than urban youth. Greater percentages attend community meetings, with, for example, 27 percent more rural Ghanaian youth than urban Ghanaian youth reporting this activity. More rural youth than urban youth also report active membership in a community group, though the percentage differences are not as large. Such reported behavior, though, does not elucidate what citizenship means for rural youth. How do rural youth relate citizenship to particular notions of obligation and sociality in rural spaces? For example, rural Nigerian youth help mediate herder–farmer conflicts, acts they may view as citizen contributions (Adzande 2022). Rural youth also seem less legalistic than urban youth, at least in terms of tax paying, with Tanzanian rural youth being the least willing to support this legal obligation: 74 percent agree or strongly agree that tax authorities have the right to require this action versus 86 percent of urban youth (data not shown). Tanzanian views may relate to the ways that the colonial state and Ujamaa policies extracted from peasants (Phillips 2018; Scott 1998). In turn, 4 percent fewer rural youth than urban youth in Uganda agree or strongly agree that people must obey the law (data not shown). Given the relatively strong economy of affection in rural communities (Hyden 1980), and the overall weakness of the state in rural people's lives (Lund 2006), rural youth may be even more likely than urban youth to define citizenship as local acts that foster reputations and reciprocities rather than as acts that meet legal obligations to the state.

In terms of political participation, voter turnout rates tend to be higher in rural populations (Bleck and van de Walle 2018, 239). This may be because brokers (e.g., traditional leaders) mobilize rural voters (Koter 2013), voting is perceived as a collective endeavor, incumbents often campaign in rural areas, and elections may generate prorural policies (Harding 2020). In Tanzania, 9 percent more rural than urban youth report voting, but in Ghana the difference is only 2 percent. Qualitative research could investigate how rural youth perceive voting

Table C.1 *Select acts of citizenship for youth, by location and country*

Country	Location	Attended community meetings (%)*	Active membership in voluntary or community group (%)	Voted (%)**	Joined others to request govt action (%)*	Attended a demonstration or protest(%)***	N
Ghana	Urban	20	13	79[a]	7	5	733
	Rural	47	25	81[b]	9	6	590
Tanzania	Urban	51	19	80[c]	12	>1	439
	Rural	73	25	89[d]	18	2[g]	827
Uganda	Urban	34	25	79[e]	14	8	209
	Rural	49	29	86[f]	18	3	498

* Percentage answering "several times" or "often"
** Percentage of youth aged twenty-six to thirty-five. The other columns are the weighted average of all youth.
*** Percentage answering "once or twice"
[a] N = 388; [b] N = 310; [c] N = 244; [d] N = 442; [e] N = 115; [f] N = 264; [g] N = 823
Source: Data from Afrobarometer (2016/2018), compiled by the authors

in terms of everyday citizen moral expectations, relational obligations, and/or economic interests. How do rural youth both respond to elders' mobilization efforts in elections and stake their own citizen identity? Higher percentages of rural youth than urban youth report joining with others to request government action. Although one might predict that rural youth would not engage in protest because of the logistical difficulties of mobilization, in Ghana 6 percent report this action. Information on how these activities relate to everyday concerns of family, economy, employment, or friendship networks would elucidate these behaviors.

Survey data does not capture the creative, agentic nature of rural youth citizenship, the tensions across generations, or the contestation of citizenship based on various identities. For example, how might rural youth consider economically driven activities such as seasonal migration to be acts of citizenship? How does gendered citizenship play out in rapidly changing villages that face environmental and economic challenges? We anticipate that, just like urban youth, rural youth contest the meaning of citizenship from their particular vantage points and through distinct acts related to their context and relational ties. Future analyses might even question how views of urban and rural citizenship inform one another. Despite minimal contact with rural communities, some urban youth may view rural sites as arenas of belonging and places to act out citizenship as building the nation (Cheney 2004). In turn, rural youth may link their citizenship to the economic opportunities assumed to exist in the city.

C.3 Urban Youth Citizens: Active, Creative, Optimistic

This book's objective has been to privilege the voice of African youth as they grapple with the meaning of citizenship in their everyday lives. Our interpretive approach shines light on the complex and at times contradictory experiences of youth citizenship. We have tried to provide a launchpad from which future scholars can build interpretive work or scientific, causal explanations. In keeping with our effort to privilege youth voices, we conclude with our respondents' overarching views on citizenship. Despite some youth frustration and anger (see Chapter 7), most urban youth we met had a deep belief that their citizenship meant making their lives, the lives of those around them, and their countries better. They were active, creative, and hopeful for the future.

For our respondents, citizenship was an active rather than a passive identity. They did not shy from discussing their country's problems, envisioning solutions, and striving to implement them. A Tanzanian man said, "We [youth] are the ones who are complaining [more] than any other group!" (TZ FGD 8). They hustled for new social or economic opportunities, raised their voices despite patriarchy and gerontocracy, and, when possible, used their connections to elders to achieve goals. A South African stated, "A good citizen fights for change. It's someone who doesn't sit and expect things to happen!" (SA VYLTP 10). Many youth citizens were not satisfied with the status quo, and, although their spaces for action could be limited, they rarely just "sat" in waithood.

Urban youth repeatedly demonstrated a creative citizenship. This observation does not deny the contexts of significant income inequality, poverty, unemployment, corruption, and authoritarian governance in which many maneuvered. Their efforts were sometimes frustrated and their goals unmet. Despite this reality, we encountered youth who tackled new issues that elite elders were too afraid or complacent to discuss (e.g., environmental issues, HIV, mental health, GBV). Youth tapped into a variety of skills and pools of expertise to build the nation (e.g., starting businesses that employed others, blogging about health). They leaned on their friends and neighbors to approach citizenship collectively and differently (e.g., spraying graffiti with peace messages, *toyi-toying* for land access, praying for the nation). Yet, as one Ugandan angrily expressed, their elders often just didn't get it. They chose to be blind to youth's ingenuity and energy. She said, "The other day the president talked about how we have no solutions in Uganda ... And I said to myself, 'Are you kidding me? Do you know how many, just here at Makerere University alone, the number of young people with amazing solutions that could change lives?' And then you have the audacity to say there are no solutions?" (UG Interview 20).

As the speaker hinted at, youth are eager citizens. For our respondents, youth were not *future* leaders to build the nation: They were citizens engaged in the nation-building project *right now*. Waiting on the margins in positions of limited status discounted the real facts on the ground. As one Tanzanian said, "Youth who are called 'tomorrow's generation' are the ones who are fighting for the development of their country [today], not the elders who are considered 'today's nation.' Youth are ready" (TZ FGD 5). The desire of youth to distinguish themselves from their elders through their energy, new ideas, relations of care, and everyday actions embodies how citizenship is never static or devoid of power struggles. In these struggles, youth are not innocent bystanders – they have material and status interests too in their desire for greater recognition. They are not victims of generational machinations, nor are they devoid of hope for the future.

The world is a different place now than it was in 2018 when we began our fieldwork. The COVID-19 pandemic and the Ukraine war with their knock-on effects of inflation, food shortages, high national debt, and economic downturns present significant challenges for youth citizens in low-income countries (IMF 2022). Youth must maneuver in new ways in these increasingly constrained spaces, and we anticipate that, given such spaces, elders will be even less inclined to fully embrace the citizenship contributions of youth. But subsequent visits to Ghana, Tanzania, and Liberia (not a study country) in 2021 and 2022 make us believe youth continue through a balance of realism and optimism to contest citizenship in their everyday relations and actions. A Liberian youth saw his citizenship contribution as establishing a Whatsapp hotline for other youth facing mental health crises during the pandemic lockdown.[1] The youth organization Arise Ghana took to the streets in June 2022 to protest inflation and high fuel prices (Hanspal and Nyabor 2022), while #FixTheCountry sought to mobilize ordinary Ghanaian youth for political change.[2] For these youth, citizenship is more than a national identification card: It is an identity rooted in hope, and, to reiterate the takeaway from the above-cited Ghanaian, "how you live every day."

---

[1] Interview, executive board member, Mental Care Liberia, Monrovia, May 13, 2022.
[2] See #AriseGhana! and https://fixthecountrygh.com.

Appendix 1
Thematic Categories for Content Analysis*

Thematic category	Description	Words, phrases, word roots	Average number words/ focus group discussion
Communal	Actions/attitudes/ emotions geared toward the local community and its inhabitants; ways that individuals are situated within a local context	problem solve, love, help, respect, honor, commun-, care, support, neighbor, contribut-, volunteer, collaborat-, cooperat-, work with, share, together, trust, relate, watch out for, responsib-, kind (21 terms)	45.7
Build the nation	Actions that occur at the family, community, or national level that are perceived to help the country economically, promote stability, and/ or foster social welfare; may be framed in terms of future generations and investments	develop, build the country, build the nation, job creat-, contribute to economy, defend country, protect country, service, provide for others, work, wellbeing of country, welfare of country, future generation, helps country develop, develop the country,	51.4

(*cont.*)

Thematic category	Description	Words, phrases, word roots	Average number words/ focus group discussion
		help country move forward, needs of country, ensure betterment of country, sacrifice, contribute to country, making country progress, industry, entrepreneur, farm, secur-, self-employment, producti-, blood donat- (28 terms)	
Moral	Behaviors that lead to positive or negative relations with others; behaviors that are usually viewed negatively, some of which are illegal	Behav-, conduct, character, honest, deeds, alcohol, drink, drugs, marijuana, ganja, drunk, homo [sexual], abortion, sex, prostitution, adultery, bibl-, God, gambl-, example, conform, moral (22 terms)	34.1
Legalistic	Legal aspects of citizenship; actions done in relation to government laws or regulations	Constitution, legal, law, tax, rules, regula-, crime, criminal, theft, steal, rob, order, civic duty, civic, national ID, regist-, residen-, security, weapon, report to authorit- (20 terms)	29.5

(*cont.*)

Thematic category	Description	Words, phrases, word roots	Average number words/ focus group discussion
Participatory	Actions to influence state policies, resource allocation, and officials	protest, community meeting, contact, participat-, involve-, pressurize, vote, organize, input, march, monitor government, watchdog, creating awareness, holding government accountable, riot, demonstrate-, speak the truth (17 terms)	2.6
Rights	Expectations of particular rights; conveys how the state protects or encroaches on those rights	Speech, educat-, human rights, media, information, know rights, claim rights, freedom, social media, opportunit-, rights, right to association (12 terms)	6.7
Patriotic	Emotional attachment to the country	love of country, love your country, proud of country, respect the country, love of nation (5 terms)	1.6

*In response to the question, "What does it mean to be a good citizen?"

Appendix 2
Fieldwork Questions

Questions for Focus Group Discussions (FGDs)

1 In your opinion, what does it mean to be a good citizen?
2 Does being a good citizen differ for men and women? Why or why not?
3 How does being a good citizen affect your actions in your local community? in/for your country? [If churchgoing youth] in your church?
4 How interested are you in what the national government is doing in the country? or what the local government is doing in your community, or elsewhere?
   a What interests you about these things?
   b Why are you interested/not interested in these things?
5 Does anyone at your church [or community] talk about voting or engaging in public affairs? [modify if churchgoing youth]
   a What do they say?
   b What do you think of their ideas?
6 Does anyone at your church [or in the community] talk about how we should serve or help our communities? [Fill in items from earlier conversations about helping the community.]
   a What do they say?
   b What are your opinions about that?
7 Can you describe a time when you felt close to your community? [If applicable] your church? What made you feel that way?

Questions for Youth Activist Interviews

1 Tell me a little about your position. What does your job entail?
2 How did you come to be in this position/work?
3 Who influenced or mentored you to become involved in this position/work?

4 Tell me a little about your childhood.
   a Where did you grow up?
   b Who were the people who influenced you growing up?
5 How do you define being a good citizen?
6 How does your work in this position relate to your understanding of citizenship?
7 Does being a good citizen differ for men and women? Why/why not?
8 What role has religion played in your life? [If applicable] How does religion affect your views of citizenship?
9 Have you ever heard religious leaders in this country talk about public affairs? or about citizenship?
   a What did they say?
   b What did you think about that?

Questions for Religious Leader Interviews

1 What is your position in this organization or church, and how long have you worked here?
2 Describe, if you can, the history of this organization and its mission.
3 What are your organization's (or your church's) theological perspectives or biblical insights on political engagement and citizen mobilization?
4 Describe in your own words what it means to be a good citizen. How does the organization or church employ this view of citizenship?
5 How do you encourage your parishioners to be engaged civically? Do you think churches and Christian organizations should be involved in efforts of civic engagement? Why or why not?
6 Do you think being a good citizen looks different for men and women? What do men need to do to be good citizens? What do women need to do to be good citizens?
7 In your opinion, what is the role of youth (aged eighteen to thirty-five) in public affairs at the national and local levels in this country? What should their role be?
8 How is youth involvement in the public realm viewed by people in this organization/church?
9 How is youth involvement in the church viewed by people in this organization/church?

10 What type of youth programs does this organization/church have? How do these programs help youth engage in public affairs (either locally or nationally)?
11 What have been the outcomes of these programs for youth?

Appendix 3
Fieldwork Interviews and Focus Group Discussions (FGDs)

Ghana Fieldwork in Accra

Ghana FGDs

1 Frequent churchgoers, mainline, men, lower-income, June 18, 2018
2 Frequent churchgoers, mainline, women, lower-income, June 18, 2018
3 Frequent churchgoers, renewalist, men, lower-income, June 23, 2018
4 Frequent churchgoers, renewalist, women, lower-income, June 23, 2018
5 Frequent churchgoers, renewalist, mixed gender, higher-income, June 24, 2018
6 Frequent churchgoers, mainline, mixed gender, higher-income, June 24, 2018
7 Infrequent churchgoers, men, lower-income, June 18, 2018
8 Infrequent churchgoers, women, lower-income, June 18, 2018
9 Infrequent churchgoers, men, lower-income, June 23, 2018
10 Infrequent churchgoers, women, lower-income, June 23, 2018
11 Infrequent churchgoers, men, higher-income, June 21, 2018
12 Infrequent churchgoers, women, higher-income, June 21, 2018
13 Infrequent churchgoers, men, higher-income, June 24, 2018
14 Infrequent churchgoers, women, higher-income, June 28, 2018

Ghana Interviews

1 Presbyterian chaplain at Ghanaian university, June 25, 2018
2 Christian Council of Ghana official, June 26, 2018
3 ICGC pastor, June 28, 2018
4 National Association of Charismatic and Christian Churches official, June 29, 2018

5 National Catholic Secretariat official, July 3, 2018
6 Action Chapel International pastor, July 5, 2018
7 Ghanaian university residence hall leader, June 18, 2018
8 NPP student branch president, June 21, 2018
9 NDC student branch general secretary, June 22, 2018
10 NDC student branch president, June 25, 2018
11 CBO founder 1, June 27, 2018
12 Advocacy organization founder, June 28, 2018
13 CBO founder 2, July 2, 2018
14 Good governance advocate, July 2, 2018
15 CBO founder 3, July 2, 2018
16 NPP civil servant, July 4, 2018
17 CBO founder 4, July 5, 2018

Ghana Case Study – International Central Gospel Church (GH ICGC)

1 ICGC FGD 1, women, July 18, 2021
2 ICGC FGD 2, women, July 18, 2021
3 ICGC FGD 3, women, July 18, 2021
4 ICGC FGD 4, men, July 18, 2021
5 ICGC FGD 5, men, July 18, 2021
6 ICGC youth facilitator 1, interview, July 18, 2021
7 ICGC youth facilitator 2, interview, July 18, 2021
8 ICGC youth facilitator 3, interview, July 18, 2021
9 ICGC youth facilitator 4, interview, July 18, 2021
10 ICGC youth pastor, interview, July 18, 2021
11 Observations, Sunday youth service, July 18, 2021
12 Infrequent churchgoers FGD 1, women, July 22, 2021
13 Infrequent churchgoers FGD 2, men, July 22, 2021

Ghana Case Study – Stand Up! (GH Stand Up!)

1 Stand Up! member 1, interview, July 20, 2021
2 Stand Up! leader 1, interview, July 20, 2021
3 Stand Up! member 2, interview, July 23, 2021
4 Stand Up! leader 2, interview, July 23, 2021
5 Stand Up! leader 3, interview, August 2, 2021

  6 Nonmember FGD 1, women, July 22, 2021

  7 Nonmember FGD 2, men, July 22, 2021

South Africa Fieldwork in Hermanus and Khayelitsha

South Africa Case Study – Volmoed Youth Leadership Training Programme (SA VYLTP)

  1 VYLTP FGD 1, men, June 17, 2019

  2 VYLTP FGD 2, women, June 23, 2019

  3 VYLTP director, interview, June 17, 2019

  4 VYLTP cofounder, June 19, 2019

  5 VYLTP seminar observations, May 21–July 5, 2019 (intermittent)

  6 Nonmember FGD 1, women, June 6, 2019

  7 Nonmember FGD 2, men, June 6, 2019

  8 Nonmember FGD 3, mixed gender, June 5, 2019

  9 Nonmember FGD 4, mixed gender, June 5, 2019

10 SJC activist 1, interview, May 29, 2019

11 SJC activist 2, interview, May 29, 2019

12 SJC activist 3, interview, June 4, 2019

13 SJC activist 4, interview, June 4, 2019

Tanzania Fieldwork in Dar es Salaam

Tanzania FGDs

  1 Frequent churchgoers, renewalist, mixed gender, lower-income, April 3, 2018

  2 Frequent churchgoers, mainline, mixed gender, lower-income, April 15, 2018

  3 Infrequent churchgoers, women, lower-income, April 25, 2018

  4 Infrequent churchgoers, women, lower-income, April 19, 2018

  5 Infrequent churchgoers, men, lower-income, April 19, 2018

  6 Infrequent churchgoers, men, lower-income, April 19, 2018

  7 Frequent churchgoers, mainline, mixed gender, higher-income, April 15, 2018

  8 Frequent churchgoers, mainline, mixed gender, higher-income, April 26, 2018

  9 Infrequent churchgoers, men, higher-income, April 24, 2018

Tanzania Interviews

1 Council of Pentecostal Churches in Tanzania official, April 4, 2018
2 Catholic priest, April 11, 2018
3 Christian Professionals of Tanzania official, March 28, 2018
4 Christian Council of Tanzania official, April 5, 2018
5 ELCT pastor, April 5, 2018
6 Pentecostal pastor, April 3, 2018
7 Christian Council of Tanzania official, April 17, 2018
8 ELCT youth program official, April 18, 2018
9 ELCT pastor, April 21, 2018
10 Catholic priest, March 29, 2018
11 CCM official 1, April 28, 2018
12 Member of Parliament for CCM, March 29, 2018
13 University of Dar es Salaam student government official, April 17, 2018
14 CHADEMA student organization official, April 10, 2018
15 CHADEMA official, April 10, 2018
16 CCM youth league official 1, April 28, 2018
17 CHADEMA youth council official, April 10, 2018
18 CCM youth league official 2, April 23, 2018
19 CCM official 2, April 28, 2018
20 CCM official 3, April 28, 2018

Tanzania Case Study – Evangelical Lutheran Church of Tanzania Youth Programs (TZ ELCT)

1 ELCT FGD 1, mixed gender, July 14, 2021
2 ELCT FGD 2, mixed gender, July 14, 2021
3 ELCT FGD 3, mixed gender, July 19, 2021
4 ELCT FGD 4, mixed gender, July 21, 2021
5 ELCT FGD 5, mixed gender, July 24, 2021
6 ELCT FGD 6, mixed gender, July 25, 2021
7 ELCT youth leader 1, interview, July 15, 2021
8 ELCT youth leader 2, interview, July 16, 2021
9 ELCT pastor 1, interview, July 16, 2021
10 ELCT youth leader 3, interview, July 18, 2021
11 ELCT youth leader 4, interview, July 19, 2021

12 ELCT youth leader 5, interview, July 20, 2021
13 ELCT pastor 2, interview, July 23, 2021

Uganda Fieldwork in Kampala

Uganda FGDs

1 Infrequent churchgoers, men, lower-income, May 31, 2018
2 Infrequent churchgoers, men, lower-income, June 2, 2018
3 Infrequent churchgoers, men, higher-income, June 7, 2018
4 Infrequent churchgoers, men, higher-income, June 3, 2018
5 Infrequent churchgoers, women, lower-income, June 2, 2018
6 Infrequent churchgoers, women, higher-income, June 7, 2018
7 Infrequent churchgoers, women, higher-income, July 3, 2018
8 Infrequent churchgoers, women, lower-income, May 31, 2018
9 Frequent churchgoers, renewalist, men, lower-income, June 2, 2018
10 Frequent churchgoers, mainline, men, lower-income, May 30, 2018
11 Frequent churchgoers, renewalist, men, higher-income, June 4, 2018
12 Frequent churchgoers, mainline, men, higher-income, May 31, 2018
13 Frequent churchgoers, mainline, women, lower-income, May 30, 2018
14 Frequent churchgoers, mainline, women, higher-income, June 2, 2018
15 Frequent churchgoers, renewalist, women, lower-income, June 2, 2018
16 Frequent churchgoers, renewalist, women, higher-income, June 4, 2018

Uganda Interviews

1 Catholic Secretariat official, June 11, 2018
2 Renewalist church pastor 1, June 4, 2018
3 Renewalist church pastor 2, June 9, 2018
4 Uganda Joint Christian Council official 1, June 4, 2018
5 Uganda Joint Christian Council official 2, May 23, 2018
6 Uganda Joint Christian Council official 3, May 23, 2018
7 Uganda Joint Christian Council official 4, May 23, 2018
8 Uganda Joint Christian Council official 5, June 4, 2018
9 Uganda Joint Christian Council official 6, June 4, 2018

10 Inter-Religious Council of Uganda official, June 13, 2018
11 Mainline church pastor, June 7, 2018
12 Renewalist church pastor 3, June 2, 2018
13 CBO founder 1, May 24, 2018
14 Health NGO official, June 12, 2018
15 CBO founder 2, May 25, 2018
16 Good governance advocate 1, May 28, 2018
17 Human rights advocate, May 25, 2018
18 Local government official, May 24, 2018
19 Youth empowerment NGO official, May 25, 2018
20 Youth member of parliament 1, May 28, 2018
21 Youth member of parliament 2, May 29, 2018
22 Good governance advocate 2, May 27, 2018
23 AIDS organization leader, June 12, 2018
24 Reproductive health NGO official, May 27, 2018

Zambia Fieldwork in Various Locations

Zambia Case Study – Network of Zambian People Living with HIV/AIDS (ZA NZP+)

1 NZP+ national officer, interview, Lusaka, March 7, 2011
2 NZP+ regional coordinator 1, interview, Kabwe, April 18, 2011
3 NZP+ regional coordinator 2, interview, Ndola, May 22, 2011
4 AIDS NGO worker, interview, Kitwe, May 20, 2011
5 NZP+ FGD 1, mixed gender, Livingstone, June 21, 2011
6 NZP+ FGD 2, mixed gender, Lusaka, March 24, 2011
7 NZP+ FGD 3, mixed gender, Lusaka, May 9, 2011
8 NZP+ FGD 4, mixed gender, Ndola, May 23, 2011

References

Abbink, Jon, and Ineke van Kessel. 2005. *Vanguard or Vandals: Youth Politics and Conflict in Africa*. Leiden: Brill.

Abdulai, Abdul-Gafuru, and Sam Hickey. 2016. "The Politics of Development under Competitive Clientelism: Insights from Ghana's Education Sector." *African Affairs* 115 (458): 44–72.

Abrahamsen, Paul, and Ronald Inglehart. 1995. *Value Change in Global Perspective*. Ann Arbor: University of Michigan.

Abrahamsen, Rita, and Gerald Bareebe. 2016. "Uganda's 2016 Elections: Not Even Faking It Anymore." *African Affairs* 115 (461): 751–65.

2021. "Uganda's Fraudulent Election." *Journal of Democracy* 32 (2): 90–104.

Adams, Brian. 2004. "Public Meetings and the Democratic Process." *Public Administration Review* 64 (1): 43–54.

Adams, Melinda. 2016. "Context and Media Frames: The Case of Liberia." *Politics & Gender* 12 (2): 275–95.

Adzande, Patience. 2022. "Harnessing the Social Energies of Youths in Farming and Pastoral Communities in Managing Conflicts in Nigeria." *African Studies Review* 65 (2): 479–503.

AfDB (African Development Bank). 2011. "Market Brief – The Middle of the Pyramid: Dynamics of the Middle Class in Africa." www.afdb.org/en/documents/document/market-brief-the-middle-of-the-pyramid-dynamics-of-the-middle-class-in-africa-23582.

African Union Commission. 2006. *African Youth Charter*. www.un.org/en/africa/osaa/pdf/au/african_youth_charter_2006.pdf.

Afrobarometer. 2016/2018. "Round 7." www.afrobarometer.org/data.

2019. "More than One in Four Africans See Wife-Beating as Justifiable, Afrobarometer Finds." News Release. https://afrobarometer.org/press/more-one-four-africans-see-wife-beating-justifiable-afrobarometer-survey-finds.

2019/2021. "Round 8." www.afrobarometer.org/data.

Akor, Christopher. 2017. "From Subalterns to Independent Actors? Youth, Social Media and the Fuel Subsidy Protests of January 2012 in Nigeria." *Africa Development* 42 (2): 107–27.

Allah-Mensah, Beatrix. 2007. "Women and Politics in Ghana, 1993–2003." In *Ghana: One Decade of the Liberal State*, edited by Kwame Boafo-Arthur, 251–79. Dakar: CODESRIA.

Allen, Nathaniel. 2021. "The Promises and Perils of Africa's Digital Revolution." Brookings Institute, March 11. www.brookings.edu/tech stream/the-promises-and-perils-of-africas-digital-revolution.

Almond, Gabriel, and Sidney Verba. 1963. *The Civic Culture: Attitudes and Democracy in Five Nations*. Princeton, NJ: Princeton University Press.

Alwin, Duane, and Jon A. Krosnick. 1991. "Aging, Cohorts, and the Stability of Sociopolitical Orientations of the Life Span." *American Journal of Sociology* 97 (1): 169–95.

Ammann, Carole. 2016. "Everyday Politics: Market Women and the Local Government in Kankan, Guinea." *Stichproben. Wiener Zeitschrift für kritische Afrikastudien* 16 (30): 37–62.

Ampofo, Akosua Adomako. 2017. "Africa's Fastest Growing Pentecostal Mega-Churches Are Entrenching Old Injustices against Women." *Quartz Africa*, June 16.

Anderson, Emma-Louise, and Amy S. Patterson. 2017a. *Dependent Agency and the Global Health Regime*. New York: Palgrave.

2017b. "Instrumentalizing AIDS Empowerment Discourses in Malawi and Zambia: An Actor-Oriented View of Donor Politics." *International Affairs* 93 (5): 1185–204.

Andolina, Molly, Krista Jenkins, Cliff Zukin, and Scott Keeter. 2003. "Habits from Home, Lessons from School: Influences on Youth Civic Engagement." *PS: Political Science and Politics* 36 (2): 275–80.

Aning, Emmanuel Kwesi. 1998. "Gender and Civil War: The Cases of Liberia and Sierra Leone." *Civil Wars* 1 (4): 1–26.

Annan, James Kofi. 2016. "ICGC – 32 Years of Influencing Society." *Modern Ghana*, March 9. www.modernghana.com/news/679346/icgc-32-years-of-influencing-society.html.

Apter, David. 1968. "Ghana." In *Political Parties and National Integration in Tropical Africa*, edited by James Coleman and Carl Rosberg, 259–315. Los Angeles: University of California Press.

Armah-Attoh, Daniel, and Anna Robertson. 2014. "The Practice of Democracy in Ghana: Beyond the Formal Framework." *Afrobarometer Briefing Paper* 137. www.afrobarometer.org/wp-content/uploads/2022/02/afrobriefno137.pdf.

Arnot, Madeleine, Fatuma N. Chege, and Violet Wawire. 2012. "Gendered Constructions of Citizenship: Young Kenyans' Negotiations of Rights Discourses." *Comparative Education* 48 (1): 87–102.

Arriola, Leonardo. 2013. *Multiethnic Coalitions in Africa: Business Financing of Opposition Election Campaigns*. New York: Cambridge University Press.

Arriola, Leonardo, and Martha Johnson. 2014. "Ethnic Politics and Women's Empowerment in Africa: Ministerial Appointments to Executive Cabinets." *American Journal of Political Science* 58 (2): 495–510.

Arthur, Peter. 2009. "Ethnicity and Electoral Politics in Ghana's Fourth Republic." *Africa Today* 56 (2): 45–73.

Asante, Lewis Abedi, and Ilse Helbrecht. 2018. "Seeing through African Protest Logics: A Longitudinal Review of Continuity and Change in Protests in Ghana." *Canadian Journal of African Studies* 52 (2): 159–81.

Asante, Richard. 2006. "The Youth and Politics in Ghana: Reflections on the 2004 General Elections." In *Voting for Democracy in Ghana*, edited by K. Boafo-Arthur, 211–36. Accra: Freedom Publications.

    2013. "Growth without Security? Dilemmas of Youth and Human Security in Africa." In *African Studies and Knowledge Production*, edited by Stephen Owoahene-Acheampong, 157–76. Legon-Accra: Sub-Saharan Publishers.

Asante, Richard, Megan Hershey, Phoebe Kajubi, Tracy Kuperus, Colman Msoka, and Amy Patterson. 2021. "What Motivates Young African Leaders for Public Engagement? Lessons from Ghana, Tanzania, and Uganda." *International Journal of Culture, Politics and Society* 34: 309–33.

Asiedu-Acquah, Emmanuel. 2019. "'We Shall Be Outspoken': Student Political Activism in Post-Independence Ghana, c. 1957–1966." *Journal of Asian and African Studies* 52 (2): 169–88.

Bakari, Muhammad, and Richard Whitehead. 2013. "Tanzania: Nurturing Legacies of the Past." In *One Party Dominance in African Democracies*, edited by Renske Doorenspleet and Lia Nijzink, 93–116. Boulder, CO: Lynne Rienner.

Bangura, Ibrahim. 2018. "Young People and the Search for Inclusion and Political Participation in Guinea." *African Conflict & Peacebuilding Review* 8 (1): 54–72.

Bareebe, Gerald. 2020. "Predators or Protectors? Military Corruption as a Pillar of Regime Survival in Uganda." *Civil Wars* 22 (2–3): 313–32.

Barreto, Matt, and José Muñoz. 2003. "Reexamining the 'Politics of In-Between': Political Participation among Mexican Immigrants in the United States." *Hispanic Journal of Behavioral Sciences* 25 (4): 427–47.

Bauer, Gretchen. 2012. "'Let There Be a Balance': Women in African Parliaments." *Political Studies Review* 10 (3): 370–84.

    2018. "Ghana: Stalled Patterns of Women's Parliamentary Representation." In *Palgrave Handbook of Women's Political Rights*, edited by Susan Franceschet, Mona Krook, and N. Tan, 607–25. New York: Palgrave Macmillan.

2020. "Roles of Women." In *Understanding Contemporary Africa*, edited by Peter Schraeder, 218–38. Boulder, CO: Lynne Rienner.

Bauer, Gretchen, and Akosua Darkwah. 2022. "'The President's Prerogative'? The Cabinet Appointment Process in Ghana and the Implications for Gender Parity." *Politics & Gender* 18 (2): 546–73.

Bayat, Asef. 2010. *Life as Politics: How Ordinary People Change the Middle East*. Stanford, CA: Stanford University Press.

BBC Africa Daily. 2022. "How Has 'Mama Samia' Changed Tanzania?" March 18. www.bbc.co.uk/sounds/play/p0bw541m.

BBC News. 2021. "Tanzanian MPs Demand Apology for 'Tight' Trousers Incident." *BBC News*, June 2. www.bbc.com/news/world-africa-57329930.

Beardsworth, Nicole. 2016. "Challenging Dominance: The Opposition, the Coalition and the 2016 Election in Uganda." *Journal of Eastern African Studies* 10 (4): 749–68.

Beck, Linda. 2003. "Democratization and the Hidden Public: The Impact of Patronage Networks on Senegalese Women." *Comparative Politics* 35 (2): 147–69.

Becker, Felicitas. 2021. "Tanzania's Authoritarian Turn: Less Sudden than It Seems." *Current History* 120 (826): 189–94.

Bekker, Martin, and Carin Runciman. 2022. "The Youth Vote in the 2021 Local Government Elections in South Africa." *Center for Social Change*, University of Johannesburg. https://osf.io/preprints/socarxiv/57twh.

Berezin, Mabel. 2009. *Illiberal Politics in Neoliberal Times: Culture, Security and Populism in the New Europe*. New York: Cambridge University Press.

Beveridge, Ross, and Phillippe Koch. 2019. "Urban Everyday Politics: Politicising Practices and the Transformation of the Here and Now." *Environment and Planning D: Society and Space* 37 (1): 142–57.

Bezabeh, Samson. 2011. "Citizenship and the Logic of Sovereignty in Djibouti." *African Affairs* 11 (441): 587–606.

Bhandari, Abhit, and Lisa Mueller. 2019. "Nation-State or Nation-Family? Nationalism in Marginalized African Societies." *Journal of Modern African Studies* 57 (2): 297–322.

Bird, Gemma. 2016. "Beyond the Nation State: The Role of Local and Pan-National Identities in Defining Post-Colonial African Citizenship." *Citizenship Studies* 23 (2): 260–75.

Bjarnesen, Mariam. 2020. "Briefing: The Foot Soldiers of Accra." *African Affairs* 119 (475): 296–307.

Blais, André. 2000. *To Vote or Not to Vote? The Merits and Limits of Rational Choice*. Pittsburgh, PA: University of Pittsburgh Press.

Bleck, Jaimie. 2015. *Education and Empowered Citizenship in Mali.* Baltimore: Johns Hopkins University Press.

Bleck, Jaimie, and Nicolas van de Walle. 2019. *Electoral Politics in Africa since 1990: Continuity and Change.* New York: Cambridge University Press.

Bøås, Morten. 2009. "'New' Nationalism and Autochthony – Tales of Origin as Political Cleavage." *African Spectrum* 44 (1): 19–38.

Bob-Milliar, George. 2014. "Party Youth Activists and Low-Intensity Electoral Violence in Ghana: A Qualitative Study on Party Foot Soldiers' Activism." *African Studies Quarterly* 15 (1): 125–52.

Bob-Milliar, George, and Jeffrey Paller. 2018. "Democratic Ruptures and Electoral Outcomes in Africa: Ghana's 2016 Election." *Africa Spectrum* 53 (1): 5–35.

Bocast, Brooke. 2014. "Uganda: Mini-Skirt Ban." Council on Foreign Relations, March 6. www.cfr.org/blog/uganda-miniskirt-ban.

Bochow, Astrid. 2018. "Saving and Serving the Nation: HIV Politics and the Emergence of New Professional Classes in Botswana." In *Middle Classes in Africa: Changing Lives and Conceptual Challenges*, edited by Lena Kroeker, David O'Kane, and Tabea Scharrer, 157–76. New York: Palgrave Macmillan.

Bodewes, Christine. 2010. "Civil Society and the Consolidation of Democracy in Kenya: An Analysis of a Catholic Parish's Efforts in Kibera Slum." *Journal of Modern African Studies* 48 (4): 547–71.

Bollyky, Thomas. 2018. *Plagues and the Paradox of Progress.* Cambridge, MA: MIT Press.

Bompani, Barbara. 2016. "For God and for My Country: Pentecostal-Charismatic Churches and the Framing of a New Political Discourse in Uganda." In *Public Religion and the Politics of Homosexuality in Africa*, edited by Ezra Chitando and Adriaan van Klinken, 19–34. Aldershot: Ashgate.

Boone, Catherine, and Lydia Nyeme. 2015. "Land Institutions and Political Ethnicity in Africa: Evidence from Tanzania." *Comparative Politics* 48 (1): 67–86.

Booysen, Susan. 2015. *Domination and Decline: The ANC in the Time of Zuma.* Johannesburg: Wits University Press.

Bosch, Tanja Estella, Mare Admire, and Meli Ncube. 2020. "Facebook and Politics in Africa: Zimbabwe and Kenya." *Media, Culture & Society* 42 (3): 349–64.

Bourdieu, Pierre. 1986. "The Forms of Capital." In *The Handbook of Theory and Research for the Sociology of Education*, edited by John Richardson, 241–58. Westport, CT: Greenwood.

Boussalis, Constantine, Travis Coan, and Mirya Holman. 2021. "Political Speech in Religious Sermons." *Politics and Religion* 14: 241–68.

Bouvard, Marguerite Guzman. 2002. *The Mothers of the Plaza de Mayo*. New York: Rowman & Littlefield.

Boyd, Lydia. 2014. "Ugandan Born-Again Christians and the Moral Politics of Gender Equality." *Journal of Religion in Africa* 44 (3–4): 333–54.

2015. *Preaching Prevention: Born-Again Christianity and the Moral Politics of AIDS in Uganda*. Athens: Ohio University Press.

Brady, Henry, Sidney Verba, and Kay Schlozman. 1995. "Beyond SES: A Resource Model of Political Participation." *American Political Science Review* 89 (2): 271–94.

Branch, Adam, and Zachariah Mampilly. 2015. *Africa Uprising*. London: Zed Books.

Brass, Jennifer. 2016. *Allies or Adversaries: NGOs and the State in Africa*. New York: Cambridge University Press.

Bratton, Michael. 1989. "Beyond the State: Civil Society and Associational Life in Africa." *World Politics* 41 (3): 407–30.

1999. "Political Participation in a New Democracy: Institutional Considerations from Zambia." *Comparative Political Studies* 32 (5): 549–88.

2008. "Vote Buying and Violence in Nigerian Election Campaigns." *Electoral Studies* 27: 621–32.

2013. "Voting and Democratic Citizenship in Africa." In *Voting and Democratic Citizenship in Africa*, edited by Michael Bratton, 1–15. Boulder, CO: Lynne Rienner.

Bratton, Michael, and Nicolas van de Walle. 1997. *Democratic Experiments in Africa: Regime Transitions in Comparative Perspective*. New York: Cambridge University Press.

Brennan, James. 2006. "Youth, the TANU Youth League and Managed Vigilantism in Dar es Salaam, Tanzania, 1925–73." *Africa* 76 (2): 221–46.

Bridger, Emily. 2018. "Soweto's Female Comrades: Gender, Youth and Violence in South Africa's Township Uprisings, 1984–1990." *Journal of Southern African Studies* 44 (4): 559–74.

Briggs, Ryan. 2017. "Explaining Case Selection in African Politics Research." *Journal of Contemporary African Studies* 35 (4): 565–72.

Brisset-Foucault, Florence. 2013. "A Citizenship of Distinction in the Open Radio Debates of Kampala." *Africa* 83 (2): 227–50.

Brown, Hannah, and Ruth Prince. 2015. "Introduction: Volunteer Labor – Pasts and Futures of Work, Development, and Citizenship in East Africa." *African Studies Review* 58 (2): 29–42.

Brown, Julian. 2015. *South Africa's Insurgent Citizens: On Dissent and the Possibility of Politics*. London: Zed Books.

Brubaker, Rogers. 2017. "Why Populism?" *Theory and Society* 46 (5): 357–85.

Burchardt, Marian. 2013. "Faith-Based Humanitarianism: Organizational Change and Everyday Meanings in South Africa." *Sociology of Religion* 74 (1): 30–55.

Burgess, Richard. 2015. "Pentecostalism and Democracy in Nigeria." *Nova Religio: The Journal of Alternative and Emergent Religions* 18 (3): 38–62.

Burgess, Thomas. 1999. "Remembering Youth: Generation in Revolutionary Zanzibar." *Africa Today* 46 (2): 29–50.

2002. "Cinema, Bell Bottoms, and Miniskirts: Struggles over Youth and Citizenship in Revolutionary Zanzibar." *International Journal of African Historical Studies* 35 (2/3): 287–313.

Byte, Nii Smiley. 2020. "All Male 'Mense World' Panel Chosen to Discuss Menstruation Causes a Stir on Gh Twitter." Ghana Celebrities.com. May 28. www.ghanacelebrities.com/2020/05/28/all-male-mense-world-panel-chosen-to-discuss-menstruation-causes-a-stir-on-gh-twitter-israel-laryea-and-producers-horribly-roasted.

Caglar, Ayse. 2015. "Citizenship, Anthropology of." In *International Encyclopedia of the Social and Behavioral Sciences*. 2nd ed., Vol. 3, edited by James Wright, 637–41. Amsterdam: Elsevier.

Campbell, Catherine, Andy Gibb, Sbongile Maimane, Yugi Nair, and Zweni Sibiya. 2009. "Youth Participation in the Fight against AIDS in South Africa." *Journal of Youth Studies* 12 (1): 93–109.

Canovan, Margaret. 1999. "Trust the People! Populism and the Two Faces of Democracy." *Political Studies* 47: 2–16.

Carmody, Pádraig, and Francis Owusu. 2018. "Neoliberalism, Urbanization and Change in Africa." In *Africa under Neoliberalism*, edited by Nana Poku and Jim Whitman, 61–75. London: Routledge.

Casey, Conerly. 2008. "'Marginal Muslims': Politics and the Perceptual Bounds of Islamic Authenticity in Northern Nigeria." *Africa Today* 54 (3): 66–92.

2009. "Mediated Hostility: Media, Affective Citizenship, and Genocide in Northern Nigeria." In *Genocide: Truth, Memory, and Representation*, edited by Alexander Laban and Kevin Lewis O'Neill, 247–78. Durham, NC: Duke University Press.

Chabal, Patrick, and Jean-Pascal Daloz. 1999. *Africa Works: Disorder as Political Instrument*. Bloomington: Indiana University Press.

Chazan, Naomi. 1992. "Ethnicity and Politics in Ghana." *Political Science Quarterly* 97 (3): 461–85.

Chazan, Naomi, Robert Mortimer, John Ravenhill, and Donald Rothchild. 1988. *Politics and Society in Contemporary Africa*. Boulder, CO: Lynne Rienner.

Cheeseman, Nic. 2015. *Democracy in Africa: Successes, Failures, and the Struggle for Political Reform*. New York: Cambridge University Press.

Cheeseman, Nic, and Jonathan Fisher. 2021. *Authoritarian Africa: Repression, Resistance, and the Power of Ideas*. New York: Oxford University Press.

Cheeseman, Nic, and Robert Ford. 2007. "Ethnicity as a Political Cleavage." Afrobarometer Working Paper 83. www.afrobarometer.org/wp-con tent/uploads/migrated/files/publications/Working%20paper/ AfropaperNo83.pdf.

Cheeseman, Nic, and Marja Hinfelaar. 2009. "Parties, Platforms, and Political Mobilization: The Zambia Presidential Election of 2008." *African Affairs* 109 (434): 51–76.

Cheeseman, Nic, and Miles Larmer. 2015. "Ethnopopulism in Africa: Opposition Mobilization in Diverse and Unequal Societies." *Democratization* 22 (1): 22–50.

Cheeseman, Nic, Gabrielle Lynch, and Justin Willis. 2017. "Ghana: The Ebbing Power of Incumbency." *Journal of Democracy* 28 (2): 92–104.

2020. *The Moral Economy of Elections in Africa: Democracy, Voting and Virtue*. New York: Cambridge University Press.

Cheney, Kristen. 2004. "Village Life Is Better than Town Life: Identity, Migration, and Development in the Lives of Ugandan Child Citizens." *African Studies Review* 47 (3): 1–23.

Chitando, Ezra. 2007. "A New Man for a New Era? Zimbabwean Pentecostalism, Masculinities and the HIV Epidemic." *Missionalia* 35 (3): 112–27.

Chiweshe, Manase Kudzai. 2017. "Social Networks as Anti-Revolutionary Forces: Facebook and Political Apathy among Youth in Urban Harare, Zimbabwe." *Africa Development* 42 (2): 129–47.

Christiansen, Catrine, Mats Utas, and Henrik Vigh, eds. 2006. *Navigating Youth, Generating Adulthood: Social Becoming in an African Context*. Uppsala: Nordiska Afrikainstitutet.

Chutel, Lyndsey. 2022. "South Africa's Corruption Inquiry Leaves Few of the Nation's Powerful Unscathed." *New York Times*, June 23. www .nytimes.com/2022/06/23/world/africa/south-africa-corruption-jacob-zuma-cyril-ramaphosa.html.

Citizen. 2021. "Museveni Names Women as Vice President and Prime Minister." *Citizen*, June 9. www.thecitizen.co.tz/tanzania/news/east-africa-news/museveni-names-women-as-vice-president-and-prime-minis ter-3431078.

Clapham, Christopher. 2006. "The Political Economy of Population Change." *Population and Development Review* 32: 96–114.

Clark-Kazak, Christina. 2009. "Towards a Working Definition and Application of Social Age in International Development Studies." *Journal of Development Studies* 45 (8): 1307–24.

Clarke, John, Kathleen Coll, Evelina Dagnino, and Catherine Neveu. 2014. *Disputing Citizenship*. Bristol, UK: Policy Press.

Cole, Jennifer. 2012. "The Love of Jesus Never Disappoints: Reconstituting Female Personhood in Urban Madagascar." *Journal of Religion in Africa* 42 (4): 384–407.

Coleman, James. 1988. "Social Capital in the Creation of Human Capital." *American Journal of Sociology* 94: S95–S120.

Collord, Michaela. 2016. "From the Electoral Battleground to the Parliamentary Arena: Understanding Intra-Elite Bargaining in Uganda's National Resistance Movement." *Journal of Eastern African Studies* 10 (4): 639–59.

2019. "Drawing the Wrong Lessons from Magufuli's Rule in Tanzania." *Africa Is a Country*. https://africasacountry.com/2019/05/drawing-the-wrong-lessons-from-the-magufuli-experience-in-tanzania.

Congressional Research Service. 2018. "Uganda." https://sgp.fas.org/crs/row/IF10325.pdf.

Conroy-Krutz, Jeff. 2020. "The Squeeze on African Media Freedom." *Journal of Democracy* 31 (2): 96–109.

Council on Europe. n.d. "What Is Gender-Based Violence?" www.coe.int/en/web/gender-matters/what-is-gender-based-violence.

Croke, Kevin, Guy Crossman, Horacio Larreguy, and John Marshall. 2016. "Deliberate Disengagement: How Education Can Decrease Political Participation in Electoral Authoritarian Regimes." *American Political Science Review* 110 (3): 579–600.

Crossouard, Barbara, and Máiréad Dunne. 2015. "Politics, Gender and Youth Citizenship in Senegal: Youth Policing of Dissent and Diversity." *International Review of Education* 61 (1): 43–60.

Crothers, Lane. 2018. "Why *Populism*? Why Now? An Introduction." *Populism* 1: 3–13.

Cruise O'Brien, Donald. 1996. "A Lost Generation: Youth Identity and State Decay in West Africa." In *Postcolonial Identities in Africa*, edited by Richard Webner and Terrence Ranger, 55–74. London: Zed Books.

Cyr, Jennifer. 2016. "The Pitfalls and Promise of Focus Groups as a Data Collection Method." *Sociological Methods & Research* 45 (2): 231–59.

2017. "The Unique Utility of Focus Groups for Mixed-Method Research." *PS: Political Science and Politics* 50 (4): 1238–42.

Dalton, Russell. 2000. *The Decline of Party Identification*. New York: Oxford University Press.

Darkwa, Linda. 2015. "In Our Father's Name in Our Motherland: The Politics of Women's Political Participation in Ghana." In *Constitutionalism, Democratic Governance and the African State*, edited by Boni Yao Gebe, 239–74. Accra: Black Mask.

Darvas, Peter, Shang Gao, Yijun Shen, and Bilal Bawany. 2017. *Sharing Higher Education's Promise beyond the Few in Sub-Saharan Africa*. Washington, DC: World Bank.

Davenport, Christian. 2015. *How Social Movements Die*. New York: Cambridge University Press.

Dawson, Hannah. 2014. "Youth Politics: Waiting and Envy in a South African Informal Settlement." *Journal of Southern African Studies* 40 (4): 861–82.

de Kadt, Daniel. 2017. "Voting Then, Voting Now: The Long-Term Consequences of Participation in South Africa's First Democratic Election." *Journal of Politics* 79 (2): 670–87.

de Kadt, Daniel, Ada Johnson-Kanu, and Melissa Sands. 2021. "State Violence, Party Formation and Electoral Accountability: The Political Legacy of the Marikana Massacre." https://osf.io/preprints/socarxiv/5uxzv.

de Paredes, Marta, and Thierry Desrues. 2021. "Unravelling the Adoption of Youth Quotas in African Hybrid Regimes: Evidence from Morocco." *Journal of Modern African Studies* 59 (1): 41–58.

de Tocqueville, Alexis. 2002. *Democracy in America*, trans. Harvey Mansfield and Delba Winthrop. Chicago: University of Chicago Press.

Dennis, Jack. 1968. "Problems of Political Socialization Research." *Midwest Journal of Political Science* 12 (1): 85–114.

Di Gregorio, Michael, and Jessica L. Merolli. 2016. "Introduction: Affective Citizenship and the Politics of Identity, Control, Resistance." *Citizenship Studies* 20 (8): 933–42.

Diamond, Larry. 2010. "Liberation Technology." *Journal of Democracy* 21 (3): 69–83.

　2015. "Facing up to the Democratic Recession." *Journal of Democracy* 26 (1): 141–55.

Dickovick, J. Tyler. 2008. "Legacies of Leftism: Ideology, Ethnicity and Democracy in Benin, Ghana and Mali." *Third World Quarterly* 29 (6): 1119–37.

Dietrich, Simone. 2013. "Bypass or Engage? Explaining Donor Delivery Tactics in Foreign Aid Allocation." *International Studies Quarterly* 57 (4): 698–712.

Diouf, Mamadou. 1999. "Urban Youth and Senegalese Politics: Dakar 1988–1994." In *Cities and Citizenship*, edited by James Holston, 42–66. Durham, NC: Duke University Press.

2003. "Engaging Postcolonial Cultures: African Youth and Public Space." *African Studies Review* 46 (1): 1–12.

Djupe, Paul, and Christopher Gilbert. 2009. *The Political Influence of Churches*. New York: Cambridge University Press.

Djupe, Paul, and Tobin Grant. 2001. "Religious Institutions and Political Participation in America." *Journal of the Scientific Study of Religion* 40 (2): 303–14.

Dorman, Sara R. 2016. "'We Have Not Made Anybody Homeless': Regulation and Control of Urban Life in Zimbabwe." *Citizenship Studies* 20 (1): 84–98.

2020. "Citizenship." In *Routledge Handbook of Democratization in Africa*, edited by Gabrielle Lynch and Peter VonDoepp, 460–72. London: Routledge.

Dorman, Sara, Daniel Hammett, and Paul Nugent. 2007. *Making Nations, Creating Strangers: States and Citizenship in Africa*. Leiden: Brill.

Dowd, Robert. 2015. *Christianity, Islam, and Liberal Democracy*. New York: Oxford University Press.

Dowd, Robert, and Ani Sarkissian. 2017. "The Roman Catholic Charismatic Movement and Civic Engagement in Sub-Saharan Africa." *Journal for the Scientific Study of Religion* 56 (3): 536–57.

Downie, Richard. 2015. "Religion and the State in Uganda – Co-Option and Compromise." In *Religious Authority and the State in Africa*, edited by Jennifer Cooke and Richard Downie, 49–63. Washington, DC: Center for Strategic and International Studies.

Doyle, Kevin. 2021. "Co-Opted Social Media and the Practice of *Active Silence* in Cambodia." *Contemporary Southeast Asia* 43 (2): 293–320.

Driscoll, Barry. 2020. "Democratization, Party Systems, and the Endogenous Roots of Ghanaian Clientelism." *Democratization*. 27 (1): 119–36.

du Plessis, Carien. 2021. "South Africa: Local Elections Outcome Could Be a 'Watershed Moment' for ANC." *Africa Report*, November 11. www .theafricareport.com/145436/south-africa-local-elections-outcome-could-be-a-watershed-moment-for-anc.

Dungey, Claire, and Lotte Meinert. 2017. "Learning to Wait: Schooling and the Instability of Adulthood for Young Men in Uganda." In *Elusive Adulthoods: The Anthropology of New Maturities*, edited by Deborah Durham and Jacqueline Solway, 83–104. Bloomington: Indiana University Press.

Dunning, Thad, and Lauren Harrison. 2010. "Cross-Cutting Cleavages and Ethnic Voting: An Experimental Study of Cousinage in Mali." *American Political Science Review* 104 (1): 21–39.

Durham, Deborah. 2000. "Youth and the Social Imagination in Africa." *Anthropological Quarterly* 73 (3): 113–20.

2004. "Disappearing Youth: Youth as a Social Shifter in Botswana." *American Ethnologist* 31 (4): 589–605.

2017. "Introduction." In *Elusive Adulthoods: The Anthropology of New Maturities*, edited by Deborah Durham and Jacqueline Solway, 1–38. Bloomington: Indiana University Press.

Dyck, Christopher. 2011. "Football and Post-War Reintegration: Exploring the Role of Sport in DDR Processes in Sierra Leone." *Third World Quarterly* 32 (3): 395–415.

Ekeh, Peter. 1975. "Colonialism and the Two Publics in Africa: A Theoretical Statement." *Comparative Studies in Society and History* 17 (1): 91–112.

Ellis, Stephen, and Gerrie Ter Haar. 2007. "Religion and Politics: Taking African Epistemologies Seriously." *Journal of Modern African Studies* 45 (3): 385–401.

Ellis, Stephen, and Ineke van Kessel. 2009. *Movers and Shakers: Social Movements in Africa*. Leiden: Brill.

Englebert, Pierre. 2009. *Africa: Unity, Sovereignty and Sorrow*. Boulder, CO: Lynne Rienner.

Escobar, Arturo. 1995. *Encountering Development*. Princeton, NJ: Princeton University Press.

Essop, Tasneem. 2015. "Populism and the Political Character of the Economic Freedom Fighters – a View from the Branch." *Labour, Capital and Society* 48 (1/2): 212–38.

Fallon, Kathleen. 2008. *Democracy and the Rise of Women's Movements in Sub-Saharan Africa*. Baltimore: Johns Hopkins University Press.

Fatton, Robert. 1995. "Africa in the Age of Democratization: The Civic Limitations of Civil Society." *African Studies Review* 38 (2): 67–100.

Faustine, Ngila. 2022. "These Are the African Countries That Censor the Internet the Most." *Quartz Africa*, July 20. https://qz.com/africa/2165371/these-are-the-african-countries-that-censor-internet-the-most.

Fenio, Kenly Greer. 2011. "Tactics of Resistance and the Evolution of Identity from Subjects to Citizens: The AIDS Political Movement in Southern Africa." *International Studies Quarterly* 55: 717–35.

Ferguson, James. 2010. "The Uses of Neoliberalism." *Antipode* 41 (1): 166–84.

Ferree, Karen. 2010. *Framing the Race in South Africa: The Political Origins of Racial-Census Elections*. New York: Cambridge University Press.

Ferree, Karen, and James Long. 2016. "Gifts, Threats and Perceptions of Ballot Secrecy in African Elections." *African Affairs* 115 (461): 621–45.

Fortier, Anne-Marie. 2008. *Multicultural Horizons: Diversity and the Limits of the Civil Nation*. London: Routledge.

2010. "Proximity by Design? Affective Citizenship and the Management of Unease." *Citizenship Studies* 14 (1): 17–30.

2016. "Afterword: Acts of Affective Citizenship? Possibilities and Limitations." *Citizenship Studies* 20 (8): 1038–44.

Foucault, Michel. 2002. "Governmentality." In *Michel Foucault – Power. Essential Works of Foucault 1954–1984*. Vol. 3, edited by James Faubion, 201–22. London: Penguin.

Fox, Jonathan. 2018. *An Introduction to Religion and Politics*. London: Routledge.

Fox, Louise. 2015. "Are African Households Heterogeneous Agents?" IMF, April. www.imf.org/external/pubs/ft/wp/2015/wp15102.pdf.

Franck, Raphaël, and Ilia Ranier. 2012. "Does the Leader's Ethnicity Matter? Ethnic Favoritism, Education, and Health in Sub-Saharan Africa." *American Political Science Review* 106 (2): 294–325.

Fraser, Alastair. 2017. "Post-Populism in Zambia: Michael Sata's Rise, Demise, and Legacy." *International Political Science Review* 38 (4): 456–72.

Fredericks, Rosalind. 2014. "'The Old Man Is Dead': Hip Hop and the Arts of Citizenship of Senegalese Youth." *Antipode* 46 (1): 130–48.

Freedom House. 2022. *Freedom in the World 2022: The Global Expansion of Authoritarian Rule*. https://freedomhouse.org/report/freedom-world/2022/global-expansion-authoritarian-rule.

Freire, Maria, Lall Somik, and Danny Leipziger. 2014. "Africa's Urbanization: Challenges and Opportunities." The Growth Dialogue Working Paper 7. http://growthdialogue.org/africas-urbanization-challenges-and-opportunities.

Freston, Paul. 2001. *Evangelicals and Politics in Asia, Africa and Latin America*. New York: Cambridge University Press.

Fukuyama, Francis. 1995. *Trust: The Social Virtues and the Creation of Prosperity*. New York: Free Press.

Gallego, Jorge, and Leonard Wantchekon. 2020. "Clientelism." In *Routledge Handbook of Democratization in Africa*, edited by Gabrielle Lynch and Peter VonDoepp, 205–16. London: Routledge.

Gamson, William. 1992. *Talking Politics*. New York: Cambridge University Press.

Gandhi, Dhruv. 2018. "Figures of the Week: Female Property Ownership in Sub-Saharan Africa." Brookings Institution, September 14. www.brookings.edu/blog/africa-in-focus/2018/09/14/figures-of-the-week-female-property-ownership-in-sub-saharan-africa.

Ganti, Tejaswini. 2014. "Neoliberalism." *Annual Review of Anthropology* 43: 89–104.

Garner, Robert. 2000. "Religion as a Source of Social Change in the New South Africa." *Journal of Religion in Africa* 30 (1): 310–43.

Geiger, Susan. 1987. "Women in the Nationalist Struggle: TANU Activists in Dar es Salaam." *International Journal of African Historical Studies* 20 (1): 1–26.

Gerber, Alan, Jonathan Gruber, and Daniel Hungerman. 2016. "Does Church Attendance Cause People to Vote? Using Blue Laws' Repeal to Estimate the Effect of Religiosity on Voter Turnout." *British Journal of Political Science.* 46 (3): 481–500.

Geschiere, Peter. 2009. *The Perils of Belonging: Autochthony, Citizenship and Exclusion in Africa and Europe.* Chicago: University of Chicago Press.

Ghana Web. 2021. "Akufo-Addo's Cabinet Lacks Gender Sensitivity – MP." *Ghana Web,* January 23. www.ghanaweb.com/GhanaHomePage/NewsArchive/Akufo-Addo-s-new-cabinet-lacks-gender-sensitivity-MP-1162108.

Giddens, Anthony. 1991. *Modernity and Self-Identity.* Cambridge: Polity Press.

Gifford, Paul. 1998. *African Christianity: Its Public Role.* London: C. Hurst Publishers.

    2004. *Ghana's New Christianity: Pentecostalism in a Globalizing African Economy.* Bloomington: Indiana University Press.

Gladwell, Malcolm. 2010. "Why the Revolution Will Not Be Tweeted." *New Yorker* 4: 1–9.

Global Fund. 2021. "Financial Disbursements, Zambia." https://data.theglobalfund.org/viz/signed/treemap.

Goldstein, Warren, and Jean-Pierre Reed, eds. 2022. *Religions in Rebellions, Revolutions, and Social Movements.* London: Routledge.

Gondwe, Kennedy. 2021. "Zambia Election: Young Voters May Hold the Cards." *BBC News,* August 11. www.bbc.com/news/world-africa-58146384.

Gould, Deborah. 2009. *Moving Politics: Emotion and ACT UP's Fight against AIDS.* Chicago: University of Chicago Press.

Gouws, Amanda, ed. 2005. *(Un)thinking Citizenship: Feminist Debates in Contemporary South Africa.* London: Routledge.

Government of Ghana. 2020. *Ghana beyond Aid Charter and Strategy Document.* Accra: Government of Ghana.

Green, Maia. 2010. "Ujamaa? Cultures of Governance and the Representation of Power in Tanzania." *Social Analysis: The International Journal of Anthropology* 54 (1): 15–34.

Greenhouse, Carol. 1999. "Commentary." *Political and Legal Anthropology Review* 22 (2): 104–9.

Grossman, Guy. 2015. "Renewalist Christianity and the Political Saliency of LGBTs: Theory and Evidence from Sub-Saharan Africa." *Journal of Politics* 77 (2): 337–51.

Guillaume, Xavier, and Jef Huysmans. 2018. "The Concept of 'The Everyday': Ephemeral Politics and the Abundance of Life." *Cooperation and Conflict* 54 (2): 278–96.

Gunner, Liz. 2015. "Song, Identity and the State: Julius Malema's *Dubul' Ibhunu* Song as Catalyst." *Journal of African Cultural Studies* 27 (3): 326–41.

Gupta, Akil, and James Ferguson. 2002. "Spatializing States: Toward an Ethnography of Neoliberal Governmentality." *American Ethnologist* 28 (4): 981–1002.

Gusman, Alessandro. 2009. "HIV/AIDS, Pentecostal Churches and the 'Joseph Generation' in Uganda." *Africa Today* 56 (1): 67–86.

Gyimah-Boadi, E. 1994. "Ghana's Uncertain Political Opening." *Journal of Democracy* 5 (2): 75–86.

   1995. "Ghana: Adjustment, State Rehabilitation and Democratization." In *Between Liberalisation and Oppression: The Politics of Structural Adjustment in Africa*, edited by Thandika Mkandawire and Adebayo Olukoshi, 217–29. Dakar: CODESRIA.

   1996. "Civil Society in Africa." *Journal of Democracy* 7 (2): 118–32.

   2001. "A Peaceful Turnover in Ghana." *Journal of Democracy* 12 (2): 103–17.

   2009. "Another Step Forward for Ghana." *Journal of Democracy* 20 (2): 138–52.

   2015. "Africa's Waning Democratic Commitment." *Journal of Democracy* 26 (1): 101–12.

Haggard, Stephan, and Robert Kaufman. 2021. "The Anatomy of Democratic Backsliding." *Journal of Democracy* 32 (4): 27–41.

Halisi, C. R. D., Paul Kaiser, and Stephen Ndegwa. 1998. "The Multiple Meanings of Citizenship – Rights, Identity and Social Justice in Africa." *Africa Today* 45 (3–4): 337–50.

Hamidu, Jamilla. 2015. "Are Ghanaian Diaspora Middle Class? Linking Middle Class to Political Participation and Stability in Ghana." *Africa Development* 40 (1): 139–57.

Hanspal, Jaysim, and Jonas Nyabor. 2022. "Police Now Hunt for Arise Ghana! Leaders after Protests Turn Violent." *Africa Report*, June 29. www.theafricareport.com/218884/police-now-hunt-for-arise-ghana-leaders-after-protests-turn-violent.

Hara, Blessings. 2021. "Zambian Youth Breathe New Life in Their Democracy." *Youth Voices: Their Perspective*. November 8. www

.yourcommonwealth.org/governance/zambias-youth-breathe-new-life-in-their-democracy.

Harding, Robin. 2020. *Rural Democracy: Elections and Development in Africa*. New York: Oxford University Press.

Harrison, Graham. 2005. "Economic Faith, Social Project and a Misreading of African Society: The Travails of Neoliberalism in Africa." *Third World Quarterly* 26 (8): 1303–20.

Harriss, John, and Paolo de Renzio. 1997. "'Missing Link' or Analytically Missing? The Concept of Social Capital: An Introductory Bibliographic Essay." *Journal of International Development* 9 (7): 919–37.

Hart, Gillian. 2013. *Rethinking the South African Crisis: Nationalism, Populism, Hegemony*. Athens: University of Georgia Press.

Harvard International Review. 2020. "The Rise of Bobi Wine: How a Rapper from the Slums Is Igniting a Revolution in Uganda." November 16. https://hir.harvard.edu/who-is-bobi-wine.

Harvey, David. 2007. *A Brief History of Neoliberalism*. New York: Oxford University Press.

Hassim, Shireen. 2006. *Women's Organizations and Democracy in South Africa*. Madison: University of Wisconsin Press.

Hauser, Ellen. 1999. "Ugandan Relations with Western Donors in the 1990s: What Impact on Democratization?" *Journal of Modern African Studies* 37 (4): 621–41.

Haynes, Jeff. 1996. *Religion and Politics in Africa*. London: Zed Books.

Hearn, Julie. 2002. "The 'Invisible' NGO: US Evangelical Missions in Kenya." *Journal of Religion in Africa* 32 (1): 32–60.

Heffernan, Anne. 2016. "Blurred Lines and Ideological Divisions in South African Youth Politics." *African Affairs* 115 (461): 664–87.

2019. *Limpopo's Legacy: Student Politics & Democracy in South Africa*. London: James Currey.

Hendriks, H. Jurgens, Elna Mouton, Len Hansen, and Elisabet le Roux. 2012. *Men in the Pulpit, Women in the Pew?* Stellenbosch, South Africa: Sun Press.

Herbst, Jeffrey. 2000. *States and Power in Africa*. Princeton, NJ: Princeton University Press.

Hern, Erin Acampo. 2019. *Developing States, Shaping Citizenship: Service Delivery and Political Participation in Zambia*. Ann Arbor: University of Michigan Press.

Hershey, Megan. 2013. "Explaining the Non-Governmental Organization (NGO) Boom: The Case of HIV/AIDS NGOs in Kenya." *Journal of Eastern African Studies* 7 (4): 671–90.

2019. *Whose Agency: The Politics and Practice of Kenya's HIV-Prevention NGOs*. Madison: University of Wisconsin Press.

Hirschman, Albert. 1970. *Exit, Voice and Loyalty.* Cambridge, MA: Harvard University Press.

Hodgkinson, Dan, and Luke Melchiorre. 2019. "Introduction: Student Activism in an Era of Decolonization." *Africa* 89 (1): 1–14.

Hodgson, Dorothy. 2017. "Africa from the Margins." *African Studies Review* 60 (2): 37–49.

Holmes, Carolyn. 2020. *The Black and White Rainbow: Reconciliation, Opposition, and Nation-Building in Democratic South Africa.* Ann Arbor: University of Michigan Press.

Honwana, Alcinda. 2012. *The Time of Youth: Work, Social Change, and Politics in Africa.* Boulder, CO: Kumarian Press.

Honwana, Nyeleti, and Alcinda Honwana. 2021. "Covid-19 in Africa – Youth at the Fore." *AllAfrica.com.* April 14.

Human Rights Watch. 2022. "'I Only Need Justice': Unlawful Detention and Abuse in Unauthorized Places of Detention in Uganda." March 22. www.hrw.org/report/2022/03/22/i-only-need-justice/unlawful-deten tion-and-abuse-unauthorized-places-detention.

Hunger, Sophia, and Fred Paxton. 2022. "What's in a Buzzword? A Systematic Review of the State of Populism Research in Political Science." *Political Science Research and Methods* 10 (3): 617–33.

Hunter, Mark. 2020. "Heroin Hustles: Drugs and the Laboring Poor in South Africa." *Social Science & Medicine* 265 (November): 113329.

Hyden, Goran. 1980. *Beyond Ujamaa in Tanzania: Underdevelopment and an Uncaptured Peasantry.* Berkeley: University of California Press.

ICGC (International Central Gospel Church). n.d. "About Us." https://centralgospel.com.

Ichikowitz Foundation. 2020. "African Youth Survey 2020." February 20. https://ichikowitzfoundation.com/african-youth-survey-2020-press-release/.

Ifeka, Caroline. 2006. "Youth Cultures & the Fetishization of Violence in Nigeria." *Review of African Political Economy* 33 (110): 721–36.

IMF (International Monetary Fund). 2020. *Regional Economic Output: Sub-Saharan Africa.* Washington: IMF.
    2021. *Regional Economic Output: Sub-Saharan Africa.* Washington: IMF.
    2022. *Regional Economic Output: Sub-Saharan Africa.* Washington: IMF.

Index Mundi. 2021. "Country Facts." www.indexmundi.com.

Ingelhart, Ronald, and Christian Welzel. 2005. *Modernization, Cultural Change and Democracy.* New York: Cambridge University Press.

International IDEA. 2021. *Women's Political Participation. African Barometer 2021.* www.idea.int/sites/default/files/publications/womens-political-participation-africa-barometer-2021.pdf.

Interparliamentary Union. 2021. Women in Parliament, Monthly Ranking, April 1. https://data.ipu.org/women-ranking?month=4&year=2021.

Isbell, Thomas, and Lulu Olan'g. 2021. "Troubling Tax Trends: Fewer Africans Support Taxation." Afrobarometer Dispatch 428. https://afrobarometer.org/sites/default/files/publications/Dispatches/ad428-tax_trends_in_africa-weaker_legitimacy_more_avoidance-afrobarom eter_dispatch-20feb21.pdf.

Isin, Engin. 2009. "Citizenship in Flux: The Figure of the Activist Citizen." *Subjectivity* 29: 367–88.

Isin, Engin, and Greg Nielsen. 2008. *Acts of Citizenship*. London: Zed Books.

Isin, Engin, and Bryan Turner. 2007. "Investigating Citizenship: An Agenda for Citizenship Studies." *Citizenship Studies* 11 (1): 5–17.

Iwilade, Akin. 2013. "Crisis as Opportunity: Youth, Social Media and the Renegotiation of Power in Africa." *Journal of Youth Studies* 16 (8): 1054–68.

2020. "Everyday Agency and Centred Marginality: Being "Youth" in the Oil-Rich Niger Delta of Nigeria." *Ateliers d'anthropologie* 47. doi.org/10.4000/ateliers.12277.

Jabri, Vivienne. 2013. *The Postcolonial Subject: Claiming Politics/ Governing Others in Late Modernity*. London: Routledge.

Jacobs, Carolien, and Nadia Sonneveld. 2021. "Empirical Understandings of Informal Citizenship and Membership: Internally Displaced Persons in the Democratic Republic of Congo." *Citizenship Studies* 25 (8): 1112–27.

Jennings, M. Kent, and Jan van Deth, eds. 1990. *Continuities in Political Action*. Berlin: de Gruyter.

Johnson, Carol. 2010. "The Politics of Affective Citizenship: From Blair to Obama." *Citizenship Studies* 14 (5): 495–509.

Johnson, Martha, and Melanie Phillips. 2020. "Gender Politics." In *Routledge Handbook of Democratization in Africa*, edited by Gabrielle Lynch and Peter VonDoepp, 302 16. London: Routledge.

Jones-Correa, Michael, and David Leal. 2001. "Political Participation: Does Religion Matter?" *Political Science Quarterly* 54 (4): 751–70.

Joseph, Richard. 2003. "Nation-State Trajectories in Africa." *Georgetown Journal of International Affairs* 4 (2): 13–20.

Jua, Nantang. 2003. "Differential Responses to Disappearing Transitional Pathways: Redefining Possibility among Cameroonian Youth." *African Studies Review* 46 (2): 13–36.

Jungar, Katarina, and Elina Oinas. 2011. "Beyond Agency and Victimization: Re-Reading HIV and AIDS in African Contexts." *Social Dynamics* 16 (3): 248–62.

Justesen, Mogens, and Christian Bjørnshov. 2014. "Exploiting the Poor: Bureaucratic Corruption and Poverty in Africa." *World Development* 58 (June): 106–15.

Kabeer, Naila. 2005. *Inclusive Citizenship: Meanings and Expressions.* London: Zed Books.

Kabogo, Grace. 2021. "Opinion: Tanzanians Must End Row on President Samia's Titles." *DW*, March 27. www.dw.com/en/opinion-tanzanians-must-end-row-on-president-samias-titles/a-57020589.

Kagwanja, Peter. 2005. "'Power to *Uhuru*': Youth Identity and Generational Politics in Kenya's 2002 Elections." *African Affairs* 105 (418): 51–75.

Kahl, Colin. 2006. *States, Scarcity and Civil Strife in the Developing World.* Princeton, NJ: Princeton University Press.

Kalu, Ogbu. 2008. *African Pentecostalism: An Introduction.* New York: Oxford University Press.

Kalyango, Yusuf, and Benjamin Adu-Kumi. 2013. "Impact of Social Media on Political Mobilization in East and West Africa." *Global Media Journal* 12 (22): 1–20.

Kamau, Samuel. 2017. "Democratic Engagement in the Digital Age: Youth, Social Media and Participatory Politics in Kenya." *Communication* 43 (2): 128–46.

Kang, Alice, and Aili Mari Tripp. 2018. "Coalitions Matter: Citizenship, Women, and Quota Adoption in Africa." *Perspectives on Politics* 16 (1): 73–91.

Karinge, Sarah. 2013. "The Elite Factor in Sub-Saharan Africa's Development: The Urgency in Bridging Disparity." *Journal of Developing Societies* 29 (4): 435–55.

Keating, Avril, and Gabriella Melis. 2017. "Social Media and Youth Political Engagement: Preaching to the Converted or Providing a New Voice for Youth?" *British Journal of Politics and International Relations* 19 (4): 877–94.

Keating, Michael. 2011. "Can Democratization Undermine Democracy? Economic and Political Reform in Uganda." *Democratization* 18 (2): 415–22.

Keller, Edmond. 2014. *Identity, Citizenship, and Political Conflict in Africa.* Bloomington: Indiana University Press.

Kerkvliet, Benedict. 2005. *The Power of Everyday Politics. How Vietnamese Peasants Transformed National Policy.* Ithaca, NY: Cornell University Press.

Kershaw, Paul. 2010. "Caregiving for Identity Is Political: Implications for Citizenship Theory." *Citizenship Studies* 14 (4): 395–410.

Kigambo, Gaaki. 2018. "Church and State Relations in Uganda Worsening." *East African Standard.* January 13.

Kim, Sohee, and Taekyoon Kim. 2018. "Tax Reform, Tax Compliance and State-Building in Tanzania and Uganda." *Africa Development* 43 (2): 35–64.

King, Elisabeth. 2018. "What Kenyan Youth Want and Why It Matters for Peace." *African Studies Review* 61 (1): 134–57.

Kirwin, Matthew, and Wonbin Cho. 2009. "Weak States and Political Violence in Sub-Saharan Africa." Afrobarometer Working Paper 111. www.afrobarometcr.org/wp-contcnt/uploads/migrated/files/publications/Working%20paper/AfropaperNo111.pdf.

Knott, Stacey. 2018. "One of Africa's Most Promising Cities Has a Trash Problem." *Quartz Africa*. March 22. https://qz.com/africa/1229079/ghana-the-worlds-fastest-growing-economy-has-a-trash-problem.

Koter, Dominika. 2013. "Urban and Rural Voting Patterns in Senegal: The Spatial Aspects of Incumbency, c. 1978–2012." *Journal of Modern African Studies* 51 (4): 653–79.

Kpessa-Whyte, Michael, and Mumuni Abu. 2021. "A Comparative Analysis of the Social and Demographic Factors in Ghanaian Political Party Affiliations." *Politikon* 48 (3): 427–49.

Kramon, Eric, and Daniel N. Posner. 2016. "Ethnic Favoritism in Education in Kenya." *Quarterly Journal of Political Science* 11 (1): 1–58.

Krőnke, Matthias. 2022. "Broad Support for Multiparty Elections, Little Faith in Electoral Institutions." Afrobarometer Policy Paper 79. www.afrobarometer.org/wp-content/uploads/migrated/files/publications/Policy%20papers/pp79-ugandan_support_for_multiparty_elections_and_trust_in_electoral_institutions-afrobarometer_policy_paper-8feb22.pdf.

Krook, Mona Lena. 2017. "Violence against Women in Politics." *Journal of Democracy* 28 (1): 74–88.

Kuenzi, Michelle. 2006. "Nonformal Education, Political Participation and Democracy: Findings from Senegal." *Political Behavior* 28 (1): 1–31.

Kuenzi, Michelle, and Gina Lambright. 2007. "Voter Turnout in Africa's Multiparty Regimes." *Comparative Political Studies* 40 (6): 665–90.

2011. "Who Votes in Africa? An Examination of Electoral Participation in 10 African Countries." *Party Politics* 17 (6): 767–99.

Kuperus, Tracy. 2011. "The Political Role and Democratic Contribution of Churches in Post-Apartheid South Africa." *Journal of Church and State* 53 (2): 278–306.

2018. "Democratization, Religious Actors, and Political Influence: A Comparison of Christian Councils in Ghana and South Africa." *Africa Today* 64 (3): 29–51.

Kuperus, Tracy, and Richard Asante. 2021. "Christianity, Citizenship, and Political Engagement among Ghanaian Youth." *African Studies Quarterly* 20 (2): 37–61.

La Fontaine, Jean. 1986. "An Anthropological Perspective on Children in Social Worlds." In *Children of Social Worlds*, edited by Martin Richards and Paul Light, 11–27. Cambridge, MA: Harvard University Press.

Laclau, Ernesto. 2005. *On Populist Reason*. London: Verso.

Lalloo, Kiran. 1998. "Citizenship and Place: Spatial Definitions of Oppression and Agency in South Africa." *Africa Today* 45 (3–4): 439–60.

Lambert, Michael. 2016. "Changes: Reflections on Senegalese Youth Political Engagement." *Africa Today* 63 (2): 33–51.

Lardies, Carmen Alpin, Dominique Dryding, and Carolyn Logan. 2019. "Gains and Gaps: Perceptions and Experiences of Gender in Africa." Afrobarometer Paper 61. https://afrobarometer.org/publications/pp61-gains-and-gaps-perceptions-and-experiences-gender-africa.

Latendresse, Anne, and Lisa Bornstein. 2012. "Urban Developments: Cities and Slums in the Global South." In *Introduction to International Development*, edited by Paul Haslam, Jessica Schafer, and Pierre Beaudet, 355–72. New York: Oxford University Press.

Lawless, Jennifer, and Richard Fox. 2001. "Political Participation of the Urban Poor." *Social Problems* 48 (3): 362–85.

Legatum Institute. 2021. "Prosperity Index, 2021." www.prosperity.com/rankings.

Lekalake, Rorisang, and E. Gyimah-Boadi. 2016. "Does Less Engaged Mean Less Empowered? Political Participation Lags among African Youth, Especially Women." Afrobarometer Policy Paper 34. http://afrobarometer.org/sites/default/files/publications/Policy%20papers/ab_r6_policypaperno34_youth_political_engagement_in_africa_youth_day_release_eng2.pdf.

Lieberman, Evan. 2009. *Boundaries of Contagion: How Ethnic Politics Have Shaped Government Responses to AIDS*. Princeton, NJ: Princeton University Press.

Lieberman, Evan, and Rorisang Lekalake. 2022. "South Africa's Resilient Democracy." *Journal of Democracy* 33 (2): 103–17.

Lindberg, Staffan. 2003. "'It's Our Time to Chop': Do Elections in Africa Feed Neo-Patrimonialism Rather than Counter-Act It?" *Democratization* 10 (2): 121–40.

2010. "What Accountability Pressures Do MPs in Africa Face and How Do They Respond? Evidence from Ghana." *Journal of Modern African Studies* 48 (1): 117–42.

Lindberg, Staffan, and Minion Morrison. 2008. "Are African Voters Really Ethnic or Clientelistic? Survey Evidence from Ghana." *Political Science Quarterly* 123 (1): 95–122.

Lindemann, Stefan. 2011a. "The Ethnic Politics of Coup Avoidance: Evidence from Zambia and Uganda." *Africa Spectrum* 46 (2): 3–41.

2011b. "Just Another Change of Guard? Broad-Based Politics and Civil War in Museveni's Uganda." *African Affairs* 110 (440): 387–416.

Lister, Ruth. 1997. "Citizenship: Towards a Feminist Synthesis." *Feminist Review* Autumn (57): 28–48.

Lodge, Tom. 2014. "Neo-Patrimonial Politics in the ANC." *African Affairs* 113 (450): 1–23.

Lofchie, Michael. 2014. *The Political Economy of Tanzania: Decline and Recovery*. Philadelphia: University of Pennsylvania Press.

Long, Norman. 1990. "From Paradigm Lost to Paradigm Regained? The Case for an Actor-Oriented Sociology of Development." *European Review of Latin American and Caribbean Studies* 49 (December): 3–24.

Longman, Timothy. 2010. *Christianity and Genocide in Rwanda*. New York: Cambridge University Press.

Lonsdale, John. 2000. "Agency in Tight Corners: Narrative and Initiative in African History." *Journal of African Cultural Studies* 13 (1): 5–16.

2009. "Compromised Critics: Religion in Kenya's Politics." In *Religion and Politics in Kenya*, edited by Ben Knighton, 57–94. New York: Palgrave Macmillan.

López, Matias, and Juan Luna. "Assessing the Risk of Democratic Reversal in the United States: A Reply to Kurt Weyland." *PS: Political Science & Politics* 54 (3): 421–26.

Lund, Christian. 2006. "Twilight Institutions: Public Authority and Local Politics in Africa." *Development and Change* 37 (4): 685–705.

Lundåsen, Susanne. 2022. "Religious Participation and Civic Engagement in a Secular Context: Evidence from Sweden on the Correlates of Attending Religious Services." *Voluntas* 33: 627–40.

Lynch, Gabrielle. 2014. "Electing the 'Alliance of the Accused': The Success of the Jubilee Alliance in Kenya's Rift Valley Province." *Journal of Eastern African Studies* 8 (1): 93–114.

Lynch, Gabrielle, Nic Cheeseman, and Justin Willis. 2019. "From Peace Campaigns to Peaceocracy: Elections, Order and Authority in Africa." *African Affairs* 118 (473): 603–27.

MacLean, Lauren. 2010. *Informal Institutions and Citizenship in Rural Africa: Risk and Reciprocity in Ghana and Côte d'Ivoire*. New York: Cambridge University Press.

2011. "State Retrenchment and the Exercise of Citizenship in Africa." *Comparative Political Studies* 44 (9): 1238–66.

MacLean, Lauren, George Bob-Milliar, Elizabeth Baldwin, and Elisa Dickey. 2016. "The Construction of Citizenship and the Public Provision of

Electricity during the 2014 World Cup in Ghana." *Journal of Modern African Studies* 54 (4): 555–90.

Maclean, Ruth. 2022. "Five African Countries, Six Coups." *New York Times*, January 28. www.nytimes.com/article/burkina-faso-africa-coup.html.

Mama, Amina, and Margo Okazawa-Ray. 2012. "Militarism, Conflict and Women's Activism in the Global Era: Challenges and Prospects for Women in Three West African Contexts." *Feminist Review* 101: 97–123.

Mamdani, Mahmood. 1996. *Citizen and Subject: Contemporary Africa and the Legacy of Late Colonialism*. Princeton, NJ: Princeton University Press.

Manby, Bronwen. 2009. *Struggles for Citizenship in Africa*. London: Zed Books.

2021. "Naturalization in African States: Its Past and Potential Future." *Citizenship Studies* 25 (4): 514–42.

Manglos, Nicolette, and Alexander Weinreb. 2013. "Religion and Interest in Politics in Sub-Saharan Africa." *Social Forces* 92 (1): 195–219.

Manning, Carrie. 2005. "Assessing African Party Systems after the Third Wave." *Party Politics* 11 (6): 707–27.

Manqoyi, Ayanda. 2019. "Inclusive Citizenship: Review of Literature." In *Citizenship in Motion: South African and Japanese Scholars in Conversation*, edited by Itsuhiro Hazama, Kiyoshi Umeya, and Francis Nyamnjoh, 63–86. Buea, Cameroon: Langaa RPCIG.

Mare, Admire. 2018. "Politics Unusual? Facebook and Political Campaigning during the 2013 Harmonised Elections in Zimbabwe." *African Journalism Studies* 39 (1): 90–110.

Mares, Isabela, and Lauren Young. 2016. "Buying, Expropriating, and Stealing Votes." *Annual Review of Political Science* 19: 267–88.

Marshall, Ruth. 2009. *Political Spiritualities: The Pentecostal Revolution in Nigeria*. Chicago: University of Chicago Press.

Marshall-Fratani, Ruth. 2006. "The War of 'Who Is Who': Autochthony, Nationalism, and Citizenship in the Ivorian Crisis." *African Studies Review* 49 (2): 9–43.

Mattes, Robert. 2012. "The 'Born Frees': The Prospects for Generational Change in Post-Apartheid South Africa." *Australian Journal of Political Science* 47 (1): 133–53.

2020. "Lived Poverty on the Rise." Afrobarometer Policy Paper 62. www .afrobarometer.org/wp-content/uploads/migrated/files/publications/Policy %20papers/ab_r7_pap13_lived_poverty_on_the_rise_in_africa_1.pdf.

Mattes, Robert, and Dangalira Mughogho. 2009. "The Limited Impacts of Formal Education on Democratic Citizenship in Africa." Afrobarometer Working Paper 109. https://afrobarometer.org/sites/default/files/publica tions/Working%20paper/AfropaperNo109.pdf.

Mazuri, Ali. 1991. "The Polity as an Extended Family: An African Perspective." *International Journal of Sociology of the Family* 21 (2): 1–14.

McAdam, Doug. 1986. "Recruitment to High-Risk Activism: The Case of Freedom Summer." *American Journal of Sociology* 92 (1): 64–90.

McCauley, John. 2012. "Africa's New Big Man Rule? Pentecostalism and Patronage in Ghana." *African Affairs* 112 (446): 1–21.

2015. "The Political Mobilization of Ethnic and Religious Identities in Africa." *American Political Science Review* 108 (4): 801–16.

McClendon, Gwendolyn. 2018. *Envy in Politics.* Princeton, NJ: Princeton University Press.

McClendon, Gwendolyn, and Rachel Beatty Riedl. 2015a. "Individualism and Empowerment in Pentecostal Sermons: New Evidence from Nairobi, Kenya." *African Affairs* 115 (458): 119–44.

2015b. "Religion as a Stimulant of Political Participation: Experimental Evidence from Nairobi, Kenya." *Journal of Politics* 77 (4): 1045–57.

2019. *From Pews to Politics: Religious Sermons and Political Participation in Africa.* New York: Cambridge University Press.

2021. "Using Sermons to Study Religions' Influence on Political Behavior." *Comparative Political Studies* 54 (5): 779–822.

McDonnell, Terence. 2010. "Cultural Objects as Objects: Materiality, Urban Space, and the Interpretation of AIDS Campaigns in Accra, Ghana." *American Journal of Sociology* 115 (6): 1800–52.

McEvoy-Levy, Siobhan. 2013. *Troublemakers or Peacemakers? Youth and Post-Accord Peace Building.* South Bend, IN: University of Notre Dame Press.

McGregor, JoAnn, and Kudzai Chatiza. 2020. "Partisan Citizenship and Its Discontents: Precarious Possession and Political Agency on Harare City's Expanding Margins." *Citizenship Studies* 24 (1): 17–39.

Medie, Peace. 2013. "Fighting Gender-Based Violence: The Women's Movement and the Enforcement of Rape Law in Liberia." *African Affairs* 112 (448): 377–97.

Melber, Henning. 2018. "Populism in Southern Africa under Liberation Movements as Governments." *Review of African Political Economy* 45 (158): 676–86.

Melchiorre, Luke. 2021. "The Generational Populism of Bobi Wine." ROAPE, February 12. https://roape.net/2021/02/12/the-generational-populism-of-bobi-wine.

Melucci, Alberto. 1995. "The Process of Collective Identity." In *Social Movements and Culture*, edited by Hank Johnston and Bert Klandermans, 41–63. Minneapolis: University of Minnesota Press.

Meyer, Birgit. 2007. "Pentecostalism and Neo-Liberal Capitalism: Faith, Prosperity and Vision in African Pentecostal–Charismatic Churches." *Journal for the Study of Religion* 20 (2): 5–28.

Miguel, Edward. 2004. "Tribe or Nation? Nation Building and Public Goods in Kenya Versus Tanzania." *World Politics* 56 (3): 327–62.

Milanovic, Branko. 2016. *Global Inequality*. Cambridge, MA: Harvard University Press.

Miniru, Alhassan Baba. 2016. "Saving Ghana from Its Own Waste." *DW*, August 29. www.dw.com/en/saving-ghana-from-its-own-waste/a-19503010.

Mittermaier, Amira. 2014. "Beyond Compassion: Islamic Voluntarism in Egypt." *American Ethnologist* 41 (3): 518–31.

Mkandawire, Thandika. 2015. "Neopatrimonialism and the Political Economy of Economic Performance in Africa: Critical Reflections." *World Politics* 67 (3): 563–612.

Moffitt, Benjamin. 2017. *The Global Rise of Populism*. Stanford, CA: Stanford University Press.

Mohamed, Miraji Hassan. 2021. "Dangerous or Political? Kenyan Youth Negotiating Political Agency in the Age of 'New Terrorism'." *Media, War, and Conflict* 14 (3): 303–21.

Mood, Carina, and Jan O. Jonsson. 2016. "The Social Consequences of Poverty: An Empirical Test on Longitudinal Data." *Social Indicators Research* 127 (2): 633–52.

Moriguchi, Gaku. 2019. "In and out of Family: Family Affairs and Deep Play at Nightclubs in Kampala, Uganda." In *Citizenship in Motion: South African and Japanese Scholars in Conversation*, edited by Itsuhiro Hazama, Kiyoshi Umeya, and Francis Nyamnjoh, 217–37. Buea, Cameroon: Langaa RPCIG.

Morse, Yonatan. 2018. *How Autocrats Compete: Parties, Patrons, and Unfair Elections in Africa*. New York: Cambridge University Press.

Motani, Pankti, Anais van de Walle, Richmond Aryeetey, and Roosmarijn Verstraeten. 2019. "Lessons Learned from Evidence-Informed Decision-Making in Nutrition and Health (EVIDENT) in Africa: A Project Evaluation." *Health Research Policy and Systems* 17 (12). doi.org/10.1186/s12961–019-0413-6.

Mudde, Cas. 2007. *Populist Radical Right Parties in Europe*. New York: Cambridge University Press.

Mudde, Cas, and Cristobal Rovira Kaltwasser. 2013. "Exclusionary vs. Inclusionary Populism: Comparing Europe and Latin America." *Government and Opposition* 48 (2): 147–74.

2017. *Populism: A Very Short Introduction*. New York: Oxford University Press.

Mueller, Lisa. 2018. *Political Protest in Contemporary Africa*. New York: Cambridge University Press.

2020. "Popular Protest and Accountability." In *Routledge Handbook of Democratization in Africa*, edited by Gabrielle Lynch and Peter VonDoepp, 392–403. London: Routledge.

Mueller, Valerie, and James Thurlow. 2019. *Youth and Jobs in Rural Africa: Beyond Stylized Facts*. New York: Oxford University Press.

Mukhopadhyay, Maitrayee. 2007. "Gender Justice, Citizenship and Development: An Introduction." In *Gender Justice, Citizenship and Development*, edited by Maitrayee Mukhopadhyay and Navsharan Singh, 1–14. Delhi: Zubaan.

Muriaas, Ragnhild, and Vibeke Wang. 2012. "Executive Dominance and the Politics of Quota Representation in Uganda." *Journal of Modern African Studies* 50 (2): 309–38.

Musinguzi, Laban Kashaija. 2016. "The Role of Social Networks in Savings Groups: Insights from Village Savings and Loan Associations in Luwero, Uganda." *Journal of Community Development* 51 (4): 499–516.

Mutsvairo, Bruce, and Lys-Anne Sirks. 2015. "Examining the Contribution of Social Media in Reinforcing Political Participation in Zimbabwe." *Journal of African Media Studies* 7 (3): 329–44.

Mwenda, Andrew. 2007. "Personalizing Power in Uganda." *Journal of Democracy* 118 (October): 23–28.

Nathan, Noah. 2019. *Electoral Politics and Africa's Urban Transition*. New York: Cambridge University Press.

Ndegwa, Stephen. 1997. "Citizenship and Ethnicity: An Examination of Two Transition Moments in Kenyan Politics." *American Political Science Review* 91 (3): 599–616.

Negi, R. 2008. "Beyond the Chinese Scramble: The Political Economy of Anti-Chinese Sentiment in Zambia." *African Geographical Review* 27: 41–63.

News24. 2016. "Watch: Ugandan Youths Drop Piglets at Parliament in Protest." September 16. www.news24.com/news24/Africa/News/watch-ugandan-youths-drop-piglets-at-parliament-in-protest-20160915-2.

Ngozwana, Nomazulu. 2014. *Understandings of Democracy and Citizenship in Lesotho: Implications for Civic Education*. Unpublished doctoral dissertation. University of KwaZulu–Natal, South Africa. https://researchspace.ukzn.ac.za/handle/10413/12110.

Nie, Norman, Sidney Verba, and Jae-on Kim. 1974. "Political Participation and the Life Cycle." *Comparative Politics* 6 (3): 319–40.

Nkrumah, Bright. 2021. "Beyond Tokenism: The 'Born Frees' and Climate Change in South Africa." *International Journal of Ecology*. doi.org/10.1155/2021/8831677.

Norris, Pippa. 2002. *Democratic Phoenix: Reinventing Political Activism.* New York: Cambridge University Press.

2004. *Electoral Engineering: Voting Rules and Political Behavior.* New York: Cambridge University Press.

Norris, Pippa, and Ronald Inglehart. 2011. *Sacred and Secular: Religion and Politics Worldwide.* New York: Cambridge University Press.

NTV Uganda. 2021. "The Rise of Uganda's First Female Prime Minister: Robinal Nabbanja." YouTube, June 10. www.youtube.com/watch?v=dQ2qr6DGvmc.

Nugent, Paul. 2001. "Winners, Losers and Also Rans: Money, Moral Authority and Voting Patterns in the Ghana 2000 Election." *African Affairs* 100 (400): 405–28.

Nyabola, Nanjala. 2018. *Digital Democracy, Analogue Politics: How the Internet Era Is Transforming Kenya.* London: Zed Books.

Nyamnjoh, Francis. 2007. "From Bounded to Flexible Citizenship: Lessons from Africa." *Citizenship Studies* 11 (1): 73–82.

2016. *#RhodesMustFall: Nibbling at Resilient Colonialism in South Africa.* Buea, Cameroon: Langaa RPCIG.

Nyamu-Musembi, Celestine. 2007. "Addressing Formal and Substantive Citizenship: Gender Justice in Sub-Saharan Africa." In *Gender Justice, Citizens and Development*, edited by Maitrayee Mukhopadhyay and Navsharan Singh, 171–233. Delhi: Zubaan.

Obadare, Ebenezer. 2011. "Revalorizing the Political: Towards a New Intellectual Agenda for African Civil Society Discourse." *Journal of Civil Society* 7 (4): 427–42.

2016. *Humor, Silence and Civil Society in Nigeria.* Rochester, NY: University of Rochester Press.

Ochieng' Opalo, Ken. 2019. *Legislative Development in Africa: Politics and Postcolonial Legacies.* New York: Cambridge University Press.

Oduro, Franklin. 2009. "The Quest for Inclusion and Citizenship in Ghana: Challenges and Prospects." *Citizenship Studies* 13 (6): 621–39.

Oinas, Elina, Henri Onodera, and Leena Suurpää. 2018. *What Politics? Youth and Political Engagement in Africa.* Leiden: Brill.

Okia, Opolot. 2019. "Introduction: Communal Forced Labor as a Mask of Tradition." In *Labor in Colonial Kenya after the Forced Labor Convention, 1930–1963*, edited by Opolot Okia, 1–24. London: Palgrave Macmillan.

Olaiya, Taiwo. 2014. "Youth and Ethnic Movements and Their Impacts on Party Politics in ECOWAS Member States." *Sage Open*, January–March: 1–14.

Olaoluwa, Azeezat. 2020. "End SARS Protests: The Nigerian Women Leading the Fight for Change." *BBC News*, December 1. www.bbc.com/news/world-africa-55104025.

Oldfield, Sophie, Netsai Sarah Matshaka, Elaine Salo, and Ann Schlyter. 2019. "In Bodies and Homes: Gendering Citizenship in Southern African Cities." *Urbani Izziv* 30 (February): 37–51.

Oloka-Onyango, Joseph. 2004. "'New Breed' Leadership, Conflict, and Reconstruction in the Great Lakes Region of Africa: A Sociopolitical Biography of Uganda's Yoweri Kaguta Museveni." *Africa Today* 50 (3): 29–52.

Oloka-Onyango, Joseph, and Josephine Ahikire, eds. 2017. *Controlling Consent: Uganda's 2016 Elections.* Trenton, NJ: Africa World Press.

Olorunnisola, Anthony, and Aziz Douai, eds. 2013. *New Media Influence on Social and Political Change in Africa.* Hershey, PA: IGI Global.

Omelicheva, Mariya, and Ranya Ahmed. 2018. "Religion and Politics: Examining the Impact of Faith on Political Participation." *Religion, State, and Society* 46 (1): 4–25.

O'Neill, Kevin L. 2009. "But Our Citizenship Is in Heaven: A Proposal for the Future Study of Christian Citizenship in the Global South." *Citizenship Studies* 13 (4): 333–48.

Onwuegbuzie, Anthony, Wendy Dickinson, Nancy Leech, and Annmarie Zoran. 2009. "A Qualitative Framework for Collecting and Analyzing Data in Focus Group Research." *International Journal of Qualitative Methods* 8 (3): 1–21.

Ortiz-Ospina, Estaban, and Max Roser. 2016. "Trust." http://ourworldindata.org/trust.

Osei, Anya. 2016. "Formal Party Organisation and Informal Relations in African Parties: Evidence from Ghana." *Journal of Modern African Studies* 54 (1): 37–66.

2018. "Elite Theory and Political Transitions: Networks of Power in Ghana and Togo." *Comparative Politics* 51 (1): 21–40.

Otiono, Nduka. 2021. "Dream Delayed or Dream Betrayed: Politics, Youth Agency and the Mobile Revolution in Africa." *Canadian Journal of African Studies* 55 (1): 121–40.

Ottaway, Marina. 1999. *Africa's New Leaders: Democracy or State Reconstruction?* New York: Carnegie Endowment.

Paget, Daniel. 2020a. "Again, Making Tanzania Great: Magufuli's Restorationist Developmental Nationalism." *Democratization* 27 (7): 1240–60.

2020b. "Mistaken for Populism: Magufuli, Ambiguity and Elitist Plebeianism in Tanzania." *Journal of Political Ideologies* 26 (2): 121–41.

2021. "Tanzania: The Authoritarian Landslide." *Journal of Democracy* 32 (2): 61–76.

2022. "Lone Organizers: Opposition Party-Building in Hostile Places in Tanzania." *Party Politics* 28 (2): 223–35.

Pailey, Robtel Neajai. 2016. "Birthplace, Bloodline and Beyond: How 'Liberian Citizenship' Is Currently Constructed in Liberia and Beyond." *Citizenship Studies* 20 (6–7): 811–29.

2021. *Development, (Dual) Citizenship and Its Discontents in Africa: The Political Economy of Belonging in Liberia*. New York: Cambridge University Press.

Paller, Jeffrey. 2018. "From Urban Crisis to Political Opportunity." In *Africa under Neoliberalism*, edited by Nana Poku and Jim Whitman, 76–94. London: Routledge.

2019. *Democracy in Ghana: Everyday Politics in Urban Africa*. New York: Cambridge University Press.

2021. "Everyday Politics and Sustainable Urban Development in the Global South." *Area Development and Policy* 6 (3): 319–36.

Paret, Marcel. 2018. "Beyond Post-Apartheid Politics: Cleavages, Protest and Elections in South Africa." *Journal of Modern African Studies* 56 (3): 471–96.

Parsitau, Damaris. 2011. "'Arise, O Ye Daughters of Faith': Women, Pentecostalism and Public Culture in Kenya." In *Christianity and Public Culture in Africa*, edited by Harri Englund, 131–45. Athens: Ohio University Press.

Pateman, Carol. 1989. *The Disorder of Women*. Cambridge: Polity Press.

Patterson, Amy S. 1999. "The Dynamic Nature of Citizenship and Participation: Lessons from Three Rural Senegalese Case Studies." *Africa Today* 46 (1): 3–27.

2006. *The Politics of AIDS in Africa*. Boulder, CO: Lynne Rienner.

2011. *The Church and AIDS in Africa: The Politics of Ambiguity*. Boulder, CO: Lynne Rienner.

2016. "Training Professionals and Eroding Relationships: Donors, Aids Care and Development in Urban Zambia." *Journal of International Development* 28 (6) 827–44.

2019. "'To Save the Community': Carework as Citizenship in Liberia's Ebola Outbreak and Zambia's AIDS Crisis." *Africa Today* 66 (2): 29–54.

2022. "The Tanzanian State Response to COVID-19: Why Low Capacity, Discursive Legitimacy and Twilight Authority Matter." WIDER Working Paper Series 2022–34. United Nations University. doi.org/10.35188/UNU-WIDER/2022/165-5.

Patterson, Amy S., and Tracy Kuperus. 2016. "Mobilizing the Faithful: Organizational Autonomy, Visionary Pastors, and Citizenship in South Africa and Zambia." *African Affairs* 115 (459) 318–41.

Perullo, Alex. 2005. "Hooligans and Heroes: Youth Identity and Hip-Hop in Dar es Salaam, Tanzania." *Africa Today* 51 (4) 75–101.

Pfeiffer, James, and Rachel Chapman. 2010. "Anthropological Perspectives on Structural Adjustment and Public Health." *Annual Review of Anthropology* 39 (October): 149–65.

Phillips, Anne. 1991. *Engendering Democracy*. Cambridge: Polity Press.

Phillips, Kristin. 2018. *An Ethnography of Hunger: Politics, Subsidence, and the Unpredictable Grace of the Sun*. Bloomington: Indiana University Press.

Piper, Laurence, and Bettina von Lieres. 2015. "Mediating between State and Citizens: The Significance of the Informal Politics of Third-Party Representation in the Global South." *Citizenship Studies* 19 (6–7): 696–713.

Pitcher, Anne, Mary Moran, and Michael Johnston. 2009. "Rethinking Patrimonialism and Neopatrimonialism in Africa." *African Studies Review* 52 (1): 122–56.

Piven, Frances Fox, and Richard Cloward. 1977. *Poor People's Movements: How They Succeed, Why They Fail*. New York: Random House.

Population International. 2010. "The Effects of a Very Young Age Structure in Uganda." www.issuelab.org/resources/4998/4998.pdf.

Posel, Deborah. 2014. "Julius Malema and the Post-Apartheid Public Sphere." *Acta Academica* 46 (1): 32–54.

Posner, Daniel. 2005. *Institutions and Ethnic Politics in Africa*. New York: Cambridge University Press.

Preston, Jesse, Erika Salomon, and Ryan Ritter. 2013. "Religious Prosociality: Personal, Cognitive, and Social Factors." In *Religion, Personality, and Social Behavior*, edited by Vassilis Saroglu, 149–69. London: Psychology Press.

Putnam, Robert. 1994. *Making Democracy Work: Civic Traditions in Modern Italy*. Princeton, NJ: Princeton University Press.

Puumala, Eeva, and Reiko Shindo. 2021. "Exploring the Links between Language, Everyday Citizenship, and Community." *Citizenship Studies* 25 (6): 739–55.

Quaynor, Laura J. 2015a. "'I Do Not Have the Means to Speak': Educating Youth for Citizenship in Post-Conflict Liberia." *Journal of Peace Education* 12 (1): 15–36.

　2015b. "Researching Citizenship Education in Africa: Considerations from Ghana and Liberia." *Comparative & International Education* 10 (1): 120–34.

Rabe, Marlize. 2017. "Care, Family Policy and Social Citizenship in South Africa." *Journal of Comparative Family Studies* 48 (3): 327–38.

Radelet, Steven. 2010. "Success Stories from 'Emerging Africa.'" *Journal of Democracy* 21 (4): 87–101.

Rasmussen, Louise Mubanda. 2013. "'To Donors, It's a Program, but to Us, It's a Ministry': The Effects of Donor Funding on a Community-Based Catholic HIV/AIDS Initiative in Kampala." *Canadian Journal of African Studies* 47 (2): 227–47.

Ratcliffe, Rebecca, and Samuel Okiror. 2019. "Millions of Ugandans Quit Internet Services as Social Media Tax Takes Effect." *Guardian*, February 27. www.theguardian.com/global-development/2019/feb/27/millions-of-ugandans-quit-internet-after-introduction-of-social-media-tax-free-speech.

Republic of Uganda. 2001. "The National Youth Policy." www.youthpolicy .org/national/Uganda_2001_National_Youth_Policy.pdf.

Resnick, Danielle. 2010. "Populist Strategies in African Democracies." UNU–WIDER Working Paper 2010/114.

    2015. "The Political Economy of Africa's Emergent Middle Class: Retrospect and Prospects." *Journal of International Development* 27: 573–87.

    2022. "How Zambia's Opposition Won." *Journal of Democracy* 33 (1): 70–84.

Resnick, Danielle, and Daniela Casale. 2014. "Young Populations in Young Democracies: Generational Voting Behavior in Sub-Saharan Africa." *Democratization* 21 (6): 1172–94.

Resnick, Danielle, and James Thurlow, eds. 2015. *African Youth and the Persistence of Marginalization: Employment, Politics, and Prospects for Change*. London: Routledge.

Riker, William, and Peter Ordeshook. 1968. "A Theory of the Calculus of Voting." *American Political Science Review* 62 (1): 25–42.

Rizzo, Matteo. 2017. *Taken for a Ride: Grounding Neoliberalism, Precarious Labour, and Public Transport in an African Metropolis*. New York: Oxford University Press.

Robins, Steven. 2004. "'Long Live Zackie, Long Live': AIDS Activism, Science and Citizenship after Apartheid." *Journal of Southern African Studies* 30 (3): 651–72.

    2014. "The 2011 Toilet Wars in South Africa: Justice and Transition between the Exceptional and Everyday after Apartheid." *Development and Change* 45 (3): 479–501.

Rocca, Camilla, and Ines Schultes. 2020. "Africa's Youth: Action Needed Now to Support the Continent's Greatest Assets." Briefing for Mo

Ibrahim Foundation. August. https://mo.ibrahim.foundation/sites/default/files/2020-08/international-youth-day-research-brief.pdf.

Rogers, Wendy. 2003. "What Is a Child?" In *Understanding Childhood: A Multidisciplinary Approach*, edited by Martin Woodhead and Heather Montgomery, 1–23. Open University Online.

Rosander, Eva Evers. 1997. "Women in Groups in Africa: Female Associational Patterns in Senegal and Morocco." In *Organizing Women: Formal and Informal Women's Groups in the Middle East*, edited by Dawn Chatty and Annika Rabo, 101–23. New York: Berg Publishers.

Ross, Michael. 2015. "What Have We Learned about the Resource Curse?" *Annual Review of Political Science* 18: 239–59.

Rotberg, Robert. 2013. *Africa Emerges: Consummate Challenges, Abundant Opportunities*. Cambridge: Polity Press.

Runciman, Carin, Martin Bekker, and Terri Maggott. 2019. "Voting Preferences of Protesters and Non-Protesters in Three South African Elections (2014–2019): Revisiting the 'Ballot and the Brick'." *Politikon* 46 (4): 390–410.

Rushton, Simon, and Owain David Williams. 2012. "Frames, Paradigms and Power: Global Health Policy-Making under Neoliberalism." *Global Society* 26 (192): 147–67.

Ryder, Norman. 1965. "The Cohort as a Concept in the Study of Social Change." *American Sociological Review* 30 (6): 843–61.

Sackey, Brigid. 2006. *New Directions in Gender and Religion: The Changing Status of Women in African Independent Churches*. Lanham, MD: Lexington Books.

Sadgrove, Joanna. 2014. "Global Moralities, Local Responses: Interpreting Sexual Morality and Social Belonging in Uganda." In *Strings Attached: AIDS and the Rise of Transnational Connections in Africa*, edited by Nadine Beckmann, Alessandro Gusman, and Catrine Shroff, 79–103. New York: Oxford University Press.

Sadurni, Sumy. 2018. "Women Activists Take to the Streets of Kampala to Demand More Police Action." *PRI's the World*, July 3. www.pri.org/stories/2018-07-03/women-activists-take-streets-kampala-demand-more-police-action.

Schaffer, Frederic. 2000. *Democracy in Translation*. Ithaca, NY: Cornell University Press.

Schatzberg, Michael. 2001. *Political Legitimacy in Middle Africa: Father, Family, Food*. Bloomington: Indiana University Press.

Schertz, China. 2014. *Having People, Having Heart*. Chicago: University of Chicago Press.

Scheye, Eric, and Eric Pelser. 2020. "Emerging Crimes: Africa's Development Models Must Change." *ENACT Observer*, November 17. https://enactafrica.org/enact-observer/africas-development-models-must-change.

Schmidt, Elizabeth. 2005. "Top down or Bottom up? Nationalist Mobilization Reconsidered with Special Reference to Guinea (French West Africa)." *American Historical Review* 11 (4): 975–1014.

Schneider, Leander. 2014. *Government of Development: Peasants and Politicians in Postcolonial Tanzania*. Bloomington: Indiana University Press.

Scott, James. 1998. *Seeing Like a State: How Certain Schemes to Improve the Human Condition Have Failed*. New Haven, CT: Yale University Press.

Seekings, Jeremy. 1993. *Heroes or Villains? Youth Politics in the 1980s*. Johannesburg: Raven Press.

Selnes, Florence Namasinga, and Kristin Skare Orgeret. 2020. "Social Media in Uganda: Revitalising News Journalism?" *Media, Culture and Society* 42 (April): 380–97.

Semboja, Joseph, and Ole Therkildsen, eds. 1995. *Service Provision under Stress in East Africa: The State, NGOs and People's Organizations in Kenya, Tanzania and Uganda*. Copenhagen: Centre for Development Research.

Senay, Banu. 2008. "How Do the Youth Perceive and Experience Turkish Citizenship?" *Middle Eastern Studies* 44 (6): 963–76.

Shirazi, Roozbeh. 2012. "Performing the 'Knights of Change': Male Youth Narratives and Practices of Citizenship in Jordanian Schools." *Comparative Education* 48 (1): 71–85.

Shivji, I. G. 2012. "Nationalism and Pan-Africanism: Decisive Moments in Nyerere's Intellectual and Political Thought." *Review of African Political Economy* 39 (131): 103–16.

Silberman, Israella. 2005. "Religion as a Meaning System: Implications for the New Millennium." *Journal of Social Issues* 61 (4): 641–63.

Sinyangwe, Chiwoyu. 2021. "Zambia: Young, Urban and Disgruntled PF Supporters, Can Lungu Woo Them Back?" *Africa Report*, July 13. www.theafricareport.com/107675/zambia-young-urban-and-disgruntled-pf-supporters-can-lungu-woo-them-back.

Sklar, Richard. 1979. "The Nature of Class Domination in Africa." *Journal of Modern African Studies* 17 (4): 531–52.

Sloam, James. 2011. "Introduction: Youth, Citizenship and Politics." *Parliamentary Affairs* 65 (1): 4–12.

Smith, Christian. 1996. *Disruptive Religion: The Force of Faith in Social Movement Activism*. London: Routledge.

Smith, Daniel Jordan. 2003. "Patronage, Per Diems and the 'Workshop Mentality': The Practice of Family Planning Programs in Southeastern Nigeria." *World Development* 31: 703–15.

Smith, Lahra. 2013. *Making Citizens in Africa: Ethnicity, Gender and National Identity in Ethiopia.* New York: Cambridge University Press.

Snow, David, Sarah Soule, and Hanspeter Kriesi. 2004. *The Blackwell Companion to Social Movements.* London: Blackwell Publishing.

Soifer, Hillel. 2020. "Shadow Cases in Comparative Research." *Qualitative and Multi-Method Research* 18 (2): 9–18.

Solomon, Ryan. 2019. "Xenophobic Violence and the Ambivalence of Citizenship in Post-Apartheid South Africa." *Citizenship Studies* 23 (2): 156–71.

Sommers, Marc. 2010. "Urban Youth in Africa." *Environment & Urbanization* 22 (2): 317–32.

2015. *The Outcast Majority: War, Development and Youth in Africa.* Athens: University of Georgia Press.

Sperber, Elizabeth, and Erin Hern. 2018. "Pentecostal Identity and Citizen Engagement in Sub-Saharan Africa: New Evidence from Zambia." *Politics and Religion* 11: 830–62.

Sperber, Elizabeth, O'Brien Kaaba, and Gwyneth McClendon. 2022. "Increasing Youth Political Engagement with Efficacy Not Obligation: Evidence from a Workshop-Based Experiment in Zambia." *Political Behavior* 44: 1933–58.

Squire, Peverill, Raymond E. Wolfinger, and David P. Glass. 1987. "Residential Mobility and Voter Turnout." *American Political Science Review* 81 (1): 45–65.

Ssenkaaba, Stephen. 2021. "Uganda: Violence against Women Unabated despite Laws." *Africa Renewal.* www.un.org/africarenewal/news/uganda-violence-against-women-unabated-despite-laws-and-policies.

Statista. 2021. "Youth Unemployment Rate in Africa from 2012 to 2021." www.statista.com/statistics/1266153/youth-unemployment-rate-in-africa.

Stats SA. 2022. "Quarterly Labour Force Survey." June. www.statssa.gov.za.

Stites, Elizabeth. 2013. "A Struggle for Rites: Masculinity, Violence, and Livelihoods in Karamoja, Uganda." In *Gender, Violence, and Human Security: Critical Feminist Perspectives,* edited by Aili Mari Tripp, Myra Marx Ferree, and Christina Ewig, 132–61. New York: New York University Press.

Stockemer, Daniel. 2011. "Women's Parliamentary Representation in Africa: The Impact of Democracy and Corruption on the Number of Female Deputies in National Parliaments." *Political Studies* 59 (3): 693–712.

Stoeltje, Beverly. 2003. "Asante Queen Mothers: Precolonial Authority in a Postcolonial Society." *Research Review* 19 (2): 1–19.

Stolzenberg, Ross, Mary Blair-Loy, and Linda J. Wait. 1995. "Religious Participation in Early Adulthood: Age and Family Life Cycle Effects on Church Membership." *American Sociological Review* 60 (1): 84–103.

Taggart, Paul. 2000. *Populism*. Buckingham: Open University Press.

Tamale, Sylvia. 2009. "Law, Sexuality, and Politics in Uganda: Challenges for Women's Human Rights NGOs." In *Human Rights NGOs in Africa: Political and Normative Tensions*, edited by Makau Mutua, 51–74. Philadelphia: University of Pennsylvania Press.

2016. "Profile: 'Keep Your Eyes off My Thighs': A Feminist Analysis of Uganda's 'Mini-Skirt Law'." *African Feminist* 21: 83–90.

Tapscott, Rebecca. 2017. "Local Security and the (Un)Making of Public Authority in Gulu, Northern Uganda." *African Affairs* 116 (462): 39–59.

Taylor, Charles F. 2017. "Ethnic Politics and Election Campaigns in Contemporary Africa: Evidence from Ghana and Kenya." *Democratization* 24 (6): 951–69.

Taylor, Liam. 2021. "Millions of Ugandans Denied Services over Digital ID Cards." *Reuters*, June 8. www.reuters.com/article/us-uganda-tech-rights/millions-of-ugandans-denied-vital-services-over-digital-id-cards-idUSKCN2DK28W.

Thieme, Tatiana. 2013. "The 'Hustle' amongst Youth Entrepreneurs in Mathare's Informal Waste Economy." *Journal of Eastern African Studies* 7 (3): 389–412.

Thiong'o, Julius. 2021. "President John Magufuli: A Man after Julius Nyerere's Own Heart." *Standard*, October 21. www.standardmedia .co.ke/politics/article/2001406767/magufuli-in-the-footsteps-of-julius-nyerere-with-nationalist-agenda.

Thompson, Lisa, Chris Tapscott, and Pamela T. De Wet. 2018. "An Exploration of the Concept of Community and Its Impact on Participatory Governance Policy and Service Delivery in Poor Areas of Cape Town, South Africa." *Politikon* 48 (2): 276–90.

Tipple, Graham, and Suzanne Speak. 2009. *The Hidden Millions: Homelessness in Developing Countries*. London: Routledge.

Transparency International. 2021. "Corruption Perception Index." www .transparency.org/en/cpi/2021.

Treanor, Paul. 2005. "Neoliberalism: Origins, Theory." http://web.inter.nl .net/users/Paul.Treanor/neoliberalism.html.

Tripp, Aili Mari. 2000. *Women and Politics in Uganda*. Oxford: James Currey.

2006. "Uganda: Agents of Change for Women's Advancement?" In *Women in African Parliaments*, edited by Gretchen Bauer and Hannah Britton, 111–32. Boulder, CO: Lynne Rienner.

2010. *Museveni's Uganda: Paradoxes of Power in a Hybrid Regime.* Boulder, CO: Lynne Rienner.

Tsikata, Dzodzi. 2009. "Women's Organizing in Ghana since the 1990s: From Individual Organizations to Three Coalitions." *Development* 52 (2): 185–92.

Tuğul, Cihan. 2021. "Populism Studies: The Case for Theoretical and Comparative Reconstruction." *Annual Review of Sociology* 47: 327–47.

Uganda Bureau of Statistics. 2016. "Uganda: 2016 Demographic and Health Survey Key Findings." https://dhsprogram.com/pubs/pdf/SR245/SR245.pdf.

UN Department of Economic and Social Affairs. 2022. "World Population Prospects." https://population.un.org/wpp.

UNAIDS (Joint United Nations Programme on HIV/AIDS). 2021. "UNAIDS Data 2021." www.unaids.org/sites/default/files/media_asset/JC3032_AIDS_Data_book_2021_En.pdf.

UNDP (United Nations Development Programme). 2017. *Income Inequality Trends in Sub-Saharan Africa.* New York: UNDP.

2021. "Human Development Index Ranking 2021." https://hdr.undp.org.

United Nations. 2022. "Who Are Youth?" www.un.org/en/global-issues/youth.

United Republic of Tanzania, Ministry of Labour, Employment, and Youth Development. 2007. "National Youth Development Policy." www.youthpolicy.org/national/Tanzania_2007_National_Youth_Policy.pdf.

US Embassy of Zambia. 2021. "PEPFAR in Zambia." https://zm.usembassy.gov/our-relationship/pepfar/pepfar-in-zambia.

USAID (US Agency for International Development). 2011. *YouthMap Uganda.* www.youthpolicy.org/national/Uganda_2011_Youth_Mapping_Volume_1.pdf.

2021. *Country Development Cooperation Strategy, 2020–2025.* www.usaid.gov/sites/default/files/documents/CDCS-Ghana-August-2025.pdf.

Utas, Mats. 2005. "Agency of Victims: Young Women's Survival Strategies in the Liberian Civil War." In *Makers and Breakers: Children and Youth in Postcolonial Africa*, edited by Filip de Boeck and Alcinda Honwana, 53–80. Oxford: James Currey.

Uwalaka, Temple. 2022. "Social Media as Solidarity Vehicle during the 2020 #EndSARS Protests in Nigeria." *Journal of Asian and African Studies.* doi.org/10.1177/00219096221108737.

Uzodike, Ufo Okeke, and Ayo Whetho. 2008. "In Search of a Public Sphere: Mainstreaming Religious Networks into the African Renaissance Agenda." *Politikon* 35 (2): 197–222.

Van Allen, Judith. 1972. "'Sitting on a Man': Colonialism and the Lost Political Institutions of Igbo Women." *Canadian Journal of African Studies* 6 (2): 165–81.

2015. "What Are Women's Rights Good For? Contesting and Negotiating Gender Cultures in Southern Africa." *African Studies Review* 38 (3): 97–128.

van de Walle, Nicolas. 2001. *African Economies and the Politics of Permanent Crisis, 1979–1999*. New York: Cambridge University Press.

2007. "Meet the New Boss, Same as the Old Boss? The Evolution of Political Clientelism in Africa." In *Patrons, Clients and Policies: Patterns of Democratic Accountability and Political Competition*, edited by Herbert Kitschelt and Steven I. Wilkinson, 50–67. New York: Cambridge University Press.

Van Gyampo, Ransford. 2015. "Youth in Parliament and Youth Representation in Ghana." *Journal of Asian and African Studies* 50 (1): 69–82.

2020. "Generational Dynamics and Youth Politics." In *Routledge Handbook of Democratization in Africa*, edited by Gabrielle Lynch and Peter VonDoepp, 329–41. London: Routledge.

Van Gyampo, Ransford, and Nana Akua Anyidoho. 2019. "Youth Politics in Africa." *Oxford Research Encyclopedia*. Published online June 25. doi.org/10.1093/acrefore/9780190228637.013.716.

Van Gyampo, Ransford, and Bossman Asare. 2017. "The Church and Ghana's Drive toward Democratic Consolidation and Maturity." *Journal of Church and State* 59 (1): 1–22.

Van Gyampo, Ransford, Emmanuel Graham, and Bossman Asare. 2017. "Political Vigilantism and Democratic Governance in Ghana's Fourth Republic." *African Review* 44 (2): 112–35.

Van Gyampo, Ransford, and F. Obeng-Odoom. 2012. "Youth Participation in Local and National Development: 1620–2013." *Journal of Pan African Studies* 5 (9): 129–55.

van Klinken, Adriaan. 2013. *Transforming Masculinities in African Christianity: Gender Controversies in the Time of AIDS*. Aldershot: Ashgate.

van Stekelenburg, Jaquelien, and Bert Klandermans. 2009. "Social Movement Theory: Past, Present and Prospects." In *Movers and Shakers: Social Movements in Africa*, edited by Stephen Ellis and Ineke van Kessel, 17–43. Leiden: Brill.

Venugopal, Rajesh. 2015. "Neoliberalism as Concept." *Economy and Society* 44 (2): 165–87.

Verba, Sidney, and Norman Nie. 1972. *Participation in America: Political Democracy and Social Equality*. New York: Harper & Row.

Verba, Sidney, Kay L. Schlozman, and Henry E. Brady. 1995. *Voice and Equality: Civic Voluntarism in American Politics*. Cambridge, MA: Harvard University Press.

Vokes, Richard, and Sam Wilkins. 2016. "Party Patronage and Coercion in the NRM's 2016 Re-Election in Uganda: Imposed or Embedded?" *Journal of Eastern African Studies* 10 (4): 581–600.

von Lieres, Bettina. 2014. "Citizenship from below: The Politics of Citizen Action & Resistance in South Africa & Angola." In *Civic Agency in Africa: Arts of Resistance in the 21st Century*, edited by Ebenezer Obadare and Wendy Willems, 49–62. London: James Currey.

VonDoepp, Peter. 2020. "Liberal Visions and Actual Power in Grassroots Civil Society: Local Churches and Women's Empowerment in Rural Malawi." *Journal of Modern African Studies* 40 (2): 273–301.

VYLTP (Volmoed Youth Leadership Training Programme). 2019. "Programme Content." Organizational Brochure. Author's personal copy.

Walsh, Declan. 2022. "William Ruto, the Self-Proclaimed Champion of Kenya's 'Hustler Nation'." *New York Times*, August 9. www.nytimes .com/2022/08/09/world/africa/kenya-elections-william-ruto.html.

Ward, Kevin. 2015. "The Role of the Anglican and Catholic Churches in Uganda in Public Discourse on Homosexuality and Ethics." *Journal of Eastern African Studies* 9 (1): 127–44.

Watkins, Susan, and Ann Swidler. 2012. "Working Misunderstandings: Donors, Brokers and Villagers in Africa's AIDS Industry." *Population and Development Review* 38: 197–218.

Westheimer, Joel, and Joseph Kahne. 2004. "Educating the 'Good' Citizen: Political Choices and Pedagogical Goals." *PS: Political Science & Politics* 37 (2): 241–47.

Weyland, Kurt. 2001. "Clarifying a Contested Concept: Populism in the Study of Latin American Politics." *Comparative Politics* 34 (1): 1–22.

2020. "Populism's Threat to Democracy: Comparative Lessons for the United States." *Perspectives on Politics* 18 (2): 389–406.

2022. "Why US Democracy Trumps Populism: Comparative Lessons Reconsidered." *PS: Political Science and Politics* 55 (3): 478–83.

Whitaker, Beth Elise. 2005. "Citizens and Foreigners: Democratization and the Politics of Exclusion in Africa." *African Studies Review* 48 (1): 109–26.

White, Julie Anne. 2001. "Citizenship and the Labor of Care." *Polity* 233 (3): 487–99.

White, Sarah. 2002. "From the Politics of Poverty to the Politics of Identity? Child Rights and Working Children in Bangladesh." *Journal of International Development* 14: 725–35.

Whitehead, Richard. 2012. "Historical Legacies, Clientelism and the Capacity to Fight: Exploring Pathways to Regime Tenure in Tanzania." *Democratization* 19 (6): 1086–116.

Whiting, John. 1990. "Adolescent Rituals and Identity Conflicts." In *Cultural Psychology: Essays on Comparative Human Development*, edited by James Stigler, Richard Shweder, and Gilbert Herdt, 357–65. New York: Cambridge University Press.

WHO (World Health Organization). 2018. "Violence against Women Prevalence Estimates, 2018: Executive Summary." https://who.canto .global/s/KDE1H?viewIndex=0&column=document&id= b49pm5q72l3id8bohtnqutfg69.

Whyte, Jessica. 2019. *The Morals of the Market: Human Rights and the Rise of Neoliberalism*. New York: Verso.

Wilkins, Sam, Richard Vokes, and Moses Khisa. 2021. "Briefing: Contextualizing the Bobi Wine Factor in Uganda's 2021 Elections." *African Affairs* 120 (481): 629–43.

Williams, Beth Ann. 2018. "Mainline Churches: Networks of Belonging in Postindependence Kenya and Tanzania." *Journal of Religion in Africa* 48 (3): 255–85.

Williams, Paul, and Ian Taylor. 2000. "Neoliberalism and the Political Economy of the 'New' South Africa." *New Political Economy* 5 (1): 21–40.

Woldemichael, Andinet. 2020. "Closing the Gender Gap in African Labor Market Is Good Economics." Brookings Institution, January 23. www .brookings.edu/blog/africa-in-focus/2020/01/23/closing-the-gender-gap-in-african-labor-markets-is-good-economics.

Woolcock, Michael. 1998. "Social Capital and Economic Development: Toward a Theoretical Synthesis and Policy Framework." *Theory and Society* 27 (2): 151–208.

World Bank. 1981. *Accelerated Development in Africa: An Agenda for Action*. Washington, DC: World Bank.

2016. *Migration and Development: A Role for the World Bank Group*. Washington, DC: World Bank.

2019. "Prevalence of Severe Food Insecurity in the Population (%) – Uganda." https://data.worldbank.org/indicator/SN.ITK.SVFI.ZS?loca tions=UG.

2020a. "Literacy Rate, Adult Female (% of Females Ages 15 and above) – Sub-Saharan Africa." https://data.worldbank.org/indicator/SE.ADT .LITR.FE.ZS?locations=ZG.

2020b. "Literacy Rate, Adult Male (% of Males Ages 15 and above) – Sub-Saharan Africa." https://data.worldbank.org/indicator/SE.ADT .LITR.MA.ZS?locations=ZG.

2020c. *Uganda Vision 2040*. https://consultations.worldbank.org/sites/ default/files/materials/consultation-template/materials/vision20204011 .pdf.

2021. "Indicators." https://data.worldbank.org/indicator.

2022. "Tanzania Economic Update 17 Final Report." www.worldbank .org/en/country/tanzania/publication/tanzania-economic-update-teu.

World Prisons Brief. 2020. "World Prisons Brief Data." www.prisonstudies .org/world-prison-brief-data.

Wuthnow, Robert. 2002. "Religious Involvement and Status-Bridging Social Capital." *Journal for the Scientific Study of Religion* 41 (4): 669–75.

Yoon, Mi Yung. 2008. "Special Seats for Women in the National Legislature: The Case of Tanzania." *Africa Today* 55 (1): 61–86.

Young, Crawford. 2007. "Nation, Ethnicity and Citizenship: Dilemmas of Democracy and Civil Order in Africa." In *Making Nations, Creating Strangers: States and Citizenship in Africa*, edited by Sara Dorman, Daniel Hammett, and Paul Nugent, 241–64. Leiden: Brill.

Yuval-Davis, Nira. 2007. "Intersectionality, Citizenship and Contemporary Politics of Belonging." *Critical Review of International Social and Political Philosophy* 10 (4): 561–74.

Zembylas, Michalinos. 2014. "Affective Citizenship in Multicultural Societies: Implications for Critical Citizenship Education." *Citizenship Teaching & Learning* 9 (1): 5–18.

Zoettl, Peter Anton. 2016. "'Prison Is for Young People!' Youth, Violence, and the State in Praia and Mindelo, Cape Verde." *African Studies Review* 59 (2): 231–49.

Index

Milton Keynes UK
Ingram Content Group UK Ltd.
UKHW022350020823
426244UK00014B/137